PENGUIN BOOKS

LLOYDS BANK TAX GUIDE

Sara Williams is a financial journalist and a former investment analyst and lecturer in finance. For a number of years she wrote for *Which?*, including the *Which? Tax-Saving Guide* and the *Which? Book of Tax*. She has also contributed many articles on personal finance and tax to newspapers and magazines. She is the author of the *Lloyds Bank Small Business Guide*, *Unit Trusts* and *Breakout*. Sara Williams has been a public interest member for LAUTRO (Life Assurance and Unit Trust Regulatory Organization) and is a council member of the Consumers' Association.

John Willman is public policy editor for the *Financial Times*. He has written extensively on personal finance and tax for *Which?*, including the *Which? Tax Saving Guide* and the *Which? Book of Tax*. Formerly publications editor at Peat, Marwick, McLintock (the city accountants), he was the editor of *Assessment* and *Taxes*, published by the Inland Revenue Staff Federation. He is the author of *Make Your Will*, *How to Sort Out Someone's Will* and the *Which? Guide to Planning and Conservation*.

SARA WILLIAMS AND JOHN WILLMAN

LLOYDS BANK TAX GUIDE
1994/95

PENGUIN BOOKS

PENGUIN BOOKS

Published by the Penguin Group
Penguin Books Ltd, 27 Wrights Lane, London W8 5TZ, England
Penguin Books USA Inc., 375 Hudson Street, New York, New York 10014, USA
Penguin Books Australia Ltd, Ringwood, Victoria, Australia
Penguin Books Canada Ltd, 10 Alcorn Avenue, Toronto, Ontario, Canada M4V 3B2
Penguin Books (NZ) Ltd, 182–190 Wairau Road, Auckland 10, New Zealand

Penguin Books Ltd, Registered Offices: Harmondsworth, Middlesex, England

First published 1987
Second edition 1988
Third edition 1989
Fourth edition 1990
Fifth edition 1991
Sixth edition 1992
Seventh edition 1993
Eighth edition 1994
10 9 8 7 6 5 4 3 2 1

CONTENTS

SECTION V SPENDING YOUR MONEY

SECTION VI OTHER TAXES

THE LLOYDS BANK TAX GUIDE TREASURE TROVE – YOUR CHANCE TO WIN A PSION HAND-HELD COMPUTER

Ever wished you could be better organized? Here's a chance to fulfil that longing – this year we've got 20 Psion hand-held computers available as prizes. Seize your opportunity to win this valuable prize by trying to crack some simple clues which are scattered through the Guide.

The Psion Series 3 is a pocket-sized computer which comes complete with a range of software. So you will be able do your own word processing, build your own database of information, sort out your diary and appointments, organize the jobs you have to do, carry out calculations and lots more. There can be no more excuses about being disorganized! It's also great fun to use.

WHAT YOU HAVE TO DO

There are eleven Treasure Trove clues hidden throughout the Guide. Each is a question about tax, the answer to which is a number. You can find the answers by reading the Guide. At the back of the Guide, on p. 381, is an entry form. Enter your answers in the spaces provided and add up all the numbers. Then explain why the total should be of interest to taxpayers in not more than 20 words. The best 20 answers will scoop the prizes!

Your entry should be made on the form at the end of the Guide – no photocopies acceptable! Make sure you send your entry to arrive by 31 December 1994. The authors are the judges and their decision is final. The terms and conditions for the Treasure Trove are overleaf.

Happy hunting!

TERMS AND CONDITIONS FOR THE LLOYDS BANK TAX GUIDE TREASURE TROVE

1.   Entries will be accepted only on the entry form on p. 381. Photocopies will not be accepted.

2.   Illegible, damaged or defaced entries will not be accepted.

3.   The closing date for entry is 31 December 1994.

4.   Proof of posting of an entry form will not be taken as proof of receipt and no responsibility is accepted for entries lost or delayed in the post.

5.   Employees of Lloyds Bank Plc or its subsidiaries and Penguin Books Ltd, or of associated companies of any of these, or the immediate families of such employees, are not eligible to enter this competition.

6.   This competition will be judged by the authors whose decisions will be final. No correspondence will be entered into.

7.   Winners will be notified by post by 15 February 1995.

8.   A list of winners and the solutions to the clues can be obtained by writing to Lloyds Bank Tax Guide Competition Solutions, Penguin Books, 27 Wrights Lane, London W8 5TZ after 1 April 1995.

9.   There will be no cash equivalent or substitute prizes available.

10.   The competition should not be taken as an endorsement of any supplier or its products by Lloyds Bank Plc, Penguin Books Ltd or the authors.

EASY FIVE-POINT PLAN TO CUT YOUR TAX BILL

Reading this Guide will help you understand the tax system and should suggest plenty of ways to save tax. There's a list of 50 tax-saving tips which can save you money at the end of the Guide (see p. 352). But as a start, follow this five-point plan to identify the commonest ways of ensuring that you pay not a penny more in tax than you should.

POINT 1: Keep tabs on your tax – mistakes do happen!

The average tax bill is £4,000 a year, yet most people spend less than an hour a year checking their tax bill. It could pay to keep an eye on your tax:

● if you're sent a PAYE Notice of Coding, make sure you're getting the allowances you're entitled to (p. 149)

● a Notice of Assessment is the Inland Revenue's calculation of your tax bill – check it carefully (p. 73)

● spend some time after the end of the tax year checking that you've paid the right amount (see Chapter 10 on p. 78 for how to do this)

● look at the chapters of this Guide which apply to your circumstances – you could find ways of saving tax.

POINT 2: If you are married, make sure that you take advantage of independent taxation to minimize the tax you both pay:

● arrange for interest on savings accounts, share dividends and other investment income to be paid to the partner with the lower rate of tax (see p. 263)

● make sure that allowances which can be switched between partners go to the partner with the higher rate of tax (see p. 50 and p. 106)

● remember that a husband and wife can each make over £5,800 this year in tax-free gains (see p. 311)

● sharing your wealth between you can cut the inheritance tax payable on what you pass on to your children (see p. 342).

POINT 3: You can save huge amounts of tax by saving through pensions.

There are big tax reliefs for saving through an employer's pension scheme or via a personal pension. For example, you can get as much as a third of your income tax-free if you contribute to a personal pension – and begin to cash it in any time after the age of 50. See Chapter 25 on p. 219 for details of the tax savings on offer.

POINT 4: If you are over 65 (or your spouse is if you're married), you can get higher tax allowances provided your 'total income' is below a certain level – £14,200 for 1994/95.

If your income is above this level, the higher allowances are gradually withdrawn until you get the same allowances as under-65s. If you're in this income trap, look at tax-free investments (see p. 264). And if you're married, juggling your investment income between you might bring the total income of at least one of you – and perhaps both – below the £14,200 limit (p. 136).

POINT 5: Don't miss out on the expenses and allowances you can claim against various types of income to minimize your tax bill.

See Chapter 18 if you work for an employer (p. 144), Chapter 23 if you're self-employed (p. 195), Chapter 27 if you let out property (pp. 249, 251).

A message from Brian Pitman, Chief Executive, Lloyds Bank

I am delighted that Lloyds Bank has, once again, worked in conjunction with Sara Williams, John Willman and Penguin Books to produce the ninth edition of the Lloyds Bank Tax Guide.

Over the years, the Lloyds Bank Tax Guide has gained a reputation for providing clear, concise, relevant and up-to-date information on a subject that many readers had previously found extremely difficult to understand.

Indeed, this edition has been published earlier in the year than previous editions to reflect the important changes announced in the Chancellor's Autumn Budget in time for the new tax year.

Lloyds Bank is dedicated to building long-term relationships with its customers by anticipating and meeting their changing needs. Our aim is to differentiate ourselves from our competitors by better products, innovation and, above all, a high level of service.

We were, for example, among the first to summarise credit interest for the whole tax year on account statements, thus helping customers to complete their tax returns.

More recently, we produced a summary of the Chancellor's Autumn Budget for our Gold Service account customers. The text was prepared as the Chancellor spoke and customers received their complimentary copies within two days.

I hope that you will find the Lloyds Bank Tax Guide useful.

Brian Pitman

Brian Pitman

ACKNOWLEDGEMENTS

We should like to convey our gratitude to a number of people without whom this book could not have appeared. Foremost among those is Brian Clutterbuck of Lloyds Private Banking who cast his expert eye over the text to eradicate any little slips. Emma Hodgson was also involved in research and verification for this year's guide.

We are also delighted to acknowledge the help we've received from Sally Berry and Nigel Jeacock-Fewtrell at Lloyds Retail Banking. The Marketing department at Penguin, under John Bond's enthusiastic guidance, have been especially helpful in promoting the Guide this year. On the production side Tony Garrett, Moira Greenhalgh, Image Setting Ltd and Julia West have provided expert support and service.

Our thanks go the Controller of Her Majesty's Stationery Office for permission to reproduce Inland Revenue Forms P1, 11P, 11, P2 and P70. These forms are Crown Copyright.

Writing the Guide inevitably dislocates normal family life in our household. Our thanks to Margaret and Peter for covering out tracks, and to Charles, Michael, Kate, Freddie and Claire for agreeing to be scandalously neglected.

NOTE

As with every edition of the Guide, both of us – along with everyone at Lloyds Bank and Penguin Books – have made strenuous efforts to check the accuracy of the information. If, by chance, a mistake or omission has occurred, we are sorry that we can't take responsibility if you suffer any loss or problem as a result of it. But please write to us c/o Penguin Books if you have any suggestions about how we can improve the content of the Guide.

HAD A TAX WINDFALL?

If you've made a tax saving as a result of reading this Guide – or you've discovered a new tax tip – write and tell us about it. There's a bottle of champagne for the best two letters sent in by 31 December 1994.

Send your entries to: Sara Williams and John Willman, Lloyds Bank Tax Guide, Penguin Books, 27 Wrights Lane, London W8 5TZ.

1 • THE BASIC TAX SYSTEM

This is the ninth edition of the Lloyds Bank Tax Guide – how the tax system has changed from that very first edition. In 1986/87, there was no independent taxation, capital gains were taxed at a different rate from income, there were far more allowances which you could claim against tax and the rates of tax on income were higher. Today, the income tax system is more streamlined and straightforward. But compared to the very first imposition of income tax, all those years ago, the system remains complex.

Income tax was first introduced in Britain in 1799 by William Pitt to finance the Napoleonic Wars. The tax was 10d. in the pound (roughly 4p at today's rate). Today Pitt would probably be astounded at how tax of one sort or another embraces most economic activities and at what it is all used for.

One reason why the system is complicated is that over the last two centuries it hasn't grown in a planned and orderly fashion; its development has been higgledy-piggledy. As public spending increased, successive governments wanted to raise more money from taxes. So, at regular intervals, Chancellors of the Exchequer looked for ways to increase the rates of taxation and to spread the net wider. For example, before the Second World War there were fewer than four million income taxpayers. In recent years, the number has risen to over thirty million.

Another reason the system remains complex is that taxpayers, not surprisingly, don't want to pay tax. So they look for ways to cut their tax bills. Every so often, the government has to step in to block a loophole which taxpayers have been utilizing. Hence, tax law is rather piecemeal.

A third reason which explains part of the complication is the desire of governments to be fair. So, for example, when the rules change for some particular part of the system, some people may be allowed to carry on using the old rules for a while. One particular example of this was the change in the taxation of maintenance which occurred in 1988.

There are different rules depending on whether the maintenance agreement was made on or after a certain date or before that date. This makes for confusion.

Further complications in the income tax system arise when it is tinkered with to stimulate certain activities in the economy. For example, there are special schemes to encourage you to invest in certain ways.

Finally, the system remains difficult to understand because there is still one hangover from the very early days – the way the tax system divides income up into a system of Schedules. There seem to be some strange bedfellows and odd omissions. Schedules were first introduced in 1803. It's hardly surprising that a way of grouping income which was suitable nearly two hundred years ago does not come up to scratch today.

Income tax is not the only tax, of course. Other taxes have been introduced in an attempt to raise more money. There have been three attempts to tax people's wealth, culminating in the latest: inheritance tax. And in 1965 a tax was introduced on gains you might make on certain items as they increase in value; this tax is called capital gains tax.

HOW THE TAX RULES ARE CHANGED

Nowadays, most changes in the tax rules are announced once a year in the Budget. This year the Budget was earlier, at the same time as the old Autumn Statement, in November 1993. This Finance Bill will be published and after debate in Parliament, the Finance Act will be passed before 5 May 1994.

The Finance Act can run to a large number of pages, one or two hundred or more, which means a lot of changes to what happens in the tax system. And there are Acts which consolidate all the changes which take place year by year.

HOW THE TAX RULES ARE PUT INTO PRACTICE

The tax system is operated by the Inland Revenue. The system at present is that Tax Inspectors are responsible for assessing how much tax each taxpayer should pay. The taxpayer has the responsibility for providing the information which the Tax Inspector needs to do the assessment. This is done by filling in a Tax Return; even if you do not receive a Tax Return it is nevertheless your responsibility to tell your Tax Inspector about any new source of income. From 1996/97 some eight million people will be able to assess their own tax bill. This will generally be the self-employed, people whose main source of income is investments, and employees and pensioners who receive tax returns. This system is known as self-assessment.

Under the present system, Tax Inspectors are not allocated to certain taxpayers. Instead, they are allocated according to the type of income. This can lead to confusion for the taxpayer. If you change your jobs frequently, it's also likely that you will have frequent changes in Tax Inspectors.

If you get income from different places in a tax year, you could be dealing with more than one Tax Inspector at a time. For example, if you have a job and also run a business on the side, only by pure coincidence would both these sources of income be dealt with by the same person. It is far more likely that for the earnings from your job, you are corresponding with one Tax Inspector located at one end of the country, while the earnings from your business are dealt with by a local Tax Inspector.

However this will change under the new system and you should only get one bill for all your income.

TYPES OF TAXES

There is a variety of different taxes. The taxes included in this Guide are:

● *income tax*

● *capital gains tax:* this is a tax on the increase in the value of certain assets you own, payable when you dispose of them

● *inheritance tax:* this attempts to tax money being passed from one person to another on death and sometimes in gifts before death

● *National Insurance:* this is a tax on people who work.

There are other taxes which are beyond the scope of this Guide. These include:

● *corporation tax:* the government raises money from companies through this tax

● *value added tax:* it is charged on most goods and services which you buy as a consumer and it is passed on through the sellers of the goods, rather than straight to the government

● *excise duties:* these will be paid by everyone who smokes, drinks or drives a car. It is also an indirect tax, like VAT, which is paid by the consumer

● *council tax:* this is the replacement for community charge or poll tax.

2 • HOW TO USE THIS GUIDE

The Guide is written in simple, everyday language to help you sort out your tax affairs. You will not find the normal complicated tax jargon that is in other books or used by the professionals. Instead, the intricacies of the tax system are laid bare so that you and your family can understand what's going on. However, the Guide also helps you to understand the words used by the tax people; these are explained in the text and there is a Glossary on p. 346.

The Guide covers all the important tax points which the vast majority of taxpayers need to know, but it can't cover the minute details of the more unusual problems. However, even if you hand over your tax affairs to a tax adviser, because you quake at the very thought of the tax system, this Guide will help you keep an eye on what your tax adviser says or does.

There are a number of specific tasks which this Guide will enable you to do.

TASK 1: *Filling in your Tax Return*. In Chapter 9, 'The Forms', p. 64 the Guide explains the different sorts of Tax Return there are and who has to fill one in; it uses an illustration of a Tax Return to show you where to find the particular points that *you* need to know to fill in your Tax Return. Each chapter covers a different tax topic. At the end of each chapter there is a summary of what you should put in your Tax Return.

The Guide uses as an illustration the form which you should fill in at the start of the 1994/95 tax year.

TASK 2: *Checking your PAYE code*. For taxpayers who do not have to fill in a Tax Return every year, it is vital to keep track of what is going on. The Guide shows you how to check your Notice of Coding and your PAYE code, so you can ensure that you are not paying too much tax. It is a common fallacy to believe that if your tax affairs are very simple you will not be able to save tax. Do not fall into this trap. Use this Guide to check that you are getting all the reliefs and allowances that you can.

TASK 3: *Checking your tax bill.* Whether you get a Tax Return to fill in or not, it is important to check at the end of the tax year that you have not paid too much tax. If you use this Guide, you should be able to make sure that your Tax Inspector has not included income which should not have been included or left out allowances or reliefs you should have had. Do not forget to check the arithmetic, too. Chapter 10, 'Checking Your Income Tax Bill', p. 78, will help you work out what your tax should be for the tax year 1993/94. If your affairs are a bit more complicated, you may be sent a Notice of Assessment; Chapter 9, 'The Forms', p. 64, shows you how to understand this.

TASK 4: *Saving tax.* There may be simple steps you can take to rearrange your affairs to help you cut the amount of tax you pay. The Guide is packed with lots of useful tips to help you do that. And on p. 352, there is a list of the more common tax-saving tips.

TASK 5: *Dealing with your Tax Inspector.* Finding your way around the Inland Revenue can be difficult. It can be very confusing if, for example, you find yourself corresponding with more than one Inspector at a time. Chapter 8, 'Your Tax Inspector', p. 55, explains why this might happen to you; it tells you who is the right person to go to for queries, problems, claiming relief, or appealing against decisions. Throughout the book are practical hints on the best method of presenting information to your Tax Inspector to achieve what you want.

TASK 6: *Checking specific tax points.* If you are puzzled about a particular tax treatment, you will find the answers to virtually all of your queries here in this book. Use the Index as your starting point.

HOW THIS GUIDE IS ORGANIZED

There are six sections to this Guide. In each section is a number of chapters; the individual chapter headings are on pp. 5 and 6. Here is a brief description of what you can find in each section.

SECTION 1 · AN OUTLINE OF INCOME TAX

This section starts off by explaining how the tax system has developed (Chapter 1, p. 15) and gives a summary of how the income tax system works (Chapter 3, p. 23). Next, it outlines in simple detail what makes up income (Chapter 4, p. 28) and what can be deducted from it to reduce your tax bill (Chapters 5 and 6, pp. 43 and 49). Finally, it describes the changes which occurred in the November Budget (Chapter 7, p. 52).

SECTION II · YOU AND YOUR TAX INSPECTOR

This gives an explanation of how the Inland Revenue works and how you should communicate with your Tax Inspector (Chapter 8, p. 55). The next chapter, Chapter 9, p. 6444, describes the process of filling in Tax Returns and checking other forms. You can use this to find out where each specific entry in your Tax Return is covered in detail in the Guide. Chapter 10, p. 78, shows you a simple way of checking that you are paying the right tax. Finally, Chapter 11, p. 92, explains how you can appeal against a tax bill and what happens if you are investigated.

SECTION III · HOW THE FAMILY IS TAXED

You can find here clear details of what happens if you are single (Chapter 12, p. 100), marry (Chapter 13, p. 104) and subsequently separate or divorce (Chapter 14, p. 113). The tax affairs of the widowed (Chapter 15, p. 124), children and students (Chapter 16, p. 128) and the elderly (Chapter 17, p. 132) are also explained.

SECTION IV · IN WORK OR OUT OF WORK

The income which you earn from your work is the main source of income taxed by the UK system. This section looks at how your income from work is treated. Employees can be paid earnings (Chapter 18, p. 140) and fringe benefits (Chapter 19, p. 161). What happens when you start or leave a job is explained in Chapter 20, p. 177. When unemployment strikes, Chapter 21, p. 181, should help you organize your financial affairs (details of other benefits are also given here). How you will be taxed if you work abroad is explained in Chapter 22, p. 188.

Earning money on the side as a freelance can be useful (Chapter 4, p. 80). And if you set up in business it can be on your own (Chapter 23, p. 192) or in partnership (Chapter 24, p. 214).

SECTION V · SPENDING YOUR MONEY

This section explains how your money is taxed if you invest it (Chapter 28, p. 262) or give it to charity (Chapter 30, p. 233). Some investments are dual purpose, such as your home (Chapter 26, p. 233) or life insurance (Chapter 29, p. 287). The best way of saving for your retirement is through a pension scheme (Chapter 25, p. 219) and there are other ways of investing in property, as well as buying your home (Chapter 27, p. 248).

SECTION VI • OTHER TAXES

Income tax may not be the only tax you have to pay. You may find yourself having to pay capital gains tax (Chapter 31, p. 301) or inheritance tax (Chapter 32, p. 327).

3 • HOW INCOME TAX WORKS

The government gets much of *its* income by taxing *your* income. Income tax is likely to make the biggest hole in your pay packet: bigger than your mortgage payments, bigger than fuel bills, bigger than your food budget. So why pay more than you have to? Spend some of your time keeping your tax affairs organized, checking that you are not paying too much income tax and claiming it back if you are. There may be ways you can alter your tax bill by following the tax-saving tips on p. 352. But as a first step, try to understand how the income tax system works.

Cutting through all the complexities, income tax works like this:

STEP 1: Calculate your income from your job, investments, self-employment or other sources. Chapter 4, 'Income', p. 28, tells you what is, and what is not, income and which income is, or is not, taxed.

STEP 2: From your income for tax purposes, deduct the items on which you get tax relief. These are known as 'deductions' and are listed in Chapter 5, 'Deductions', p. 43. After you have done this, you will be left with a figure which in most cases will be what the taxman calls 'total income' – quite a misnomer. But if you are retired, or nearing retirement, knowing what your 'total income' is can be important.

STEP 3: Deduct the personal allowances you can claim; these also give you tax relief and reduce the amount of income on which you must pay tax. This leaves you with taxable income.

STEP 4: Work out how much tax you are going to pay on your taxable income. For the 1993/94 tax year, you will pay tax at 20 per cent on the first £2,500 and at 25 per cent on the next £21,200. For the 1994/95 tax year, tax is at 20 per cent on the first £3,000 and at 25 per cent on the next £20,700. On the next page are the rates of tax charged for the tax years 1993/94 and 1994/95.

TAX RATES FOR 1994/95

INCOME BAND £	SIZE OF BAND £	TAX RATE %	TAX ON BAND £
1-3,000	3,000	20	750
3,001-23,700	20,700	25	5,175
Over 23,700		40	

TAX RATES FOR 1993/94

INCOME BAND £	SIZE OF BAND £	TAX RATE %	TAX ON BAND £
1–2,500	2,500	20	500
2,501–23,700	21,200	25	5,300
Over 23,700		40	

EXAMPLE

In the tax year 1994/95, Freddie Noble's earnings from his job are £32,000. Before he is paid, his employer deducts pension contributions of £1,500. He can claim the personal and married couple's allowance for those aged under 65 for the year. How much tax will he pay?

Income		£32,000
less deductions:		
pension contributions		£1,500
Total income		£30,500
less personal allowance		£3,445
Taxable income		£27,055
Tax: £3,000 at 20%	£600	
£20,700 at 25%	£5,175	
£3,355 at 40%	£1,342	
		£7,117
less married couple's allowance		
£1,720 at 20%		£344
TOTAL TAX		£6,773

WHEN DO YOU PAY INCOME TAX?

Taxpayers pay their tax bills on different days during the tax year. For 1994/95:

TAXABLE INCOME	WHEN IS TAX DUE
Earnings from a job, pensions from employer	Tax deducted as you are paid, for example, weekly, monthly
Profits from self-employment, a partnership, normally furnished holiday accommodation, and Enterprise Allowance	First instalment 1 January 1995; second equal instalment 1 July 1995
Taxable investment income paid without deduction of tax, for example, maintenance received under the old rules (see p. 110), interest on National Savings investments	1 January 1995
Rents which are unearned income	1 January 1995
Higher-rate tax due on income from investments received after deduction of tax; other payments received with basic-rate tax deducted, for example, annuities	1 December 1995
Taxable social security benefits	Normally after you return to work, weekly or monthly

If you are an employee and the bulk of your income comes from your job, you may find that your Tax Inspector includes your other bits of income in your PAYE code and may estimate what these are for the current year. Tax will be collected on these bits of income weekly or monthly rather than on the dates shown. Sometimes, however, your Tax Inspector may include it in next year's calculation of your PAYE code which means that this is the best way for you to pay.

On occasion the amount of income tax you are supposed to pay may not have been settled by the dates above. In this case, you don't have to pay until 30 days after you receive what's called a Notice of Assessment from your Tax Inspector, but you might like to do so to avoid interest (see p. 63). A Notice of Assessment shows your Tax Inspector's calculation of the income tax you owe or are owed, if you have paid too much.

The 1993 Budget proposed a great simplification in the way tax bills are organized, to be introduced in 1996/97. The intention is that every taxpayer will have just one tax statement with only one tax bill for all their income.

THE IMPORTANCE OF TIME

As you read through the Guide, you will find that there are some deadlines to meet if you want a bit of income to be taxed in one way rather than another or if you want to tell your Tax Inspector that your tax bill is wrong. Here are some of the important income tax deadlines:

WITHIN 30 DAYS

- appealing against a Notice of Assessment p. 61
- applying for a postponement of tax due p. 62

WITHIN 60 DAYS

- telling your tax office you disagree with the statement p. 182
of taxable social security benefits you receive from
the benefit office
- returning a joint 'declaration of beneficial interests' p. 109
(Form 17) to your Tax Inspector after you have completed
and signed it (a husband and wife use this to show how the
ownership of jointly held investments is split between
them)

BEFORE 31 OCTOBER

- returning your Tax Return to your Tax Inspector in p. 63
sufficient time to avoid paying interest on any tax due

BEFORE 6 APRIL 1995

- applying to allocate the married couple's allowance to the p. 105
wife or to split it equally between husband and wife

WITHIN A YEAR OF THE END OF THE TAX YEAR

WITHIN TWO YEARS OF THE END OF THE TAX YEAR

WITHIN SIX YEARS OF THE END OF THE TAX YEAR

GETTING HELP AND ADVICE

This Guide cannot cover every single point of income tax. For a few specialized areas, for example, if you are a director or a partner or if you are not resident or domiciled in the UK, you will need further advice. The obvious people to turn to are an accountant or your bank. If you want help on some fairly easy problem, you could try your Citizens' Advice Bureau to see if it can handle it.

4 • INCOME

The first step in working out how much income tax you are going to have to pay is to sort out what your income is for the tax year. This is not as obvious as it may seem; income is not necessarily the same as money. For example, what you get from selling some unit trusts is not income (but may be a capital gain), but the value your Tax Inspector puts on your company car counts as income for tax purposes. Since 1988/89, the distinction between income and capital gains is not quite as important as in previous years, because the tax rates on the two are the same. However, there is still an advantage for a capital gain, see p. 301. In any case, the tax system still makes the distinction between the two.

Once you have worked out what counts as income (see opposite), you may find that not all of it is taxed. Some income is specifically excluded from the calculation because it is said to be tax-free (p. 30). You do not have to include it when working out your tax bill.

Even more confusing for the ordinary taxpayer can be the question of which income is being taxed. In most cases, the income your Tax Inspector is interested in is what you get during the current tax year between 6 April in one year and 5 April in the next. So, for the tax year 1994/95, this is what you earn or receive between 6 April 1994 and 5 April 1995.

But sometimes your tax may be based on the income which you got in the preceding tax year. So, for example, if you are an employee with a part-time self-employed business you will find your tax bill based on two different years. For 1994/95, the tax bill for your earnings from your job will be based on what you receive during that year. But the tax bill for your earnings from self-employment, if it has been going a number of years, will be based on earnings made in 1993/94 (strictly, the accounting year ending during the preceding tax year – see p. 207). This confusing system is to be scrapped from the 1996/97 tax year when all income will be taxed on a current-year basis, with trading profits taxed in the year of assessment which includes the accounts year-end.

A further complication is that sometimes you receive the income without any tax deducted and on other occasions tax has been paid, at basic rate or even the higher rate, if due. So you need to sort out which is which; p. 35 gives you guidance.

WHAT IS INCOME?

Some of the commonest ways you get income are from:

● your job, including salary, bonuses, the value your Tax Inspector puts on fringe benefits, holiday pay (pp. 140, 161)

● your business, if you are self-employed (p. 192) or in partnership (p. 214)

● letting out property, such as rent (p. 248)

● investments, such as interest or dividends (p. 262)

● the state, such as the state retirement pension (p. 133) or unemployment benefit (p. 181)

● past employer, such as a pension from your employer's pension scheme (p. 133)

● casual earnings, such as occasional freelance work (p. 40)

● someone else, such as maintenance received from your ex-spouse (p. 117) under old arrangements made before 15 March 1988.

What counts as income can change from time to time. This may occur when the Chancellor announces that some particular money or proceeds will now be treated as income (or no longer treated as income). For example, the Chancellor decided that maintenance payments (paid under arrangements made on or after 15 March 1988) were not part of taxable income.

Your Tax Inspector has the power to classify proceeds from the same action as two different types of money, for example, sometimes income and sometimes gain. This might occur with buying and selling houses. Any gain you make is not normally treated as income. But if you do it too often, your Inspector may decide that you are doing this as a business and treat it as income instead.

IS IT EARNED OR UNEARNED?

The tax laws distinguish between income which is earned and income which is unearned, also called investment income. Broadly, from the list above, income from investments, rent from property (but see p. 249) and maintenance income received under old arrangements (see p. 117) are treated as unearned income. But this distinction is not as important as in earlier years.

WHAT ISN'T INCOME?

You may receive money or proceeds during the year, which the tax system does not call income. This does not mean that this money will not be taxed; it may well be, but by some other tax, not income tax.

The commonest examples are likely to be:

● gifts or presents (but there may be inheritance tax or capital gains tax to pay, p. 327 and p. 301)

● gain from selling an asset, for example, shares, antiques (but there may be capital gains tax to pay – p. 301)

● money you inherit (but there may be inheritance tax to pay – p. 327)

● premium bond prizes (no tax to pay)

● winnings from a lottery or from gambling (no tax to pay, unless it is your business)

● what you receive under maintenance agreements or covenants made on or after 15 March 1988

● money you borrow (no tax to pay, unless it is a cheap loan from your employer).

WHICH INCOME IS TAX-FREE?

There is no logical pattern to help you distinguish income which is tax-free from income which is not. Instead the government at different times has specified that taxpayers will not have to pay tax on some bits of income:

From investments
● interest on National Savings Certificates, the Yearly Plan, National

Savings Children's Bonds (and Ulster Savings Certificates for Northern Ireland inhabitants)

● what you get back at the end of SAYE contracts

● the first £70 interest each year on a National Savings Ordinary Account

● part of the income from an annuity (that is, the bit which is treated as a return of your money – p. 268)

● normally what you get from a regular-premium life insurance policy, such as a with-profits endowment policy or unit-linked one (p. 288)

● loan interest paid to members of a credit union

● income from a Personal Equity Plan (PEP), whether reinvested or paid out (p. 274)

● interest from a Tax Exempt Special Savings Account (known as 'TESSA') with a bank or building society, if some of it is reinvested in the account (see p. 276).

Pensions and benefits
● war widows' pensions and equivalent overseas pensions

● tax-free lump sum instead of part of a pension (pp. 220 and 223) and some *ex-gratia* lump sums paid on retirement or death

● some social security benefits (p. 185)

● certain compensation payments and pensions paid to victims of Nazi persecution

● wound and disability pensions

● pension paid to a former employee who retires because of a disability due to injury at work or a work-related illness

● allowances and gratuities paid for additional service in the armed forces

● additional pensions paid to holders of some awards for bravery, for example, the Victoria Cross

● rent rebates and council tax rebates

● improvement and renovation grants for your home.

From jobs

● genuine personal gifts from your employer, such as a wedding present

● some fringe benefits (p. 163)

● in special circumstances, earnings from working abroad (p. 188)

● some payments on leaving a job, up to maximum of £30,000 (p. 177). From 16 March 1993, counselling and outplacements services paid for by your employer

● all the pay received under a registered profit-related pay scheme, subject to certain limits (p. 141)

● awards from suggestion schemes available to all employees, within limits. Broadly, up to £25 tax-free can be given for any suggestion. If a suggestion is implemented, an employee can be awarded tax-free up to 50 per cent of the first year's expected net benefit to the employer or up to 10 per cent of the net benefit over five years, with a maximum of £5,000

● travelling /subsistence allowances, if public transport is disrupted

● income paid to an employee attending a full-time course (for example, sandwich course) at college, within certain limits (p. 130)

● expenses (for example, books, fees) paid by employer for attending a job-related course, or a course of general education if under a certain age

● the first 15p a day of luncheon vouchers

● statutory redundancy payments

● miners' free coal or cash allowances instead of the coal

● foreign service allowances paid to servants of the Crown, for example, diplomats

● certain payments from your employer, for reimbursement of tuition expenses, for example

● payments to employees moved to higher-cost housing areas, within certain limits. From 6 April 1993, this tax-free payment will be more limited (p. 143).

Other payments

● gambling profits (if not your business), premium bond prizes, lottery prizes and winnings on the football pools

● income from life insurance policies, such as family income benefit policies and mortgage protection policies

● income from a permanent health insurance policy paid for the first complete tax year, if you paid the premiums for the policy yourself

● what is received under some accident insurance policies (generally group ones)

● interest on a tax rebate

● interest on a delayed settlement for damages for personal injury or death

● scholarships or grants for full-time students (p. 130), but probably not if from the parent's employer (p. 166)

● increase since 1988/89 in maintenance paid under old rules; also an amount equal to the married couple's allowance is tax-free, if paid to an ex-husband or ex-wife

● from 6 April 1992, income from letting out a furnished room in your only or main home if not more than £3,250 a year (the 'rent a room scheme' – see p. 248).

WHOSE INCOME IS TAXED?

Not many escape the income tax system. Even if your child has some income, tax could be payable (although unlikely because your child can claim personal allowances, too). Broadly speaking, the system tries to tax all the income of UK residents no matter where in the world it comes from, but also the income of non-residents if the income comes from the UK. The tax treatment of non-residents is beyond the scope of this Guide and you should take professional advice.

You may also be responsible for paying tax for someone else, for example one partner for another partner who has not paid up, an executor of a will or an agent acting for someone living abroad.

EXAMPLE

During 1994/95, Peter Wong and his wife Elizabeth receive the following bits of money:

PETER:

1 £34,600 salary from his job, including a London weighting allowance, and use of a company car

2 £784 from selling some shares

3 £3,760 from selling part of a collection of antique silver

4 A £100 win on the premium bonds

5 An award of £25 for putting up a good suggestion in his firm's suggestion scheme (even though his idea was not adopted)

6 Interest of £21.46 on British Government stocks bought on the National Savings Stock Register.

ELIZABETH:

1 £8,740 salary from her job, including luncheon vouchers

2 A £2,450 lump sum, part of it pay (including holiday pay) and part of it money in lieu of notice, paid when her firm closes down the department she works for

3 £2,000 of loans to start her own business, half from her bank and half from her granny

4 The lump sum paid out when a ten-year unit-linked life insurance policy comes to an end

5 £54.60 interest on a building society account.

What is income?

Of the money Peter and Elizabeth receive, the following is income:

Salary, London weighting allowance, the award from the suggestion scheme, interest on British Government stocks, luncheon vouchers, holiday pay, money in lieu of notice, income from self-employment and interest from a building society account. The use of the company car also counts as income.

None of the other money received is income (including the prize from the premium bond, which is in any case tax-free).

Which income is tax-free?

The following income received by Peter and Elizabeth is tax-free:

Award from the suggestion scheme, first 15p a day of luncheon vouchers, money in lieu of notice (if £30,000 or less) but not the other income received when Elizabeth left.

HOW IS THE INCOME PAID TO YOU?

To work out what your income is for tax purposes, you need to tot up all the amounts you have received from various different sources. A complication arises here because some income you receive has already had tax deducted (see below); it is called 'net' income. Tax is generally deducted at the basic rate, that is 25 per cent for both 1993/94 and 1994/95. But from 6 April 1993, share dividends and unit trust distributions carry a tax credit of 20 per cent (see p. 269). If you are a higher-rate taxpayer you will have to pay an extra 20 per cent. But if you are a basic-rate taxpayer there is no more tax to pay.

Other income you receive without any tax deducted is called 'gross' income (p. 36). You may have to put both lots of income on the same footing and you do this by turning the 'net' income figure into a 'gross' figure. For income which comes after deduction of tax at 25 per cent, you turn the net income into gross income as follows:

$$\text{net income} \times \frac{100}{75} = \text{gross income}$$

For income which comes with a tax credit of 20 per cent, you turn the net income into gross income as follows:

$$\text{net income} \times \frac{100}{80} = \text{gross income}$$

There are ready reckoners on p. 358 to help you gross-up net income.

EXAMPLE

Wayne Peters has received 'net' interest of £10.55 from a building society account in the 1994/95 tax year. This is paid after tax has been deducted at the basic rate of 25 per cent. To check his tax bill, Wayne needs to know the 'gross' amount. This is:

$$£10.55 \times \frac{100}{75} = £14.07$$

INCOME PAID WITH TAX DEDUCTED: 'NET' INCOME

The following types of income will have had tax deducted before you receive them. With all these types of income there will be no more basic-rate tax to pay. If you pay tax at the higher rate, you will have to pay more tax (though in a couple of cases, higher-rate tax has also been deducted from the income before you receive it). Non-taxpayers can claim back the tax deducted. If you pay tax at the lower rate of 20 per cent only, you may be able to claim a repayment:

● what you earn in your job (any lower-rate and higher-rate tax due is also deducted before you receive it). If you receive taxable fringe benefits, tax on those may be deducted from your earnings

● pension from an employer's pension scheme (any lower-rate and higher-rate tax due also deducted before you receive it)

● interest from an account with a bank, building society, licensed deposit-taker, local authority loan (p. 266). Interest will be paid without deduction of tax to non-taxpayers if you request it on Form R85

● interest from British Government stocks, except for those bought through the post office (through the National Savings Stock Register), or War Loan

● usually income from an annuity – basic-rate tax is deducted from part of the income (p. 268)

● dividends from shares and distributions from unit trusts (pp. 269-272). If paid before 6 April 1993, these come with tax credits of 25 per cent – if you pay tax at the lower rate of 20 per cent only, you can claim a repayment of the difference. Dividends and distributions paid on or after 6 April 1993 come with a tax credit of 20 per cent which covers your tax bill if you pay tax at the lower or basic rate (so lower-rate taxpayers can no longer claim a repayment)

● until 5 April 1994, maintenance paid under the old rules to a child aged 21 or more (sometimes if child aged 18 or more – see p. 120)

● income paid out by an executor before the will is sorted out

● income from a trust – with some trusts basic-rate taxpayers may be able to claim a repayment (see p. 272).

INCOME PAID WITHOUT TAX DEDUCTED: 'GROSS' INCOME

The following types of income will be paid to you without any tax deducted from them, although the income is taxable:

● what you earn as a self-employed person, with some exceptions in the building industry

● what you earn as a partner

● social security benefits like unemployment benefit or income support paid while unemployed or on strike. If you return to work before the end of the tax year, any tax you should have paid will be deducted from your earnings (p. 182)

● the state retirement pension (but if you have other earnings taxed under PAYE, tax on the pension will be deducted from them)

● maintenance payments, unless to a child aged 18 (but less than 21 from 6 April 1994) – p. 120

● interest on British Government stock, if bought at the post office on the National Savings Stock Register, and interest on War Loan, however you buy it

● rent from property you let, unless you are resident abroad in which case your agent or tenant deducts tax before paying (and see rent a room scheme on p. 248)

● interest on some National Savings investments, such as the Investment Account, Income Bonds, Deposit Bonds, Capital Bonds

● interest from an account with a bank, building society, licensed deposit-taker, local authority loan if you are a non-taxpayer and have requested it to be paid without deduction of tax (p. 267).

EXAMPLE

Elizabeth and Peter Wong check which income they receive net and which income gross (see the example on p. 34 for what income they receive).

The following they receive after tax has been deducted:
 Salary, London weighting allowance, holiday pay, interest from a building society account (Elizabeth is a taxpayer). Although tax has obviously not been deducted from the company car and the luncheon vouchers, the tax due has been collected on these from Peter and Elizabeth's salary (p. 149 for how PAYE codes are worked out).

The following income they receive without tax deducted:
 Interest on British Government stocks bought through the National Savings Stock Register, income from self-employment. None of the tax-free income has had tax deducted.

SCHEDULES: HOW THE TAX SYSTEM GROUPS INCOME

One of the more confusing parts of the tax system is the way it divides most types of income up into what are called Schedules. In some cases, the Schedules are divided up further into Cases. These divisions can

SCHEDULES: WHICH INCOME GOES WHERE?

SCHEDULE A	Income from land or property, for example, letting a house. But income from furnished lettings is normally taxed under Schedule D Case I or Case VI. Tax is normally worked out on a current-year basis and is based on the rent due during the tax year, whether you receive it or not. Schedule A income is unearned income. Further details, including the expenses you can claim, are on pp. 249-252.
SCHEDULE B	Abolished – was for commercially managed woodlands.
SCHEDULE C	Interest on British Government stocks (also stock issued by some foreign governments). Schedule C income is unearned income. There are no expenses you can claim.
SCHEDULE D Case I, Case II	Income from a business, trade, profession or vocation. Tax is normally worked out on a preceding-year basis, but can be worked out on a current-year basis. This income is earned income. For details of the expenses you can claim, see p. 196.
SCHEDULE D Case III	Interest, for example, from loans and banks, income from annuities and other regular yearly payments, such as maintenance payments made under the old arrangements. Tax is normally worked out on a preceding-year basis if it is interest, but it can be worked out on a current-year basis (and normally is for maintenance payments). Since 6 April 1991, interest from banks, building societies and other deposit-takers has been taxed under this Case on a current-year basis – it is paid with basic-rate tax deducted, unless you are a non-taxpayer and ask for it to be paid gross. Any higher-rate tax due will be worked out on a current-year basis. Schedule D Case III income is unearned income. There are no expenses you can claim.

seem illogical and bizarre. To understand your tax bill, you do not need to know which income goes into which Schedule, except in the case of losses. So this section of the Guide is mainly for 'keenies'. Nevertheless, it may be helpful to have some idea of what is going on, as the names are sometimes used to describe taxpayers; for instance, a

SCHEDULE D Case IV Case V	Income from abroad, such as interest on foreign securities, rent, trading profits. The income is normally taxed on a preceding-year basis, but can be worked out on a current-year basis. Trading profits are earned income; the rest unearned income. There are no expenses you can claim on the unearned income; for further details of what expenses you can claim against the earned income, see p. 196.
SCHEDULE D Case VI	Odds and ends of income, such as income from occasional freelance work, Enterprise Allowance or its equivalent received from a TEC, income received after you close down a business and income from furnished lettings and furnished holiday lettings (unless it amounts to a business, in which case it comes under Schedule D Case I). Tax is normally worked out on a current-year basis. The income is unearned income, apart from Enterprise Allowance and income received after you close down a business. However, you can set personal pension payments against income from furnished holiday letting, even though it is unearned. For details of the expenses you can claim, see pp. 40, 254.
SCHEDULE E	Earnings from your job. The income is taxed on a current-year basis. For details of the expenses you can claim, see p. 144. There are three Cases, but the vast majority of you come under Case I.
SCHEDULE F	Share dividends and unit trust distributions. The income is taxed on a current-year basis. There are no expenses you can claim. For further details, see pp. 269-272.

Schedule E taxpayer is an employee. And if you get a Notice of Assessment (p. 72), knowing what the Schedules are is useful.

In practice, there are two main differences which still exist in the treatment of income under one Schedule rather than another. First, the tax is due on different dates, although this will change starting in the 1996/97 tax year. Second, you may be allowed to charge up more in expenses against the income from one Schedule rather than another.

EXAMPLE

The income received by Peter and Elizabeth Wong (pp. 34, 37) is all taxed under Schedule E, except the interest on British Government stocks and from the building society account (Schedule D Case III) and income from self-employment (Schedule D Case I).

CASUAL INCOME

The odd bit of freelance or other income from writing an article or doing a bit of dressmaking, for example, can come in handy. For employees it can be an extra bit of work you undertake in the evenings or at weekends. For the housebound it can be fitted in among other family commitments. But knowing how it will be taxed is not straightforward. The income could be taxed as if:

● it is casual income (in tax jargon, this will be taxed under Schedule D Case VI – see p. 39)

● you are self-employed (p. 192)

● you are an employee, where the work is carried out for one business, for example. On p. 211 there are some of the points your Tax Inspector will look for in deciding if you are an employee for that extra bit of income.

HOW CASUAL INCOME IS TAXED

If your Tax Inspector decides your income is casual, your earnings may be taxed on a current-year basis, that is, you will pay tax on your casual income in the same tax year as you receive it. In practice, if you get casual income every year, you may find your Tax Inspector works out your tax bill on what you earned in the previous tax year. If you are also an employee, you may find that tax is collected on this casual income through the PAYE system, that is your PAYE code includes an estimate of your casual income.

Any expenses which you necessarily incurred in getting the income can be deducted before arriving at the figure on which tax will be based. If your tax is not collected through the PAYE system, the tax is due on 1 January of the tax year or 30 days after the assessment is received, if this is later.

If you have made a loss, you can set it only against other income being taxed in the same way (that is, under Schedule D Case VI) in the current or future years. It cannot be set against income from a job, for example.

WHAT YOU MUST DO WHEN YOU RECEIVE CASUAL INCOME

You must tell your Tax Inspector when you start getting this income (within one year of the end of the tax year in which you first receive it). This still applies if you are making a loss rather than a profit. Failing to receive a Tax Return does not absolve you from this duty.

OTHER ODD BITS OF INCOME

There are some other odd bits of income taxed under Schedule D Case VI. These include:

● income from furnished holiday accommodation, which is treated as earned income (p. 254)

● Enterprise Allowance payments, now available from TECs under different titles. These payments are to provide you with some income while starting a business. They are treated as earned income (p. 210)

● income received after you close a business (p. 211)

● income from guaranteeing loans, dealing in futures and some income from underwriting

● certain capital payments from selling UK patent rights.

WHAT TO PUT IN YOUR TAX RETURN

Enter the amount of casual income received and what it is for under *All other income or profits* on page 7 of Forms 11P and 11 and under *All other income* at the bottom of page 2 of Form P1.

42

Form 11P

All other income or profits
Give sources and amounts of any other income etc which is taxable as yours and which you have not entered elsewhere on this form.

£

TREASURE TROVE CLUE No. 1

The amount of interest from a National Savings Ordinary Account that an individual can have tax-free in any year (2 digits).

5 • DEDUCTIONS

You do not have to pay income tax on all the income you have. You can get tax relief for a number of payments you make, called deductions in the 1994/95 Tax Returns (they used to be called 'outgoings'). Deductions reduce the amount of income you pay tax on. And they may also reduce the rate of tax you pay on some of your income from the higher rate of 40 per cent to the basic rate of 25 per cent or from the basic rate to the lower rate of 20 per cent. This chapter gives a checklist of the main deductions you can claim; the details are elsewhere in the Guide.

Tax relief is not given in the same way for all deductions. This chapter tells you briefly how to claim the tax relief you are entitled to. The main ways you can get your tax relief are:

● making lower payments (for example, the MIRAS system for mortgages), although this is being phased out gradually

● when your Tax Inspector works out your tax bill after the tax year in a Notice of Assessment (the form which is filled in showing the calculations)

● your Tax Inspector gives you a higher PAYE code so that less tax is deducted from your earnings.

There's a checklist of the main deductions overleaf, with details of where you can find further information.

CHECKLIST OF MAIN DEDUCTIONS FOR 1993/94 AND 1994/95

OUTGOING	HOW YOU GET TAX RELIEF	DETAILS
pension contributions	given by employer through PAYE system. The amount is deducted from your earnings before income tax is worked out	p. 221
personal pension payments (but not retirement annuities – see p. 230)	Self-employed: get tax relief through a lower tax bill after the end of the tax year. Employees: get tax relief by making lower payments to pension providers and any higher-rate tax relief through a lower tax bill after the tax year	p. 224
mortgage interest (on a loan used to buy a home occupied by you)	you make lower payments to the lender, that is, through the MIRAS system. There is no higher-rate relief, unless the mortgage is on a home you let. For home improvement loans, see p. 239. The relief is lowered to 20 per cent from 6 April 1994 and 15 per cent from 6 April 1995	p. 235
job expenses	either through a higher PAYE code or in a lower tax bill after the tax year	p. 147
some payments for training	making lower payments for study and examination fees. Any higher-rate relief through a higher PAYE code or in a lower tax bill after the tax year	p. 146
payments under a home income scheme	either by making lower payments to the lender (that is, through the MIRAS system) or by telling your Tax Inspector who will give you a higher PAYE code or give the tax relief in a lower tax bill after the tax year.	p. 134

covenant payments to a charity	making lower payments, that is, you deduct and keep basic-rate tax, giving yourself tax relief. Any higher-rate tax relief is given either through a higher PAYE code or by a lower tax bill after the tax year	p. 290
maintenance payments	either through a higher PAYE code or in a lower tax bill after the tax year	p. 115 p. 117
mortgage interest on a home you let	you get tax relief against the rental income normally by a lower tax bill after the tax year	p. 253
interest on loan to pay inheritance tax	you get tax relief either through a higher PAYE code or by a lower tax bill after the tax year	p. 340
investments in Business Expansion or Enterprise Investment Scheme	get tax certificate from the company to send to your Tax Inspector, who gives you tax relief either through a higher PAYE code or by a lower tax bill after the tax year	p. 277
single gifts to a charity (Gift Aid)	making lower payments, that is, deduct and keep basic-rate tax, giving yourself tax relief. Any higher-rate relief through a higher PAYE code or in a lower tax bill after the tax year	p. 297
private medical insurance for people aged 60 or over	making lower payments to insurance companies – that is, you deduct and keep basic-rate tax, giving yourself tax relief. No higher-rate relief is availaable after 6 April 1994	p. 137
interest on some business loans	tell your Tax Inspector; you get tax relief either through a higher PAYE code or by a lower tax bill after the tax year.	overleaf and p. 217

You can get tax relief for interest paid on various loans, of any size, taken out for business purposes, for example:

● buying a share of or putting capital into a partnership (but not if you are a limited partner)

● buying plant or machinery for use in your business (or your job if an employee)

● buying shares in a close company (but not for shares issued on or after 14 March 1989 that would also qualify for tax relief under the Business Expansion Scheme, which ended for new investment on 31 December 1993).

EXAMPLE

Charlie Barnard decides to make a lump sum payment of £1,000 into a personal pension scheme. Charlie pays tax at a rate of 40 per cent so he saves £40 of tax for each £100 of pension payment. His £1,000 payment actually costs Charlie £600.

FORGOTTEN TO CLAIM A DEDUCTION?

You can go back six years to check your tax bills and have them put right. So, if you have forgotten to claim some deduction for the last six years, do so now and get a tax rebate. If you have paid too much tax in any year, your Tax Inspector will work out the bill for that year again, but using the tax rates and rules which applied for that year, not the current ones.

Going back six years means that, for example, before 6 April 1995 you can claim relief for a deduction as far back as the 1988/89 tax year.

WHAT TO PUT IN YOUR TAX RETURN

Turn to the appropriate pages in this Guide for most deductions to find out what to put in the Tax Return. Husband and wife each claim their own deductions, or share of them, on their own Tax Return.

With interest on business loans which qualify for tax relief, you can claim the relief on page 8 of Forms 11 and 11P under *Other qualifying loans* and on page 3 of Form P1 under *Other loans qualifying for tax relief*. Put the lender's name, the purpose of the loan and the amount of interest you paid in the tax year. Enclose a certificate of loan interest paid, which you should be able to get from your lender.

Form 11P

Notes

For details of loans on which you can claim tax relief see note 40. For details on loans to buy or improve rental property see notes 24 and 25. If you have more than one qualifying loan, give details on a separate sheet of paper.

Other qualifying loans

Complete this form if you can claim tax relief on other loans. Only give details of loans not included elsewhere on this form. Enclose a certificate of interest paid from your lender. Do not include loans on your main home.

Name of lender

Purpose of loan

Give the address of the property if the loan is for the purchase or improvement of property used for letting

The number of weeks let

Amount of gross interest paid in the 1993-94 tax year £

If you pay property rents or interest to someone who normally lives outside the UK, you have to tell your Tax Inspector about it under *Payments abroad* on page 10 of Forms 11P and 11 and page 3 of Form P1. Before you pay rent or interest of this type, you have to deduct basic-rate tax which you pay to the Inland Revenue. But in the tax returns you have to give the gross amount of any rent or interest you paid in 1993/94. In Forms 11P and 11, there is a box to tick if you would like details of how much tax you should deduct. If you received Form P1 and need help with this ask your Tax Inspector.

Form 11P

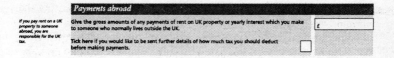

Payments abroad

If you pay rent on a UK property to someone abroad, you are responsible for the UK tax.

Give the gross amounts of any payments of rent on UK property or yearly interest which you make to someone who normally lives outside the UK. £

Tick here if you would like to be sent further details of how much tax you should deduct before making payments.

If you are following a training course leading to a National or Scottish Vocational Qualification you may be able to claim tax relief, see p. 146. You can claim tax relief on Forms 11 and 11P under *Vocational training* on page 10. Enter the name of the training organisation and the actual amount you paid for tuition fees, that is after deduction of basic rate tax. There is no space for this on Form P1, but attach details to let your tax inspector know.

48

Form 11P

Vocational training

Name of training organisation

Net amount paid in 1993-94 for training that qualifies for tax relief.

£

6 • ALLOWANCES

You may not all have deductions from your income and thus be able to reduce your tax bill that way. But nearly everybody with an income is entitled to at least one allowance, ensuring some tax-free pay.

CHECKLIST OF ALLOWANCES FOR 1993/94 AND 1994/95 TAX YEARS

ALLOWANCE	1993/94	1994/95	DETAILS
	£	£	
personal (under 65)	3,445	3,445	p. 100
personal (65–74)	4,200	4,200	p. 135
personal (75 plus)	4,370	4,370	p. 135
married couple's (under 65)*	1,720	1,720	p. 105
married couple's (65–74)	2,465	2,665	p. 135
married couple's (75 plus)	2,505	2,705	p. 135
additional personal*	1,720	1,720	p. 100
widow's bereavement *	1,720	1,720	p.124
blind person's	1,080	1,200	overleaf
income limit for age-related allowance	14,200	14,200	p. 136

* From 6 April 1994, you only get tax relief at 20 per cent on these allowances.

BLIND PERSON'S ALLOWANCE

Anyone registered as blind with a local authority can claim blind person's allowance. A registered blind person must be unable to perform any work for which eyesight is essential. No allowance is due for the partially sighted.

If your income is less than your allowances, including blind person's, and you are married and living with your husband or wife, you can transfer the unused part of this allowance to your partner. If both of you are blind, you can claim two allowances.

EXAMPLE

Alexander Groom has an income of £5,400; he automatically gets the personal allowance for under 65. The income tax he pays for 1994/95 is:

Income	£5,400
less personal allowance	£3,445
Taxable income	£1,955
Tax at lower rate (20%)	£391

But Alexander realizes that as a registered blind person he can also claim the blind person's allowance of £1,200. This reduces his taxable income to £755. Tax at the lower rate (20 per cent) is £151, a reduction of £240. So Alexander has saved tax of that amount.

FORGOTTEN TO CLAIM AN ALLOWANCE

You can go back over the last six years to 1988/89 to claim allowances, just as you can with deductions. The details are on p. 46. You will be able to claim the allowances which applied for the year you missed them, not the current one.

WHAT TO PUT IN YOUR TAX RETURN

For how to claim most allowances, turn to the pages listed in the Checklist on p. 49; the information is at the end of each chapter.

If you want to claim blind person's allowance, tick the box on the last page of the Tax Return. And if you live in England or Wales put the name of the local authority you are registered with and the date it was done. In Scotland or Northern Ireland there is no register and to claim the allowance you must be unable to perform any work for which eyesight is essential.

Form 11P

Note 62 has details.

Blind person's allowance

Tick here to claim the allowance.

Give the name of the Local Authority or equivalent body with which you have registered your blindness.

Give the date you registered | / | /19

If you cannot use up all your blind person's allowance, you can transfer the unused bit to your husband or wife (provided you live together at any time in the 1994/95 tax year) by filling in Notice of Transfer of Surplus Allowances Form 575. Do this even if you have already transferred allowances.

A copy of Form 575 may have been sent to you with the Tax Return. If not, put a cross in the *Transfer of Surplus Allowances* box on page 4 of Form P1 or page 11 of Forms 11P or 11.

Form 11P

Transfer of surplus allowances to your wife or husband

Ask your Tax Office for A Guide for Married Couples (leaflet IR80). See note 62 for blind person's allowance

To transfer any surplus allowances you must have been married and living with your wife or husband at any time in 1994-95. If you did not have enough income tax liability to use all (or any) of your married couple's allowance then you may transfer the surplus to your wife or husband.

Tick here if you need a transfer notice form.

If you have insufficient income to use all (or any) blind person's allowance you are entitled to then you may transfer any surplus to your wife or husband. If you are a husband who does not have sufficient income to use his personal allowance in some circumstances your wife may receive transitional allowance.

7 • TAX CHANGES FOR 1994/95

The November budget was the first to take place at the same time as decisions were made by the government on public spending. While, at first glance, the Budget appeared not to have raised taxes significantly, because basic and higher rates of taxes were left unchanged, a closer look made clear that the level of taxation had increased. For example, the allowances were left unchanged and not index-linked.

INCOME TAX RATES

The lower rate tax band has been increased to the first £3,000 of taxable income for 1994/95. The level of taxable income at which you will pay higher-rate tax remains the same and has not been increased in line with inflation.

ALLOWANCES

Personal tax allowances will remain the same as for 1993/94.

As from 6 April 1994, you will get tax relief for married couple's allowance (and other linked allowances, additional personal, widow's bereavement and maintenance payments) only at the lower rate of 20 per cent. From 6 April 1995, this will be cut again to 15 per cent. However, the married couple's allowance for couples aged 65 and over has been increased by £200 for 1994/95 and £330 for 1995/96. And the blind person's allowance has been put up by £120 to £1,300 for the 1994/95 tax year.

DEDUCTIONS

There is still no tax deduction for childcare, although there is a social security allowance of £28 per week to help only those on family credit with childcare costs.

Tax relief on vocational training has been extended to include National Vocational Qualifications and Scottish Vocational Qualifications up to level 5 (previously level 4). However, the relief has been withdrawn from chldren under 16, those aged 16 to 18 and in full-time education at school or training undertaken wholly or mainly for recreation or leisure.

The tax relief on private medical insurance for the over-60s has been limited to 25 per cent (was previously available at 40 per cent) from 6 April 1994.

FRINGE BENEFITS

From 1994/95 the use of company cars will be generally taxed at the rate of 35 per cent on the list price of the car, with discounts for high business mileage. If you receive free car fuel from your employer, the taxable benefit for this has risen by 6 per cent from 1994/95.

The existing treatment for cheap or free loans provided by employers as a fringe benefit has been replaced by making the first £5,000 of loans a tax-free benefit from 6 April 1994.

NEW TAXES

From October 1994 you will pay a departure tax of £5 when you fly from the UK to Europe, and £10 to other destinations. You will also have to pay tax of 3 per cent on insurance premiums, for example household and motor.

BUSINESSES

Entrepreneurs once again will benefit from further help when they sell a business on retirement. The limits for relief on gains you make when you sell a business on retirement were raised from 30 November 1993. You can now get full relief on the first £250,000 of gains and half the gain between £250,000 and £1,000,000.

The Chancellor also broadened the relief introduced in the early 1993 Budget to encourage those who sell shares in unquoted companies to reinvest them in other qualifying unquoted ones. Originally, any capital gains tax could be deferred only if entrepreneurs were selling their own company and reinvesting. The November budget has now allowed any individual and most trustees to benefit from this relief.

The Chancellor also had a couple of proposals to encourage funding for unquoted trading companies. The Enterprise Investment Scheme replaces the Business Expansion Scheme and gives tax relief at 20 per cent on investments of up to £100,000 in any tax year. And a consultation paper will be issued on a new scheme for venture capital trusts.

The VAT threshold has been raised to a level of £45,000 sales. Employers will have to pay less National Insurance contributions for their employees.

INVESTMENTS, INSURANCE AND PENSIONS

The budget introduced a Guaranteed Income Bond for pensioners, which is a five-year fixed rate investment which will pay a gross monthly income. This is of course an advantage for non-taxpayers.

The pension scheme earnings cap has been increased from £75,000 to £76,800. If you pay the premiums yourself for a permanent health insurance policy (which pays out an income if you are too ill to work), the income will now be free of income tax for twelve months only. Prevously the tax-free period varied between one and two years depending on when the income began to be paid.

CAPITAL GAINS AND INHERITANCE TAX

The threshold for inheritance tax is unchanged at £150,000. The yearly tax-free slice for capital gains has not changed at £5,800 for 1994/95. And the Chancellor is stopping the arrangement which allowed you to turn an apparent capital gain into a loss by applying indexation relief.

MORTGAGE INTEREST

From 6 April 1994, the tax relief on mortgage interest will be restricted to 20 per cent. This will be further reduced to 15 per cent from 5 April 1995.

LOOKING AHEAD

For the 1995/96 tax year there will be changes in the way the self-employed are taxed, switching from a preceding year basis to a current year basis. And there will be a move towards self-assessment of tax for the self-employed and other taxpayers who fill in a tax return every year.

8 • YOUR TAX INSPECTOR

The person with responsibility for assessing how much tax you should pay is your Tax Inspector. He or she is the local representative of the Inland Revenue, the government organization with responsibility for collecting direct taxes in the UK. With over 30 million customers on its books, the Inland Revenue is the largest financial services organization in the UK, employing more than 60,000 civil servants to collect over £76bn in tax each year.

But what sort of organization is the Inland Revenue and how will it relate to you as a taxpayer? When should *you* get in touch with your Tax Inspector and how do you find out whom to contact?

THE INLAND REVENUE

The Inland Revenue at Somerset House in London is responsible for assessing and collecting income tax, capital gains tax, inheritance tax, stamp duty, corporation tax and various petroleum royalties and taxes.

The Inland Revenue has preserved aspects of its organization in its income tax work which date back almost 200 years. In particular, the collection of income tax has been separate from the assessment of how much you should pay. Tax on different types of income is assessed under various schedules, with different rules for when the tax is due and what income it was based on (see p. 38). And the tax on various types of income might be assessed by different tax offices (see p. 59).

In addition, most taxpayers have had to do very little work in connection with their own tax bill. The Pay As You Earn system for employees allows the Inland Revenue to collect more or less the right amount of tax direct from their earnings. In many other countries, taxpayers have to work out their own tax bill and ensure that the right amount is paid each year (this is known as self-assessment).

All of this is changing, however, with a far-reaching reorganization of the way that the Inland Revenue approaches its work. These will make life simpler for the taxpayer by eliminating the various tax schedules and providing all taxpayers with a single tax bill and a single tax office to deal with. However, some taxpayers will be encouraged to take a greater responsibility for working out their own tax bills. From the 1996/97 tax year onwards, there will be a move towards self-assessment for the self-employed and taxpayers who fill in a tax return every year.

Making these changes will take several years, though offices are already being reorganized in some parts of the country – see opposite. Below are details of the traditional shape of the Inland Revenue's income tax office network.

INSPECTORS OF TAXES

The point of contact for most taxpayers is one or more of over 500 tax offices which cover most of the country and are responsible for assessing how much taxpayers should pay and liaising with them. Each tax office (or district) is headed by a District Inspector who is your Inspector of Taxes, with a team of Inspectors, most of whom specialize in either PAYE taxpayers or the self-employed. Next in order of seniority are Revenue Executives who manage the day-to-day work of the district and deal with routine cases. They are assisted by Tax Officers, and there will be a number of Revenue Assistants to send out Tax Returns, process assessments, file papers and so on.

Most tax districts in England, Wales and Northern Ireland deal with the tax affairs of both employees (that is PAYE taxpayers) and the self-employed, though different groups of staff deal with each type of work. But the tax affairs of London PAYE taxpayers are dealt with mostly by special London Provincial (LP) offices located in areas like Scotland and the North where it is easier to recruit staff. PAYE in Scotland is dealt with at the giant Centre 1 office in East Kilbride. Civil servants and members of the armed forces are dealt with by the Public Departments (PD) office at Llanishen, near Cardiff. And work on trusts is concentrated in just 50 districts.

The assessment of income tax is now done entirely by computer: eleven giant regional computer centres store taxpayers' records under conditions of strict security to keep the information confidential. Taxpayers continue to deal with their tax district, where the staff have Visual Display Unit (VDU) terminals to call up the information stored in the regional computers.

COLLECTORS OF TAXES

Tax districts are responsible for assessing your tax bill, that is, working out exactly how much you should pay. The collection of tax is handled by a separate section of the Inland Revenue known as Collectors of Taxes.

There are over 100 collectors' offices across the UK, but most tax has to be sent to the two large computerized Accounts Offices at Shipley in West Yorkshire and Cumbernauld in Scotland. If you fail to pay tax which is owed to an accounts office, you will be approached by your local Collector of Taxes, who will, if necessary, take you to court to get the money.

THE CHANGING STRUCTURE OF THE INLAND REVENUE

Over the next few years, the Inland Revenue will make fundamental changes in the way it collects income tax. These will take advantage of the new opportunities offered by computerization to merge the assessment and collection of tax, and to provide a single point of contact for taxpayers. They will also help to introduce a simplified system of tax assessing which will allow many taxpayers to work out their own tax bills.

The aim of the programme of changes will be to bring together income tax activities in a single office for most taxpayers. Your Taxpayer Service Office will send out your Tax Return, process it when you send it back and issue your PAYE code. In most cases, it will be the only tax office you need to deal with. Specialist Taxpayer District Offices will check that employers operate the PAYE system properly and chase up non-payers and tax evaders. A network of high-street Taxpayer Enquiry Centres will provide a face to face service, where taxpayers can talk to tax staff who will be able to call up their records on computer screens and deal with queries.

These new arrangements will take to the end of the century to complete. But they are already under way in 33 towns and cities, replacing the old tax districts and collectors of taxes. The first step has been to reorganize the Inland Revenue into some 30 Executive Offices, more manageable units each of which is headed by a Controller. Some of these Executive Offices are specialist units, such as the Oil Taxation Office and the Pension Schemes Office. But all the Inland Revenue's local offices are now part of 14 regional Executive Offices, so that, for example, all the local offices in Scotland are managed by a Controller based in Edinburgh.

THE INLAND REVENUE'S SPECIALIST OFFICES

There are specialist Inland Revenue offices dealing with particular taxes or aspects of taxes. Among those you might come into contact with are:

● the five specialist claims offices, which handle the repayment of tax deducted from interest and tax credits that come with share dividends – these are in Belfast, Bootle, Glenrothes, Leicester and St Austell

● the Inspector of Foreign Dividends at Thames Ditton in Surrey which specializes in investment income from abroad

● the Claims Branch at Bootle which deals with rebates for non-residents, queries over covenants and repayments of tax to charities, among other matters

● the three Capital Taxes Offices for inheritance tax (see p. 345)

● the ten Stamp Offices for the collection of stamp duty.

THE TAXPAYER'S CHARTER

In July 1991, the Prime Minister launched his Citizen's Charter, designed to help the ordinary citizen get better service out of the government, the health service and other public services. A Taxpayer's Charter sets out the standards of service taxpayers are entitled to expect from the Inland Revenue:

● prompt replies to letters – in the 1993/94 tax year, the target was to answer 93 per cent of letters within 28 days

● if a query cannot be answered within the deadline, you should be told when the reply will come

● Inland Revenue forms have been redesigned to make them easier to understand and complete

● every Inland Revenue Executive Office has appointed a customer service manager to deal with complaints.

A copy of the Charter is on the front of the Notes sent out with every Tax Return.

THE REVENUE ADJUDICATOR

The independent Revenue Adjudicator looks into complaints about the way the Inland Revenue handles tax affairs. The Adjudicator's remit covers matters such as excessive delay, errors, discourtesy or the way your Tax Inspector has exercised his or her discretion. However, complaints about the amount of your tax bill must be dealt with through the normal appeals procedure – see Chapter 11, p. 92.

The Adjudicator can look at any complaints arising from events after 5 April 1993. However, you should first take up your complaint with the tax office you are dealing with. If you are not satisfied with the response, then complain to the Controller in charge of the tax office (get the address from the tax office). If you are still dissatisfied, then ask for the case to be referred to the Adjudicator.

CONTACTING YOUR TAX INSPECTOR

You must tell your Tax Inspector if any of the following applies:

● you have a new source of income (for example, you start up as self-employed or start letting out your weekend cottage) or you make a taxable capital gain

● you are getting a tax allowance and are no longer entitled to it (for example, if the child for whom you are getting additional personal allowance leaves home).

You should also contact your Tax Inspector promptly if you have overpaid tax or are entitled to a new tax relief or allowance. If you delay, you could lose tax relief: the deadlines for claiming various allowances and reliefs are given on p. 26.

WHICH TAX OFFICE?

Before you can contact your Tax Inspector, you will have to find out which office deals with your tax affairs. This depends on the type of income you get, and you may find that you have to deal with more than one tax office. The following are the general rules:

● *employees:* normally your tax office will be the one which looks after the tax affairs of everyone working for your employer. In most cases, this will be an office near your place of work, but people in London may have to use one of the London Provincial (LP) offices well away from the capital, while Scots must communicate with Centre 1 (see p. 56). If you change employer, you may also change tax office

● *civil servants and armed forces:* Public Departments office near Cardiff (see p. 56)

● *self-employed:* your tax office will generally be near where you work (near where you live, if you work from home)

● *property income:* may be dealt with by a tax office near where the property is

● *pensioners:* if you get a pension from your former employer, a tax office near where the pension fund is administered may deal with your tax affairs (ex-civil servants and military pensioners continue to be assessed by Public Departments office in Cardiff)

● *unemployed:* the tax office of your last employer.

If in doubt about your tax office, ask your employer (your employer's pension administrators if you are retired). Otherwise, approach the tax office nearest home: you can find the address in the phone book under INLAND REVENUE.

COMMUNICATING WITH YOUR TAX INSPECTOR

You can write to or telephone your tax office, but it's probably better to write in the first place, if only to save your phone bill. Address your letter to HM Inspector of Taxes, even if you've already spoken to someone else. Always quote your reference number, if possible: you'll find it on any previous correspondence with the tax office; with a new job, your employer will tell you the reference (it's the same for all his or her employees). If you work for an employer, giving your National Insurance number will help – it's the key to your records in the computerized PAYE system.

Keep a copy of whatever you write (and of your Tax Return when you send one in). Under the Taxpayer's Charter, you should receive a reply within a month (see p. 58). If you haven't heard after a month, a follow-up telephone call might help – have your reference number ready to quote. If this is unsatisfactory, write to the Controller responsible for your tax office (the tax office will give you the name and address). If all else fails, you can complain about delays to the independent Revenue Adjudicator (p. 58).

Whatever the reason for getting in touch with your Tax Inspector, the most likely response will be to send you a Tax Return (see p. 65 for the different types). This should be completed and returned within 30 days. If you need longer, write and explain the delay.

Putting in a personal appearance may speed up communications, especially if it is a simple query which can be easily cleared up. If your tax office isn't close to home, you can arrange to discuss your tax affairs at a nearby office (they'll send for your papers, if needed). In London there are special PAYE Enquiry Offices which can liaise with the distant London Provincial offices. Lastly, you may be able to discuss your tax affairs with Inland Revenue staff in your local shopping centre when the mobile Inland Revenue enquiry centre pays a visit.

HOW YOUR TAX BILL IS WORKED OUT

When you return a completed Tax Return, it will be compared with previous returns you have sent in. The Tax Inspector will also match up what you have written with information supplied by people and organizations about payments made to you.

For example, banks, building societies and other savings organizations must tell the Inland Revenue if they pay you interest. Companies and unit trusts provide lists of dividend payments and distributions. And details of fees, commission, royalties and other payments made to you by businesses are also supplied to the Inland Revenue.

If your Tax Inspector thinks that you haven't come clean (or wants further information), you will get further letters to reply to. For details of how an investigation is carried out if the Inspector thinks you haven't told the whole truth, see p. 96.

Once your Tax Inspector is satisfied that he or she has all the information necessary, your tax bill is worked out. Many taxpayers with simple tax affairs will have paid more or less the right amount of tax on their earnings through PAYE (see p. 148). And since tax is deducted from a lot of investment income before it is paid to you, there is no further tax to pay unless you are a higher-rate taxpayer. But if there is still tax to pay, or you have paid too much tax and are entitled to a rebate, this should emerge from the assessment process.

If you have not paid the right amount of tax, your Tax Inspector is likely to issue you with a Notice of Assessment. This sets out your income, deductions and allowances, and explains how your tax bill is calculated (for how to check Notice of Assessment, see p. 73). A Notice of Assessment will also be issued if you ask for one: do this if there's something you don't understand about your tax bill.

APPEALING AGAINST AN ASSESSMENT

Whether or not you're issued with a Notice of Assessment, you can appeal against your tax bill (or any other decision by your Tax Inspector). An appeal must be made in writing within 30 days of the date of issue of a Notice of Assessment or the decision in question. After the 30-day deadline, you will be able to appeal only if you can convince your Tax Inspector that there was a good reason for the delay (for example, you were away on holiday or had moved house) or that something has happened which makes you think you have paid too much tax (for example, working through your accounts has thrown up an error).

The tax due on a Notice of Assessment must be paid even if you are appealing against the assessment, unless you also ask for a postponement of payment. The Tax Inspector is likely to agree to postpone only the amount of tax which is in dispute: for example, if the bill is £5,000 and you think it should be £3,000, £2,000 can be postponed. If you cannot agree on the amount of tax to be postponed, you can appeal to the General Commissioners (p. 92).

The tax which has not been postponed must be paid within 30 days of the postponement agreement. Once the appeal is settled, a revised assessment will be issued and any further tax which is due must be paid within 30 days of the date on this (or the date the original tax was due, if this is later). And interest will be charged on any tax which has to be paid after the appeal is decided (see opposite).

If you don't appeal against an incorrect assessment within the 30-day time limit, you won't be able to correct your tax bill later – unless you can show that something has happened to make you realize that it was wrong. So always check a Notice of Assessment quickly and put in an appeal if you are at all sceptical about its correctness. If you want to postpone payment of the tax, apply for postponement at the same time as you appeal against the assessment, within the same 30-day time limit.

ESTIMATED ASSESSMENTS

A Notice of Assessment can be issued with an estimate of your income, marked *E*, if your Tax Inspector does not have the actual figure. This will often happen because you have not replied to letters asking for information: the Inspector can use whatever assumptions he or she finds reasonable (for example, your previous income, typical income figures for people in your line of business). And Schedule A property income is usually assessed on an estimated basis, since tax bills are issued before the end of the tax year (p. 255).

You can appeal against an estimated assessment as for any other Notice of Assessment, but you will have to prove that the estimate is wrong. Issuing an estimated assessment is often a useful way of getting reluctant taxpayers to come up with the figures, and if you get one, be sure to get the appeal in quickly. You won't be able to overturn the assessment otherwise, even if the estimate is wildly exaggerated.

INTEREST ON OVERDUE TAX

If you don't pay a tax bill on time, you can be charged interest on the unpaid amount. The rate is currently 5½ per cent a year.

If you appeal against a Notice of Assessment, you have to pay the tax which has not been postponed: interest will be charged if you pay this late. And when the appeal is settled, any remaining tax must be paid within a set time (see opposite). Interest must also be paid on this, usually running from six months after the tax would have been due if there had been no appeal. Note that if the appeal ends up with your having to pay more tax than was originally assessed, you have to pay interest on the whole amount, including the bit that was not assessed in the first place.

You may also have to pay interest on tax if it is paid late because you didn't tell your Tax Inspector something which would have increased your liability (p. 59). And interest can be charged if you delay in returning a Tax Return until after 31 October following the end of the tax year for which it asks details of income.

PAYMENT OF TAX IN INSTALMENTS

If you get a large tax bill which you cannot afford to settle, you can ask the Collector of Taxes to let you pay by instalments. You will have to show that hardship would be involved in paying in one go. And interest will probably have to be paid on the tax paid late.

9 • THE FORMS

In most cases your main means of communication with your Tax Inspector will be through pre-printed forms, of which the Tax Return is the most important. The Tax Return forms have been redesigned to make them easier to fill in, though it remains a chore to complete one. And if you receive a Notice of Assessment, it is essential you check it through – and fast. This chapter looks at these two forms and how to tackle them.

THE TAX RETURN

The Tax Return asks for details of your income, deductions and capital gains for the last complete tax year and for the allowances you wish to claim for the next tax year. So the 1994/95 Tax Return, which was sent out from April 1994 onwards, asks about:

● income, deductions and capital gains for the 1993/94 tax year (ending on 5 April 1994)

● allowances for the 1994/95 tax year (beginning on 6 April 1994).

The 1995/96 Tax Return will be going out from April 1995 onwards and covers income and deductions for the 1994/95 tax year and allowances for the 1995/96 tax year.

In theory, your Tax Inspector could ask you to fill in a Tax Return every year (many taxpayers are asked to do just that). But people with relatively simple tax affairs may have to fill in a Tax Return much less frequently – many people get a Return only once every five or ten years.

If a Tax Return does land on your doormat, complete it and send it back within 30 days of the date of issue. If you're held up for any reason, write and ask for an extension. Interest can be charged if you are late sending back a Tax Return (see p. 63).

WHICH TAX RETURN?

There are several different types of Tax Return, of which the commonest are:

● *Form P1* – the simplest Return, issued to most employees who pay tax at the basic rate only and whose tax affairs are fairly straightforward

● *Form 11P* – sent to employees with more complicated tax affairs (for example, if they get substantial fringe benefits or pay tax at the higher rate)

● *Form 11* – for the self-employed, including partners in a partnership (the partnership also gets *Form 1* to give details of the partners' income as a whole).

To find out which you've been sent, check the number at the bottom left-hand corner of the first page.

Note that married couples each get their own Tax Return. Each must fill in details of his or her income and deductions and claim his or her own allowances – there is no requirement to give details on behalf of a spouse. With income from a joint account or joint holding, the Inland Revenue will assume that it is split 50:50 between the couple unless you both complete a special declaration setting out the actual ownership of joint assets (see p. 263). And with jointly incurred deductions such as mortgage interest, this will also be split 50:50 unless you both opt for a different split (see p. 263).

WHAT TO PUT IN YOUR TAX RETURN

The Tax Return is designed to provide space to enter details of most types of income. This means that you could find that there are large parts of the Return which do not apply to you. If your only sources of income are your job and a savings account, you will need to do little more than enter details of both and sign the Return (remembering to claim any allowances you might be eligible for). But if you have a number of different types of savings accounts and investments, there could be several entries to make on the Return. You may have to search out a variety of documents to fill in the details or send off with the Return (see the Checklist on p. 71). And all of this can be a time-consuming exercise.

At the end of each chapter in this Guide, there are details of what to enter in the Tax Return about your income, outgoings and capital gains and how to claim your allowances. The relevant section of Form 11P is illustrated, since it's the form you're most likely to get if your tax affairs are complicated (Form 11 is very similar in layout). What to put if you get the other Forms is also explained. Use the illustration of Form P1 on the following pages to find the information you need to complete your Return: the relevant page number is given against each heading.

When entering details of income or deductions, you can round sums of money down to the nearest whole pound (except for share dividends, unit trust distributions and tax credits). You don't need to write anything in spaces for types of income, deductions and allowances which don't apply to you. If there is insufficient room under any heading to give full details, set them out on a separate sheet of paper with the same headings as the section of the Tax Return and write 'See attached schedule' on the Return. If there are several schedules, number them.

You do not need to enter details of genuine gifts, unless made under deed of covenant (p. 299), and certain other forms of exempt income such as student grants, adoption allowances and many social security benefits. But if in doubt, give details of the income and ask your Tax Inspector for guidance.

If you've got a source of income and can't figure out where it should go on the Tax Return (or are fairly sure that it doesn't fit in under any of the headings), enter details under *All other income or profits* on page 7 of Forms 11P and 11 and *All other income* on page 2 of Form P1.

Form 11P

maintenance payments" (IR93). See note 37.	**All other income or profits** Give sources and amounts of any other income etc which is taxable as yours and which you have not entered elsewhere on this form.	£

TREASURE TROVE CLUE No. 2

The amount of the married couple's allowance for under-65s (4 digits).

Form P1

Inland Revenue

1994 Tax Return

H M Inspector of Taxes	Date of issue	Tax reference	National Insurance number

Tax Office address

What you must do with this form

You are required by law to fill in this form, sign the declaration on page 4 and send the form, and any documents asked for, back to me within 30 days.

If you don't and there is no good reason for sending this form in late, you may have to pay a penalty. You may also have to pay interest on any tax paid late because this form was not sent back in time.

However the Inland Revenue will not seek interest simply because of delay provided that the return is sent back by 31 October 1994 (or within 30 days of issue if it was sent to you after 2 October 1994). For further information please refer to the introduction in the enclosed leaflet *'Filling in your 1994 Tax Return'*, which you should use in completing this form.

What details should you give ?

You only need to fill in the sections which apply to you.

Give amounts in the Income and Deductions column and details as requested in the Details column. You may use as much of the space as you need for each item. Use a separate sheet of paper if you need more room.

You should show all the income and capital gains on which you may be charged to tax. Give details for the tax year which started on 6 April 1993 and ended on 5 April 1994 (1993-94) unless the form asks for something different.

You can also use this form to claim expenses and deductions for 1993-94 and personal allowances for the tax year which started on 6 April 1994 and ends on 5 April 1995 (1994-95).

If there is not enough space for your entries please give details on a separate sheet of paper.

Do you need help ?

If you need help please contact your Tax Office. The address and telephone number are shown above. You will need to quote your tax reference - *see above*.

Notes

Earnings etc 1993-94

		Income and (deductions)	Details

See note 1
See the form P60 from your employer and note 2

p. 158

Wages, salary, fees or bonuses etc
Give your occupation and most recent employer's name and address.

£ _____

See note 3.

pp. 158, 159

Casual earnings, tips, expense allowances
Give type of work and employer's name(s).

£ _____

See note 4. Do not include expenses from self-employment

p. 159

Employment expenses for which you wish to claim
Give type of expenses you wish to claim for.

(£ _____)

See note 5.

p. 179

Lump sum and compensation payments not included above

£ _____

pp. 160, 176

Approved profit sharing schemes
Tick if you received a taxed sum. Give scheme name.

See note 6.

p. 175

Benefits in kind
Tick if you receive any and state what they are.
Give taxable values if you know them.

£ _____

See note 7.

pp. 212, 258

Income from self-employment

Turnover   Allowable expenses

£ _____   (£ _____)

Profit (This is your turnover less allowable expenses)

£ _____

You may be able to claim a deduction. See note 8.

p. 191

Work abroad
Tick here if you were abroad for all or nearly all of a 365-day period beginning or ending during 1993-94 and you worked during that period.

See note 9. Do not claim relief already given.

p. 232

Trade union or friendly society death benefit and superannuation schemes
Give amount relating to death or superannuation benefits and name of trade union or friendly society.

(£ _____)

P1 (1994)

Form P1, continued

Notes		

Pensions and benefits for 1993-94

		Income	Details
p. 126	see note 10 for what counts as a State pension and other details.	Amount of State pension you were entitled to	£	
pp. 126, 187		Widowed mother's allowance, invalid care allowance and industrial death benefit you were entitled to	£	
pp. 127, 138	See the form P60 from the payer.	Other pensions received Give amount and the name and address of the payer.	£	
p. 187	Ask for "Income Tax and the Unemployed" (leaflet IR41).	Unemployment benefit, or income support claimed because you were unemployed. Tick here and give name of your benefit office.		

Pensions you currently receive or expect to receive before 6 April 1995

		If not currently receiving the pension, date you expect it to start	Tick if a State pension	If currently receiving a pension, whether you receive it weekly, monthly, every 4 weeks or every 3 months	Amount you currently receive each time	Tick if this is after tax
pp. 127, 138	Giving this information now will help ensure the right amount of tax is deducted. See note 10 for what counts as a State pension.	/ /19			£	
		/ /19			£	

Other income

		Gross income	Details
p. 281	See note 11 for income you do not need to include. See note 12 for joint savings and investments.	**National Savings** Ordinary Account The first £70 of interest is exempt but should be included.	£	
		Investment Account, Deposit Bonds, Income Bonds and Capital Bonds. Give the type of investment.	£	

		Net interest after tax	Tax deducted	Gross interest before tax
		First Option Bonds Give the amount you received as shown on your tax certificate.	£	£	£

Other interest from UK banks, building societies etc.

		Income after tax (leave blank if no tax was deducted)	Tax deducted (leave blank if no tax was deducted)	Gross income
pp. 281, 282	The payer can supply the details you need. See note 13	Give name of the bank, building society or other source (tick the box if you have registered to have interest paid gross)	£	£	£
			£	£	£

Dividends from shares in UK companies and income from unit trusts

			Tax credit or tax deducted	Dividend	Gross income
pp. 282, 283	See your statement or voucher and note 14. If you have not received a unit trust voucher ask your unit trust manager.	If your voucher shows a tax credit give the tax credit and the dividend. If your voucher shows tax deducted give the tax deducted and the gross income. Include unit trust income reinvested in units. Name of the company or unit trust	£	£	£
			£	£	£

Income from furnished rooms in your only or main home (UK only)
Tick one of the boxes below.

p. 258	Under the Rent-a-Room scheme, £3,250 (or £1,625 if someone else is letting rooms in your home) of income from furnished rooms in your only or main home in the UK can be tax free. See note 15	Your gross income was no more than £3,250 (or £1,625 if appropriate) and you do not opt out of the Rent-a-Room scheme. You do not need to give any more details.			
				Tax-free amount: (£3,250 or £1,625)	Gross income
		Your gross income was more than £3,250 (or £1,625 if appropriate) and you want to be assessed on the difference between the rents and this amount, with no claim for expenses.		(£)	£
		Neither of the above apply. Your rental income and expenses will be treated in the normal way. Give details under Other income from property in UK or abroad.			

		Other income from property in UK or abroad	Income	Details
pp. 260, 261	See note 16 for expenses you can claim	In the Details column give address of property including the country (if not UK), type of let (furnished, unfurnished, of land, ground rents etc), gross income including profits from supplying gas or electricity, and expenses.		
		Income less expenses	£	
p. 284	See note 17	**Foreign investment income** Give the source and country.	£	
p. 122		**Maintenance and alimony you received** Give date of original order or agreement and of any further order or agreement since 15 March 1988. Tick here if you wish to claim the exemption.	£	
p. 285	See note 18. Up to £1,720 may be exempt from tax. see note 19.	**Income from trusts or settlements funded by others** Give name of trust or settlement and the amount of gross income received in the year	£	
p. 285	See note 20	**Income from estates** Give name of deceased person and nature of your entitlement.	£	
	See note 21	**All other income** Give the source.	£	
	2			

pp. 41, 66, 131, 283, 284, 285, 293

Form P1, continued

p. 122

Notes	**Deductions: legally binding maintenance or alimony payments**

Do not include maintenance or alimony payments which cannot be legally enforced.

Give amount you were ordered to pay in 1993-94 (£   )

Give amount you actually paid (if different). (£   )

If your order/agreement is dated after 14 March 1988, give the date of any earlier order/agreement it varies, replaces, or revives.   /   /19

Your Tax Office will work out the amount you can claim. See note 22.

Date of your current order/agreement.   /   /19

Tick here if the payments are to your ex-husband/wife and he/she has remarried.

Tick if in the 1994-95 tax year you will be making payments to the Department of Social Security for your separated or divorced husband/wife, or children of the marriage, under a court order or Child Support Agency assessment.

Deductions: mortgage or loan for main home

See note 23 about loans for which you should enter details.

p. 245

Give name of lender. If the lender is a building society, give account number.

If the loan is not in the MIRAS scheme and not from a building society enclose a form Miras 5 or other certificate of interest paid from your lender. Tick here if you want your certificate returned.

See note 24 for more information about joint mortgages and shared tax relief.

If the lender is not a building society, give gross amount of interest paid in 1993-94. (£   )

Husband and wife: interest relief split
If you are married and you and your husband/wife want to change the way you share mortgage interest relief, tick and we will send you a form on which you can do this.

pp. 46, 217, 260, 345

Other deductions

See note 25 for what qualifies. For loans to buy or improve rental property see note 16.

Other loans qualifying for tax relief
Only give details of loans not included elsewhere on this form. Give name of lender and purpose of loan. If for rental property, give number of weeks let during the tax year. Enclose a certificate of interest paid from your lender.

Deductions	Details
(£)	

Give the amount you actually paid.

p. 299

Give gross amounts. See note 26. Do not include most covenants made after 14 March 1988.

Gift aid donations and covenants to charity
Give name of charity and date of any deed of covenant.

(£   )

Other covenants, settlements etc.
Give name of the person you pay and date of the deed.

(£   )

Payments abroad

You are responsible for paying the tax in this country. Ask your Tax Office for details.

p. 47

Give the gross amounts of any payments of rent on UK property or yearly interest which you make to someone who normally lives abroad.

£

Capital gains 1993-94

You may have to pay capital gains tax if you made capital gains. See note 27.

p. 324

Tick here if the total value of the assets you have disposed of in 1993-94 was more than £11,600.

Tick here if your chargeable gains were more than £5,800.

If you tick either box, give details of the assets and the gain (or loss) on each asset. If you need help contact your Tax Office.

£

Claim for personal tax allowances for 1994-95

*See note 28.
See note 37 for details of 1994-95 personal allowances.*

pp. 102, 138

You will be given the basic personal allowance automatically. You may claim other allowances below.

Allowances for those born before 6 April 1930

See note 29.

You may be able to claim a higher amount of personal allowance if you were born before 6 April 1930.

Tick here to make your claim.

Allowances to be claimed by married men.

p. 110

See note 30.

Married couple's allowance
Tick the relevant box to claim

Give your wife's full name

You are living with your wife.

Married women should see page 4.

You separated from your wife before 6 April 1990 but are still married to her and have wholly maintained her since the separation with voluntary payments for which you are not entitled to any tax relief.

If you married after 5 April 1993 give the date of your marriage   /   / 19

See note 29.

If you or your wife were born before 6 April 1930

p. 138

If you are entitled to the married couple's allowance you can claim a higher amount of allowance if you or your wife were born before 6 April 1930. **Tick here** to claim.

If your wife was born before 6 April 1930, give her date of birth   /   / 19

3

70

Form P1, continued

p. 111

Notes

See note 32.

If your wife is unable to look after herself
You may be able to claim the additional personal allowance if you are living with your wife who is totally incapacitated because of disability or illness and you have a child living with you.

Give details of the child for whom you are claiming under *If you have a child and are single, separated, divorced or widowed* below

Give your wife's illness or disability

Tick here if your wife is likely to be unable to look after herself throughout the tax year ending on 5 April 1995.

p. 111

See note 34.
See note 31.

Married couples

Allocation of married couple's allowance
A husband is responsible for claiming the married couple's allowance, but if you are living together you may choose how the allowance is to be allocated between you.
For 1995-96 one of you can ask for half the basic allowance to be given to each of you or jointly you can ask for all the basic allowance to be given to one of you.

Tick here if you wish to do this and you will be sent a form.
(You do not have to complete a form if you want the allocation for 1994-95 to continue in 1995-96).

Ask your Tax Office for 'A Guide for Married Couples '(leaflet IR80). See note 36 for blind persons allowance.

Transfer of surplus allowances to your wife or husband
To transfer any surplus allowances you must have been married and living with your wife or husband at any time in 1994-95. If you did not have enough income tax liability to use all (or any) of your married couple's allowance then you may transfer the surplus to your wife or husband.

Tick here if you need a transfer notice form.

If you have insufficient income to use all (or any) blind person's allowance you are entitled to then you may transfer any surplus to your wife or husband. If you are a husband who does not have sufficient income to use his personal allowance in some circumstances your wife may receive transitional allowance.

111

p. 126

See note 35 for details.

Allowance for widows
You may be able to claim for the year your husband died and the following year. **Tick here** to claim this allowance.

Give the date of your husband's death   /   / 19

p. 103

See notes 32 and 33 for more details.

If you have a child and are single, separated, divorced or widowed
You may be able to claim the additional personal allowance if you have a child living with you for all or part of the year and are single, separated, divorced or widowed for all or part of the year.

Details of the child
Give the name of the youngest child for whom you can claim

Give the child's date of birth   /   / 19

If the child was 16 or over on 6 April 1994 and in full-time education or training give the name of the university, college or school or type of training.

See note 34 for details of shared claims.

Tick here to confirm the child lives with you.

Shared claims
Complete this item if:
- another person is claiming for the child named above or
- you live together as husband and wife with someone you are not married to who is also entitled to this allowance.

Give the other persons's (or your partner's) name and address

State how you want the allowance to be shared (eg equally)
If you cannot agree how you want the allowance shared between you, give the number of days in the tax year that the child lives with you and the number of days the child lives with the other person.

p. 50

See note 36.

Blind person's allowance
Tick here to claim the allowance.

The date you registered   /   / 19

Give the name of the Local Authority or equivalent body with which you have registered your blindness.

Personal details

National Insurance number (if not as on front of this form)

Change of address. If you no longer live at the address shown on the front of this form, give your current address.

Date of birth (if you were born before 6 April 1935.)   /   /

Marital status. State if you are single, married, widowed, separated or divorced.

pp. 51,

Declaration

You should keep a copy of your completed form or make entries in the boxes in the leaflet 'Filling in your 1994 Tax Return'.

You must sign this statement. If you give false information or conceal any part of your income or chargeable gains, you can be prosecuted.

The information I have given on this form is correct and complete to the best of my knowledge and belief.

Signature

Date   /   / 19

4

Printed in the UK for HMSO 1/94 Dd 8407867 2804W 25038

CHECKLIST OF PAPERS NEEDED TO COMPLETE A TAX RETURN

You will need the following documents to complete your Tax Return:

● a copy of the last Tax Return you sent in as a prompt for things to enter on the new one

● Form P60 setting out your earnings from your job or income from an employer's pension scheme

● a copy of the Form P11D filled in by your employer about your fringe benefits and expense allowances if these are taxable (p. 147)

● your business accounts if you have income from self-employment

● details of rental income and allowable expenses if you let out property

● your passbooks for National Savings investments (these will need to be sent off to have the interest added – do this after 1 January for the previous calendar year)

● the Tax Deduction Certificates giving details of tax deducted from interest paid to you (ask the bank, building society or other deposit-taker for one if you have not already been sent it)

● share dividend and unit trust distribution counterfoils

● tax vouchers from stock and loan interest

● details of payments made to personal pension schemes and for additional voluntary contributions

● Form R185 or Form R185E if you get maintenance payments or alimony where tax has been deducted, or income from a trust or the estate of someone who has died

● receipts, etc. for expenses in employment and allowable professional fees and subscriptions

● certificates of interest paid for loans on which you're claiming tax relief for interest paid

● contract notes for shares you've bought and sold, and records for any other assets bought or sold on which tax may be due.

TAX CLAIM FORM

If you receive income after tax has been deducted from it, you may be able to claim back some or all of the deducted tax. This would apply, for example, to:

● non-taxpayers who get interest from banks or building societies and haven't arranged for it to be paid without deduction of basic-rate tax (p. 267)

● taxpayers who pay tax at the lower rate of 20 per cent and get interest from banks or building societies from which tax has been deducted at the basic rate of 25 per cent (p. 265)

● non-taxpayers who get share dividends or unit trust distributions (p. 270)

● beneficiaries of discretionary trusts who pay tax at less than the rate at which the trust's investment income is taxed (35 per cent for 1993/94 and 1994/95 – see p. 272).

You may be sent the rather simpler form of Return known as *Tax Claim Form R40* to claim back the tax. This asks you about the income paid after deduction of tax and for details of any other income. Send it back with the documents you got with the income which set out the tax deducted: for example, with share dividends and unit trust dividends, the tax vouchers.

You'll normally be sent a new form with the tax repayment to claim the next repayment. You can send in the completed form before the end of the tax year to get repayment as soon as possible, as long as the amount of tax involved is more than £50 and you've had all the income for the tax year which is paid after deduction of tax.

Inland Revenue leaflet IR 110, *A guide for people with savings*, gives details of when you can claim tax refunds and includes two useful forms to send off.

THE NOTICE OF ASSESSMENT

Many people will never see a Notice of Assessment throughout their taxpaying careers because more or less the right amount of tax will be deducted from their earnings through PAYE (and interest on their savings is likely to be paid after deduction of tax). But if you have several sources of income, pay tax at the higher rates or are self-employed, you'll probably be issued with a Notice of Assessment setting out your income, deductions, allowances and tax bill. Anyone with complicated tax affairs could also get one, and you can ask for one if you want to know more about how your tax bill was worked out.

There are different types of assessment notice – which you get depends on the type of income:

● *Schedule E* Notice of Assessment is sent if most of your income is taxed under PAYE (that is, you work for an employer or live off a pension). There's space for other types of income such as small amounts of investment income, property income or freelance earnings

● *Schedule A or Schedule D* Notice of Assessment will be issued if you have substantial property income, investment income or earnings from self-employment

● *Capital Gains Tax* Notice of Assessment is issued if you have a capital gains tax bill to pay

● *Form 930* may be issued if you pay tax at the higher rate, explaining how your higher-rate tax bill has been worked out.

You may get more than one Notice if you have both substantial investment income, say, and work for an employer. And you could get more than one Schedule A or Schedule D Notice if you have both investment income and earnings from self-employment.

CHECKING A NOTICE OF ASSESSMENT

Always check a Notice of Assessment as soon as you get it. Any appeal against it must normally be made within 30 days of its issue (p. 61).

An example of a Schedule E Notice of Assessment (P70) is illustrated on the following pages, completed for Philippa Grange for the 1993/94 tax year (her husband Robert gets his own Notice of Assessment to deal with his tax position). You can follow how Philippa checked her Notice as follows (it is easier to tackle the sections in this order):

Section 1 lists earned income, which includes pay, bonus, commission, the taxable value of fringe benefits and any pension (whether from an ex-employer or the state). Philippa's earnings are listed, as is the value of her company car. The tax deducted is also listed, together with any deductions allowed against the income (for example, Philippa's £120 subscription to her professional association is set off against her earnings from the job). Philippa checks that the figures are correct and that expenses have not been overlooked.

Schedule E Notice of Assessment: Sections 1–3

NOTICE OF ASSESSMENT AND STATEMENT OF TAX UNPAID OR OVERPAID FOR 1993-94

1 Income from employments, pensions, benefits etc and deductions (E=estimated			Tax Deducted or Refunded (R=Refund)
	Deductions £	Income £	£
GRIMSDALE AND GRANGE PLC		28386	7626.40
BENEFITS IN KIND		3750	
EXPENSES	120		
TOTALS	120	32136	7626.40
Less Total Deductions		120	

Amount of assessment 32016

2 Allowances etc	
	£
PERSONAL	3445
LOAN ETC INTEREST	455
Total Allowances	3900
Less allowed elsewhere	150
Allowed in this assessment	3750

28266

3 Amount chargeable to tax		
Chargeable at		£ p
Lower rate at 20.00% on	£2500	500.00
Basic rate at 25.00% on	£23100	5775.00
Higher rate(s) on	£2666	1066.40
Tax assessed for 1993-94		7341.40
Net tax due		7341.40
Less tax deducted		7626.40
Net tax underpaid at 5 April 1994		285.00

Section 2 sets out the allowances and deductions Philippa is entitled to:

● her personal allowance (her husband gets the married couple's allowance – see p. 104)

● interest on a personal loan Philippa took out several years ago to pay for home improvements – as this was taken out before 6 April 1988, it qualifies for tax relief (see p. 239).

Interest paid under MIRAS will not be included here, because the Granges have had the basic-rate tax relief on it. Philippa checks that all her allowances and deductions are included – the total comes to £3,900.

Philippa has a National Savings Investment Account and the £150 interest she got on this was paid without deduction of tax. Her total allowances of £3,900 are reduced by £150 to £3,750 in order to collect the tax due on this interest.

Section 4 shows how much of Philippa's income is taxed at the lower and basic rates of tax. For 1993/94, the first £2,500 of taxable income is taxed at the lower rate of 20 per cent and the next £21,200 at the basic rate of 25 per cent. However, the amount taxed at the basic rate can be increased or decreased to give you extra tax relief at the higher rates or to tax income at the higher rates on which tax has already been deducted at the basic rate.

Schedule E Notice of Assessment: Section 4

4 Allocation of allowances and rates of tax				
	Allowances		Rates of Tax	
		20.00%	25.00%	40.00%
Allowed elsewhere:				
UNTAXED INTEREST	150			
GROSS BSI REC'D			400	
DIVIDENDS			600	
Elsewhere total(s)	150		1000	
This assessment	3750	2500	23100	2666
TOTALS	3900	2500	24100	2666

Schedule E Notice of Assessment: Section 5

5 Explanation

YOUR BASIC RATE BAND HAS BEEN EXTENDED TO ADD
FURTHER RELIEF DUE FOR PERSONAL PENSION
CONTRIBUTIONS AS FOLLOWS:

BASIC RATE BAND	21200
PERSONAL PENSION CONTRIBUTION	2900
TOTAL CHARGE AT BASIC RATE	24100

For example, Philippa makes regular monthly contributions to a personal pension scheme, getting basic-rate tax relief by making reduced payments. The grossed-up amount of the payments is £2,900, and Philippa can be given higher-rate tax relief on this by *increasing* the amount of income taxed at the basic rate by £2,900 to £24,100 (this calculation is explained in Section 5). The total of £24,100 taxable at the basic rate is entered in Section 4 on the bottom line of the 25 per cent column.

At the same time, reducing this basic-rate band will collect higher-rate tax due on income paid after deduction of basic-rate tax. The Granges got a grossed-up amount of £800 in such income for the tax year in interest from a joint building society account: this is split 50:50 between them in the absence of a 'declaration of beneficial interest' (see p. 263), so Philippa's share is £400 ('GROSS BSI REC'D'). She also got £480 of share dividends plus £120 tax credits: making £600 of gross dividends. Interest of £400 plus gross dividends of £600 gives the £1,000 described as 'Total elsewhere' under 25 per cent in Section 4. This £1,000 is deducted from the £24,100 taxable at the basic rate to give the £23,100 to be taxed at 25 per cent.

Section 3 works out Philippa's tax bill using the results of the other four sections. It begins by deducting the £3,750 of allowances worked out in Section 2 from the total income to be taxed on this assessment of £32,016 to produce an amount chargeable to tax of £28,266. Of this, £2,500 is taxed at the lower rate of 20 per cent and £23,100 at the basic rate of 25 per cent. The rest is taxed at the higher rate of 40 per cent (the amount taxable at the higher rate is set out in Section 4). The result is a tax bill of £7,341.40, which is compared with the tax actually deducted of £7,626.40 to show that a refund of £285 is due.

If you get more than one Notice of Assessment, it won't always be obvious how the various notices relate to each other, and what allowances you've been given. Ask for Form 930 which explains how the various types of income have been taxed.

10 · CHECKING YOUR INCOME TAX BILL FOR 1993/94

During the tax year you will have opportunities to check that you are paying the right amount of income tax. These opportunities include receiving:

● your payslip, if you are an employee

● your P60, given to employees at the end of the tax year

● your Notice of Coding, which tells your employer what tax to deduct. If your outgoings and allowances have not changed from last year, you may not receive one

● a Notice of Assessment, if you receive one. If you are self-employed, this is always how your tax bill is worked out; if you are an employee, you may receive a Notice of Assessment, for example, if you are a higher-rate taxpayer.

Just because you are an employee does not mean that you should have great faith that you will have paid the correct tax at the end of the year. When the Inland Revenue have checked in the past to see if employees were paying the right amount of tax under the PAYE system, it estimated that over a quarter of employees had not. So get out your pen and paper. Gather together all the bits and pieces of information that you need to add up your income, outgoings and allowances – much the same list as you need to fill in your Tax Return, see p. 71

This chapter explains how to satisfy yourself that the income tax deducted for the 1993/94 tax year is correct. But you can also work through your Notice of Assessment to see if you have paid the right amount of tax. How to do this is explained on p. 73. The 1993/94 tax year is the fourth year that a husband and wife have been taxed independently, so you can each work out whether your tax bill is correct without checking with each other – unless you think that you may be able to transfer allowances from one to the other.

There may be some special circumstances in which you will not be able to use this chapter to check your income tax bill and you will have to check your tax using the Notice of Assessment and by doing some extra work. This applies, for example:

● if your net deductions paid after you have deducted basic-rate tax (for example covenant payments to a charity) come to more than your taxable income or leave you with a taxable income of £2,500 or less. In these cases, you will have to pay some of the tax deducted to the Inland Revenue, but you will not be able to work out how much using the method below

● if you are cashing in part or all of a single-premium bond and claiming top-slicing relief (p. 289)

● if you have dividend income and it is likely to take you from the lower to the basic rate of tax, or from the basic to the higher rate of tax.

CHECKING AN INCOME TAX BILL FOR 1993/94

We've tried to make the checking process easier for you by dividing it up into nine different sections. You may not have to fill in all sections; the information at the end and the start of each section will guide you.

You will need to follow the instructions carefully if you are to end up with an accurate figure for the amount of tax you have paid, the amount you should have paid and whether you will end up with tax to pay or an overpayment which you can reclaim.

Fill in the figures below. Note that the page number beside each entry tells you where to look for more information. Ignore pence in your calculations. Do not enter any income which is tax-free, for example any maintenance income you receive under a post-14 March 1988 arrangement (p. 115). Don't enter any earnings from abroad on which you are claiming 100 per cent tax relief.

TREASURE TROVE CLUE No. 3

The amount of higher rate tax paid on taxable income of £1,000 (3 digits).

SECTION 1: EARNED INCOME

	PAGE	£
Your before-tax earnings from job (from your P60)	141	...
Amount of all expenses and expense allowances	144	...
The taxable value of fringe benefits	161	
Amount of tips, commission, bonuses	142	...
Taxable sick pay or maternity pay	143	...
Taxable income from self-employment or a partnership (*less* expenses, capital allowances, half Class 4 NI contributions, but not loss relief) – if negative figure, put nil	193	...
Before-tax amount of taxable social security benefits such as unemployment benefit (not if included under your earnings from your job)	181	...
Before-tax pension from state, ex-employer or a personal scheme (see p. 133 for pensions from abroad)	133	...
Casual or occasional freelance income;	40	...
Furnished holiday lettings; any other earned income	254, 40	...
Amount of leaving payment over £30,000	177	...
TOTAL EARNED INCOME:		... **A**

DEDUCTIONS

	PAGE	£
Allowable expenses only in your job	144	...
Payments to employer's pension scheme*	219	...
Payments to charity through a payroll-giving scheme*	294	...
Tax-free profit-related pay*	141	...
Payments to personal pension scheme	222	...
Loss relief claimed against earned income	203	...
TOTAL DEDUCTIONS:		... **B**
NET EARNED INCOME: **A – B**		... **C**

* *may already be deducted on your P60*

SECTION 2: INVESTMENT OR UNEARNED INCOME

Enter here the amount of any investment or unearned income you receive. If the investment is in your name enter the full amount of the income. If you are married and the investment is in your joint names, enter your share of the income – 50 per cent if you have not told your Tax Inspector that the investment is owned in a different proportion. If one of you gave an investment to the other during the tax year, you will have to apportion the income correctly before and after the gift.

	PAGE	£
Investment income received without deduction of tax, such as interest from National Savings	273	...
Grossed-up value of interest from a bank, building society, deposit-taker, local authority loan (enter net amount × $100/75$ or gross amount if paid without deduction of tax)	266	...
Dividends and tax credits from UK shares and unit trusts, amount of dividend × $100/80$ (enter dividend or distribution, even if reinvested, but not any equalisation payment)	269	... D
Grossed-up value of other investment income received after deduction of tax, such as from debentures, some British Government stock, trusts and settlements (enter net amount × $100/75$)	267, 272	...
Income from property *less* expenses	248	...
The gross amount of maintenance payments received under the old rules. Enter the lower of what you received in 1988/89 or in 1993/94 *less* £1,720 if you are a spouse or ex-spouse who has not remarried (if minus figure, put zero). If child aged under 21, *do not* deduct £1,720	117	...
Taxable amount of annuity	268	...
Any other unearned income		...
TOTAL UNEARNED INCOME		... E
TOTAL OF EARNED AND UNEARNED INCOME: **C + E**		... F

SECTION 3: GROSS DEDUCTIONS

Enter here the amount of deductions which you pay gross (i.e. in full) in the 1993/94 tax year. Round your figures up to the nearest £. Deductions which you pay net of basic-rate tax will be entered in Section 4.

	PAGE	£
Loan interest paid gross which qualifies for tax relief (but not for buying or improving your home)	46	...
The amount of maintenance you paid under the old rules in 1988/89 or in 1993/94, whichever is lower	117	...
Amount of maintenance you pay under the new rules or £1,720, whichever is lower. If you paid any maintenance under the old rules, deduct this amount from £1,720	115	...
Loss relief claimed against your own investment or unearned income	203	...
The amount of contributions to a personal pension scheme, but not if you have already deducted it from your earnings in Section 1	222	...
Interest paid gross on a loan for buying and improving your home	233	... **G**
TOTAL GROSS DEDUCTIONS:		... **H**

SECTION 4: NET DEDUCTIONS

Enter here the following payments you make with basic-rate tax deducted (that is enter the actual amount you pay).

	PAGE	£
Amount of covenant you pay to a charity and any gift to charity under the Gift Aid scheme	295, 297	...
Amount of premiums for qualifying private medical insurance for people aged 60 or over	137	...
Payments for vocational training	146	...

TOTAL NET DEDUCTIONS: ... **I**

MULTIPLY **I** BY $\frac{100}{75}$ ... **J**

TOTAL DEDUCTIONS: **H + J** ... **K**

DEDUCT **G** FROM **K** ... **L**

DEDUCT **I** FROM **J** ... **M**

If you or your spouse were born before 6 April 1929, go to Section 5. Otherwise, move straight to Section 6.

SECTION 5: AGE-RELATED ALLOWANCES

If you or your husband or wife were born before 6 April 1929, you may be entitled to age-related allowances which are higher than the normal personal allowances. The amount you are entitled to depends on your 'total income', your age and the age of your spouse. In Part 1, enter the amount of mortgage interest you have chosen to have allocated to you (see p. 236 for why allocation is important).

PART 1: 'TOTAL INCOME'

	PAGE	£
Loan interest which qualifies for tax relief, paid under MIRAS	233	...
Multiply by 100/75		... **N**
Taxable gain on a life insurance policy	289	... **O**
'TOTAL INCOME': Add **F + O – K – N**		... **P**

PART 2: AGE-RELATED ALLOWANCES IF YOU ARE A MARRIED MAN LIVING WITH YOUR WIFE

(Others go to Part 3)

Your personal allowance (see Table opposite)	135	... **Q**
Your share of basic married couple's allowance £1,720 or £860 or nil	136	... **R**
Age-related bit of married couple's allowance (£745 or £785 – see Table opposite)	136	... **S**
TOTAL AGE-RELATED ALLOWANCES FOR MARRIED MAN: Q + R + S		... **T**

If 'total income' **P** is less than £14,200, enter **T** at **V** at the end of the this Section.

If **P** is £14,200 or more, enter **P** *less* £14,200	136	... **a**
Divide **a** by 2		... **b**
Deduct **b** from **T**		... **c**

Enter **c** or £5,165, whichever is higher, at **V** below

AGE-RELATED ALLOWANCES 1993/94

YOU WERE BORN	YOUR SPOUSE WAS BORN	YOUR ALLOWANCES		
		personal	*married couple's*	*including age-related bit*
On or after 6 April 1929	On or after 6 April 1929	£3,445	£1,720	nil
	Before 6 April 1929, after 5 April 1919	£3,445	£2,465	£745
	Before 6 April 1919	£3,445	£2,505	£785
Before 6 April 1929, after 5 April 1919	On or after 6 April 1919	£4,200	£2,465	£745
	Before 6 April 1919	£4,200	£2,505	£785
Before 6 April 1919	Any time	£4,370	£2,505	£785

PART 3: ALLOWANCES IF YOU ARE A SINGLE MAN OR WOMAN OR A MARRIED WOMAN

	PAGE	£
Single includes separated, divorced or widowed		
Your personal allowance (see Table above)	135	...
Add your share of basic married couple's allowance (£1,720 or £860 or nil)	136	...
Total allowances		... **U**
If 'total income' **P** is less than £14,200, enter your allowances **U** at **V** below and go to Section 6 Part 2.	136	
If **P** is £14,200 or more, enter **P** *less* £14,200		... **d**
Divide **d** by 2		... **e**
Deduct **e** from **U**		... **f**

Enter **f** or £3,445, whichever is higher, at **V** below.

TOTAL AGE-RELATED ALLOWANCES   ... **V**

Now go to Section 6 Part 2

SECTION 6: ALLOWANCES AND BUSINESS EXPANSION SCHEME

If you have filled in Section 5 to claim your age-related allowances, you should skip Part 1 and go straight to Part 2. Everyone is entitled to a personal allowance and if you are married a share of the married couple's allowance. You may also be able to claim another allowance, but you will have to check the appropriate section of the Tax Guide to see if it applies to you. If you are married you may be able to transfer blind person's allowance , from one to the other and exceptionally the husband might be able to transfer his personal allowance – see Chapter 13.

PART 1: PERSONAL AND MARRIED COUPLE'S ALLOWANCES

	PAGE	£
If you were born on or after 6 April 1929, enter the amount of personal allowance, £3,445	100	...
Enter your share of the married couple's allowance, £1,720 or £860 or nil	105	...
TOTAL PERSONAL AND MARRIED COUPLE'S ALLOWANCES:		... **W**

PART 2: TOTAL ALLOWANCES AND BUSINESS EXPANSION SCHEME

Enter total for personal allowance and married couple's allowance, **V** or **W**		...
Additional personal allowance, £1,720	100	...
Widow's bereavement allowance, £1,720	124	...
Blind person's allowance, £1,080	50	...
Friendly society/trade union benefits. Enter half the qualifying amount you paid in 1993/94	292	...
Amount of investment in Business Expansion Scheme which qualifies for tax relief	277	...
TOTAL ALLOWANCES:		... **X**

SECTION 7: TAXABLE INCOME

In this section, you work out what your total taxable income should be for 1993/94

	£
Enter total of earned and unearned income **F**	...
Enter deductions **L** (on which you can get higher-rate tax relief)	...
Income *less* deductions (**F** – **L**)	... **Y**
Enter total allowances **X**	...
Taxable income **Y** – **X**	... **Z**

SECTION 8: THE TAX YOU SHOULD PAY

From amount **Z** deduct **D**	... **ZZ**
Tax at the lower rate (20 per cent) on £2,500 or on amount **ZZ** whichever is lower	... **1**
Subtract amount **G** from **Z**	... **AA**
Tax at basic rate (25 per cent) on the lower of amount **AA** or amount **ZZ** – £2,500	... **2**
If **Z** is more than £23,700 add **D** to **ZZ**	... **BB**
Tax at higher rate (40 per cent) on **BB** – £23,700	... **3**
Total tax (add **1** + **2** + **3**)	... **CC**
Tax relief from net deductions **M**	... **M**
TOTAL TAX DUE: **CC** + **M**	... **DD**

SECTION 9: THE TAX YOU HAVE PAID

£

Tax already deducted under PAYE (for example, in
job, pensions, social security benefits, fringe
benefits, etc.) – find this from your P60 ...

Tax already paid on self-employed or
partnership income ...

Tax credits on dividends or distributions
(p. 269), 20 per cent of **D**. BUT if amount **2** is nil,
enter nil here ...

Tax deducted from interest received ...

TOTAL ... **EE**

SECTION 10: PAID TOO MUCH OR TOO LITTLE TAX?

Total tax due ... **DD**

Total tax paid ... **EE**

The difference **DD – EE** ... **FF**

If **FF** is a plus figure, you owe that amount of tax.

If **FF** is a minus figure, you can reclaim that amount of tax.

EXAMPLE

Walter Burns earns £35,000 in his job. He received expense payments of £150 (£30 of these are not allowable) and has the following fringe benefits: car (taxable value £2,310), luncheon vouchers (taxable value £351). He contributes £1,800 to a pension scheme. Walter writes the occasional article for trade magazines; in 1992/93 this amounted to £700.

Sheila Burns is self-employed. She has worked through the calculation in Chapter 23, 'The Self-Employed', p. 192, and her taxable income from self-employment for 1993/94 (based on her accounting year ending in 1992/93) is £9,500. She contributes £1,285 to a personal pension scheme.

Their investment income is as follows: interest paid on National Savings Investment Account, £250 (no tax deducted); distributions received from unit trusts, £130.65 plus tax credits of £32.66, gives a gross figure of £163.31; and net interest from a building society account of £37 (basic-rate tax deducted of £12.33 – i.e. gross interest of £49.33). These are all in Sheila's name so that the income from them is added to her lower income, thus minimising the amount of tax the two of them pay.

During the year they had the following deductions: mortgage interest of £2,280 paid net under the MIRAS scheme, a gift to charity of £1,000 made under the Gift Aid scheme (net £750) and gross maintenance payments to Walter's ex-wife under a maintenance agreement made in 1986, £4,000 (the same amount as in 1988/89).

First, Walter works through the ten sections of this chapter to find out whether he has paid the right amount of tax.

SECTION 1

Walter fills in this section: his income is £35,000 + £150 + £2,310 + £351 + £700. The total at **A** is £38,511.

He deducts certain of his decutions: allowable expenses of £120 and pension contributions £1,800 (**B** is £1,920).

The figure at **C** is £36,591.

SECTION 2

Walter has no investment income. The figure at **F** is £36,591.

SECTION 3

Walter can claim one deduction which he pays in full, the gross maintenance payments to his ex-wife of £4,000. He enters £4,000 under **H**.

SECTION 4

Walter enters the net gift to charity of £750 at **I**. Multiplying this by $100/75$ gives £1,000, which he enters at **J**. Adding **H** and **J** together gives total deductions of £5,000 (**K**). This is also amount **L**. This is the amount of deductions on which he can claim higher-rate tax relief. He works out the amount of tax relief he gets on his net deductions by subtracting **I** from **J**, which gives £250 (**M**).

SECTION 5

This section does not apply to Walter.

SECTION 6

Walter can claim personal allowance of £3,445 and married couple's allowance of £1,720, giving total allowances of £5,165 (**W**). Walter is not entitled to any other allowances under Part 2, so **X** is the same as **W**.

SECTION 7

Walter works out his taxable income for 1993/94. The amount at **F** is £36,591. He deducts deductions on which he can get higher-rate tax relief of £5,000, **L**, and total allowances of £5,165 (**X**). This gives taxable income **Z** of £36,591 − £5,000 − £5,165 = £26,42 6(**Z**).

SECTION 8

Walter's tax is worked out as follows:

Amount **D** is zero, so amount **ZZ** is £26,426

Tax is at the lower rate of 20 per cent on £2,500, ie £500 (**1**).

Tax is at the basic rate on the lower of amount **AA** or amount **ZZ** − £2,500 if less. **AA** is £21,200, which is lower than **ZZ** (£26,426). So the calculation is: 25 per cent of £21,200 = £5,300 (**2**).

Z is more than £23,700, but **D** is nil so **BB** is £26,426.

Tax is at the higher rate on **BB** − £23,700, or £26,426 − £23,700 = £2,726. So the calculation is 40 per cent of £2,726 = £1,090.40 (**3**).

So **CC** is **1** + **2** + **3** = £500 + £5,300 + £1,090.40 = £6,890.40.

Adding the £250 tax deducted from net deductions (**M**) to £6,890.40 (**CC**) gives £7,140.40 (**DD**).

SECTION 9

Walter has paid tax under the PAYE system, which has collected tax of £7,221.40 (**EE**).

SECTION 10

Total tax due **DD** is £7,140.40 and total tax paid **EE** is £7,221.40, so the difference **FF** is –£81. Walter can reclaim that amount of tax.

Sheila now works through the same process. Under Section 1, she finds **A** is £9,500 and **C** is £9,500 – £1,285 = £8,215.

Under Section 2, her investment income **E** comes to £250 + £163.31 + £49.33 = £462.64. So **F** is £8,215 + £462.64 = £8,677.64.

Sheila skips Sections 3 and 4 (she's already claimed some deductions under Section 1).

She also jumps Section 5 and goes straight to Section 6, where she claims allowances under **X** of £3,445.

Under Section 7, Sheila's taxable income is **F** less **X** equals £5,232.64 (**Z**).

In Section 8 she calculates her tax due. From amount **Z** £5,232.64 she deducts grossed-up amount of distribution **D** (£163.31) and gets **ZZ** £5,069.33. She pays tax at the lower rate on £2,500, i.e. £500 (**1**). Amount **AA** is £21,200, since amount **G** is zero. So she must pay basic-rate tax at 25 per cent of amount **ZZ** – £2,500 = £2,569.33, as this is less than **AA**. 25 per cent of £2,569.33 = £642.33 (**2**). Total tax is **1** + **2** = £500 + £642.33 = £1,142.33 (**DD**)

Section 9 helps Sheila work out how much tax she has already paid. It is £1,202 on her self-employed income and £12.33 basic-rate tax deducted from her building society interest. As amount **3** is nil, she also enters nil for tax credits on her distribution. This gives a total **EE** of £1,214.33.

In Section 10, she deducts **EE** from **DD**, £1,142.33 – £1,214.33 = –£72 (**FF**). Sheila can reclaim this amount of tax.

11 · APPEALS AND INVESTIGATIONS

Arguments with your Tax Inspector are to be avoided if at all possible. But if you think that an assessment is wrong, you should appeal against it. If you cannot sort it out with your Inspector, this chapter takes you through the appeals process.

You might also wish to claim an allowance or tax relief to which you are entitled and which you haven't claimed before. Claims can be backdated for some years, so you could reclaim tax paid in previous years. This chapter outlines the time limits for claiming such reliefs, and explains where you stand if the taxman has collected too much tax from you as the result of a mistake. It ends by looking at how the Inland Revenue carries out investigations when it probes the affairs of taxpayers who are thought to have been less than frank in filling in their Tax Returns.

APPEALS

If you get a Notice of Assessment (p. 73) which you think is wrong, you can appeal against it, in the first place to your Tax Inspector. You can also appeal against a PAYE Notice of Coding (p. 150), or any other decision made about your tax affairs by the Inland Revenue.

It may seem a little odd to appeal to the Tax Inspector who issued the notice or whatever in the first place. But the decision may have been issued by a more junior member of staff, or simply made in the absence of the full facts. Most appeals are resolved with little difficulty by negotiation between taxpayer and Inspector. If you cannot reach agreement with your Tax Inspector, you can appeal to the Commissioners, the courts and ultimately the House of Lords.

Note that if your complaint is over the handling of your tax affairs, rather than the amount of your tax bill, this should not be taken up through the appeals procedure. Instead, you should raise your complaint first with your Tax Inspector, then the Controller of the

Executive Office responsible for the tax office, and finally to the independent Revenue Adjudicator – see p. 58 for details.

APPEALS TO THE COMMISSIONERS

The Commissioners provide the first tier of appeal with which you can raise your case. Your Tax Inspector may also refer a case to the Commissioners: this is a way of pressuring you to answer letters or enquiries which the Inspector thinks is a delaying tactic.

There are two groups of Commissioners:

● *Special Commissioners:* full-time civil servants who are tax experts and who usually hear cases on their own with only a clerk to keep notes

● *General Commissioners:* unpaid lay people, serving voluntarily in the same way as magistrates. They sit in groups of two or more, with a clerk who gives expert advice, to hear cases in their locality.

Certain technical matters such as valuation of shares will automatically go to the Special Commissioners. Arguments over personal allowances or delays always go to the General Commissioners. If your appeal is not covered by any such general rule, it will automatically be heard by the General Commissioners. But you can opt for it to be heard by the Special Commissioners. This might be worth doing if your appeal is on a point of law. You must make the choice within the time limit for entering the appeal.

Once a case has been referred to the Commissioners, you will get notice of the hearing from the clerk. With delay cases (where you have failed to supply your Tax Inspector with information, say), the hearing may not take place for a year or two. Most such appeals never get as far as a formal hearing since the case will be resolved when the taxpayer comes up with the facts.

You can present your own case to the Commissioners or be represented by a lawyer or accountant (which could be expensive). If you are the party who is appealing, you open the proceedings by seeking to prove that the Inspector's decision was wrong. The Inspector replies, leaving you with a final chance to make your case and reply to the Inspector. The Commissioners' decision (which can be to increase your tax bill, as well as to reduce it or leave it as it is) will be given at the end of the hearing or in writing soon after.

APPEALING AGAINST COMMISSIONERS' DECISIONS

Either you or the Tax Inspector can appeal against the decision of the

Commissioners to the High Court, then to the Appeal Court and ultimately to the House of Lords. This becomes an expensive business, since you will need to be represented, and you may have to pay the Inland Revenue's costs if you lose.

Even if you do appeal, you must still pay the tax bill decided by the Commissioners, pending a final decision by the courts. And you cannot normally appeal on a point of fact (for example, what your expenses were), only on a point of law (whether the expense was allowable). If the Tax Inspector appeals, you have a hard decision to make: the tax at stake could be much less than the cost of fighting the case and discretion may be the better part of valour if that is so. Certainly you should try to get financial support for your appeal (for example, from your trade union or professional association).

CLAIMING A TAX REPAYMENT

If you discover that you are entitled to an allowance which you haven't been claiming, or you are entitled to tax relief on some expenditure, you should put in a claim for a tax repayment. You can claim back the tax you have overpaid for up to six complete tax years before the current one – and, perhaps, get interest on the overpaid tax.

Suppose that on reading this Guide in October 1994, you realize that you've been entitled to a tax allowance you haven't been claiming. You can claim back tax paid since 6 April 1988 – six years before the start of the 1994/95 tax year. If you became entitled to the allowance after 6 April 1988, the tax relief runs only from when you became entitled.

Although you have up to six complete tax years to discover an deduction or allowance to which you are entitled, the time limits are rather shorter in other cases:

● if you have a new source of income, you must tell your Tax Inspector about it within twelve months of the end of the tax year in which you start to get it

● to have losses from self-employment set off against income from other sources (p. 203), you must tell your Tax Inspector within two years of the end of the tax year in which you want the relief

● to set losses from a new business off against income from tax years before the business was started (p. 204), you must tell your Tax Inspector within two years of the end of the tax year in which the losses arose.

Note that it may still be worth claiming a repayment of tax even if you discover it more than six years after the event. The Inland Revenue will normally consider a claim after more than six years if the overpayment of tax was caused by its own error or that of another government department.

INTEREST ON TAX REBATES

You can get interest on rebates of overpaid tax if both the following conditions are met:

● the rebate is £25 or more

● you get the rebate more than one year after the end of the tax year to which it relates. So you won't get interest on a tax rebate paid to you in the 1994/95 tax year unless it is for tax overpaid before 6 April 1993.

The interest, called *repayment supplement*, is tax-free, and the rate is linked to interest rates in general (the current rate is 5½ per cent a year). Interest is paid for each month (complete or part) from twelve months after the end of the tax year for which it was due until the rebate is paid. But if the tax was originally paid more than twelve months after the year for which it was due, then the interest runs from the end of the tax year in which the tax was actually paid.

The Inland Revenue produces a ready reckoner which calculates the amount of interest you get. For example, if you paid £1,000 too much tax in the 1989/90 tax year, you would get interest for each part or whole month since 5 April 1991 (twelve months after the end of the 1989/90 tax year) until the rebate came through. If you got the rebate on 25 July 1994, the ready reckoner would show that the interest due is £260.90.

CHASING UP A REBATE

Time can seem to pass remarkably slowly while you await your rebate. If nothing seems to have happened after a few weeks, send a reminder. Telephone calls should follow up the reminder (ring your local PAYE Enquiry Office if you deal with a far-distant London Provincial office). If you don't feel that you're getting anywhere, write to the District Inspector. If that brings no response, then write to the controller for the executive office covering your tax office (get the address from your tax office). Once these options have been exhausted, then you can seek help from the independent Revenue Adjudicator (see p. 58), who can review your case and make recommendations which the Inland Revenue will normally accept. As a last resort, you could write to your MP. If there appears to be a case of maladministration, an MP can refer it to the ombudsman (though only a handful of taxpayers end up having to go to these lengths).

Note that replies to claims may take longer at busy times of the year (April, for example). But it is your money, so be persistent.

MISTAKES

If you discover that you have made a mistake in filling in your Tax Return (or in any other communication with your Tax Inspector), come clean quickly. If there's any suggestion that you have delayed telling the taxman, there could be penalties (p. 99).

But what happens if the mistake is the Tax Inspector's? For example, you might have told your Inspector that you were no longer entitled to an allowance, but your PAYE code wasn't altered to collect the extra tax. If the mistake is found six years later, you could be liable for tax for all six years.

Provided you've taken reasonable care to keep the Tax Inspector informed (by filling in Tax Returns, notifying new sources of income, etc.), some or all of the underpaid tax may not have to be paid. You'll be let off all the tax if your gross income is £15,500 or less. If your gross income is over £15,500, the proportion of the underpaid tax which you must pay is as follows:

GROSS INCOME	% OF TAX YOU MUST PAY
£15,501 – £18,000	25
£18,001 – £22,000	50
£22,001 – £26,000	75
£26,001 – £40,000	90
£40,000 +	100

INVESTIGATIONS

Your Tax Inspector gets information about you from many sources: your employer, your bank and building societies, companies and unit trusts you invest in and so on (p. 60). If you try to conceal a source of income, the taxman may get to hear of it and decide to make you the subject of an investigation. And information supplied by other bodies is supplemented by a greatly increased effort by the Inland Revenue itself to detect tax evasion:

● local tax offices search out businesses which don't bother to send in Tax Returns (the so-called black economy)

● regional Special Offices coordinate blitzes on hard-to-monitor trades such as builders and contractors

● the Enquiry Branch, the equivalent of the police flying squad, tackles the really sophisticated tax dodgers.

The Inland Revenue is backed by some fairly formidable powers to seize papers and search your home or office, and to demand that others hand over documents of yours. Once you have been rumbled on a tax dodge, your Tax Inspector can, in certain circumstances, have you charged in criminal proceedings. In practice, you are likely to avoid such ignominy but only by paying the tax you owe plus hefty penalties and interest.

This heavy artillery is wheeled out in only a limited number of cases each year. But an investigation can be launched into your tax affairs for much more mundane reasons (because you overlook a source of income, for example). And if you are self-employed, you may be the subject of searching enquiries about your business accounts, even if you have been entirely honest in declaring your income and claiming expenses.

UNDECLARED INCOME

If your Tax Inspector thinks that you haven't disclosed a source of income, the first shot will normally be to send you a brief letter asking you to confirm that the information given in your latest Tax Return is correct. If you get such a letter, check thoroughly that you have put everything in your Tax Return.

Start with your last Tax Return to make sure that you have left nothing out of the latest one. If you cannot immediately identify the omission, a discreet phone call to the Inspector might help. He or she might be prepared to give you some general guidance on what sort of income is under review (though he or she does not have to tell you).

If you can't find what has been missed out, don't despair: the information given to the Tax Inspector may be incorrect – for example, there may be a muddle over names. And if you do identify a mistake, come clean and quickly: your Tax Inspector can impose penalties if you have been unhelpful or obstructive.

Once a mistake of this kind has been found, you will be asked to sign a *Certificate of Full Disclosure*. This confirms that you have now made a full return of your income for the period in question, and should be signed only if you are certain that this is true. You will then have to negotiate what you must pay with your Inspector – this will be the extra tax plus, usually, penalties (see opposite).

ACCOUNTS INVESTIGATIONS

Investigations into business accounts are now targeted very carefully on areas which seem most promising. For example, businesses which deal mainly in cash or where records are rudimentary are prime candidates for scrutiny. But every business can expect a full once-over sooner or later.

Tax Inspectors monitor a wide variety of businesses and will usually have a pretty good idea of what is reasonable in the way of income for most trades. For example, they will be well-informed about the sort of tips you might get as a taxi-driver or about the profit margin on common product lines. If your income seems suspiciously low, you could be in line for investigation.

Similarly, your Tax Inspector will pay close attention to expenses which are unusually high in relation to your income. The amount of expenses which you claim for things like the use of your car which is also available for your private use will also be scrutinized. And if you are clearly living in a style which cannot be supported by your declared income, expect some searching questions.

The Inspector's first step will probably be to summon you to a meeting to go through your books and records. There may, of course, be good reason for the discrepancies identified: you might have lost income through refurbishments, for example, or have incurred high start-up costs. It is for you to justify the figures in your accounts, and well-kept books with supporting paperwork will be an essential tool in doing this.

If you use an accountant to produce your accounts, initial queries will be raised with the accountant. But if the Inspector suspects that there is more than meets the eye, a face-to-face interview will be sought. You can bring your professional adviser with you to this interview. If you don't use an accountant, consider employing one to guide you through the investigation.

Ask the Inspector for copies of the notes taken during the interview. If there are any inaccuracies, notify the Inspector immediately – these notes can be used as evidence in an appeal to the Commissioners.

BACK-TAX AND PENALTIES

Where extra tax is found to be payable, the Tax Inspector can go back up to six complete tax years before the current one and include them on the assessment. If there is neglect (that is, you have failed to reply to letters, complete a Tax Return or send in a document requested by the Tax Inspector), the tax can be collected for up to twelve complete tax years before the current one. And there is no time limit if there is fraud or wilful default.

Your Tax Inspector can also charge interest on the tax from earlier years and impose financial penalties. For example, if you submit false Returns, you can be required to pay *twice* the unpaid tax. Supplying incorrect information attracts a penalty of £3,000.

In practice, your Tax Inspector will mitigate these penalties at least to some degree, according to the circumstances of the case. For example, if you are helpful and cooperative, the penalties might be considerably reduced: if the amount of tax involved is large and you concealed the error for many years, mitigation will be less or none at all.

Once an investigation is over and you have signed a Certificate of Full Disclosure, your Inspector will suggest the amount you should pay to settle the investigation. You can either accept the suggestion or make a lower offer if you think the penalty is excessive. Your offer should be put in writing, and it will be referred with the papers to Inland Revenue Head Office. Your Inspector will make a recommendation on your offer (presumably to accept if it is for the amount suggested), but the decision rests at Head Office.

If you get involved in an investigation, you will find useful information to guide you in two Inland Revenue leaflets:

● IR72 *Investigations: the examination of business accounts*

● IR73 *Investigations: how settlements are negotiated.*

There's also a code of practice on the conduct of tax investigations, setting out your rights while undergoing an investigation. Ask your tax office for a copy.

12 • SINGLE PEOPLE

This chapter tells you how you are taxed if you are a single adult living on your own, or with someone else but unmarried. Other single people should turn to one of the following chapters:

- Chapter 14, 'Separated and Divorced', p. 113

- Chapter 15, 'Widowed', p. 124

- Chapter 16, 'Children and Students', p. 128.

Single people are taxed in the same way as married people, except that a married couple can claim the married couple's allowance. Otherwise you claim the same deductions; for example, mortgage interest relief. And your income is worked out in the same way.

You are entitled to the personal allowance, £3,445 for 1993/94 and 1994/5 if you are under 65. You get it automatically; you don't have to claim it specially in your Tax Return.

But if you are 65 or over, you can claim a higher level – and you need to do this in your Tax Return. The amount of the personal allowance if you are 65 or over during the tax year is £4,200 for 1993/94 and 1994/95; and if you are 75 or more, it becomes £4,370 for 1993/94 and 1994/95.

There are more details of how the elderly are taxed in Chapter 17, p. 132.

SINGLE PARENT

There is an additional allowance you may be able to claim, if you have a child living with you. This allowance is known as additional personal allowance – see example below. The amount of additional personal allowance is the same as the married couple's allowance and for 1993/94 and 1994/95 it is £1,720 but is restricted to 20 per cent for 1994/95.

You may be able to claim this allowance if at some time in the tax year you are:

- single

- a widow or widower

- divorced

- married but separated (and so not entitled to the married couple's allowance if a man)

- a married man but your wife is totally unable to look after herself throughout the tax year – see p. 105.

To get the allowance, you must have a child (either your own or someone else's) living with you for the whole or part of the tax year. You can only claim for a child aged 16 or over at the start of the tax year if the child is in full-time education at university, school or college or training full-time for at least two years for a trade or profession. If the child is not yours, you cannot claim if the child is 18 or over at the start of the tax year. 'Your child' includes a step-child, adopted child or legitimated child.

It is possible that two people could claim the allowance for the same child because the child lives with each of them for part of the year (who has custody is not the deciding factor). If this applies to you, you can agree with the other what proportion you can each claim. If you cannot agree, the allowance will be divided up according to the amount of time the child lives with each of you during the tax year. If there are two or more children, you may be able to claim a full allowance each.

If you are living with someone as husband and wife, but unmarried, you and your partner can claim only one additional personal allowance between the two of you and only for the youngest child. The allowance can be divided up as you wish. If you are not entitled to the allowance for the youngest child, you can't claim it at all.

EXAMPLE

Sally Jones is a single parent with two children living with her. Her income is £10,000. As well as the personal allowance she can claim the additional personal allowance although it is restricted to 20 per cent for 1994/95. Her tax bill will be:

Income	£10,000
less personal allowance	£3,445
Taxable income	£6,555
Tax due: 20% of £3,000 £600.00	
25% of £3,555 £888.75	
	£1,488.75
less additional personal allowance	
restricted to 20% of £1,720	£344.00
TOTAL TAX	£1,144.75

If Sally had not claimed the extra allowance, her tax bill would have been £1,488.75.

If you receive any social security benefits, you may find that the tax treatment varies – some are tax-free and some are taxable. A comprehensive list with an explanation of how they are taxed is in Chapter 21, 'Unemployment and Other Benefits', on p. 181.

The tax treatment of maintenance you receive or pay can depend on when you made your arrangements, how much it is and who is receiving the payment. An explanation is in Chapter 14, 'Separated and Divorced', on p. 113.

UNMARRIED COUPLE LIVING TOGETHER

There used to be tax advantages in living together rather than marrying, but these have been withdrawn. However, if you took out a mortgage to buy a home before 1 August 1988, you can carry on getting tax relief on the interest of up to £60,000 of the loan (see p. 238).

Think carefully before you move to another home, as your relief on a new mortgage would be restricted to the interest on £30,000 of this mortgage. And if you now marry this will also apply.

WHAT TO PUT IN YOUR TAX RETURN

You do not have to put anything to get the personal allowance if under 65. But if you were born before 6 April 1930 you can claim a higher amount of personal allowance. Tick the box on page 11 on Forms 11P and 11 and on page 3 of Form P1.

Form 11P

See note 55.

Allowances for those born before 6 April 1930

You may be able to claim a higher amount of personal
allowance if you were born before 6 April 1930.   Tick here to make your claim   ☐

Under *If you have a child and are single, separated, divorced or
widowed* on the back page of the Tax Return, you can claim for
additional personal allowance. Put the date of birth and the name of the
youngest child you can claim for and fill in the other details asked for.

Form 11P

Notes

See notes 59 and 60.

If you have a child and are single, separated, divorced or widowed

You may be able to claim the additional personal allowance if
you have a child living with you for at least part of the year and
you are single, separated, divorced or widowed at some time
during the year.

Give the child's date of birth   [/ /19]

Give the name of the youngest child for whom you can claim
[   ]

If the child was 16 or over on 6 April 1994 and in
full-time education or training give the name of the
university, college or the type of training.
[   ]

Tick here if the child lives with you   ☐

If you are an unmarried couple living together and you want the
allowance to be divided between you, you can choose for it to be split
in any way you like. This also applies if there is another person claiming
for the same child even if you don't live with them. Give the
information under *Shared claims*.

Form 11P

See note 61.

Shared claims
Complete this item if:
• another person is claiming for the child named above or
• you live together as husband and wife with another person,
  but you are not married to him/her, and that person is
  also entitled to claim this allowance.

Give the other person's (or your partner's) name and address
[   ]

Tick here if you want the allowance to be
shared equally between you.   ☐

If you do not want the allowance
to be shared equally, state how you   [   ]
want it to be shared

If you do not live with the other person and you cannot
agree how you want the allowance shared between you,
give the number of days in the tax year that the child lives
with you and the number of days the child lives with the
other person.
[   ]

13 • MARRIED

The tax system still blesses marriage with the wedding gift of an extra allowance – married couple's. Apart from this, since 6 April 1990 each of you is independent from a tax point of view. You each:

- have your own allowances
- are taxed on your own income
- are responsible for filling in your own Tax Return
- are responsible for paying your own tax bill
- get any tax refund due to you paid in your own name.

From 6 April 1993 you can also choose to have the married couple's allowance allocated to the husband or the wife or split equally between the two of you. Wives can ask to have half the allowance deducted from their own income if they choose without getting the agreement of their husbands, but it may result in more tax being paid in total by husband and wife, if the husband pays tax at a higher rate. So, to make your joint tax bills as low as possible, it is best to look at this together.

From 6 April 1994, the tax relief on the married couple's allowance is restricted to a rate of 20 per cent. But you could still make some savings by choosing to deduct the married couple's allowance from the higher income.

ALLOWANCES

There are three allowances. First, there is the personal allowance. Everyone is entitled to a personal allowance; it doesn't matter whether you are male or female, married or single. If you are 65 or over during the tax year you can claim a higher amount of personal allowance than most taxpayers, see p. 135.

You deduct the personal allowance from your own income before working out your tax bill. It doesn't matter whether the income is from earnings or from investments.

Secondly, there is the married couple's allowance. For 1993/94, a married man living with his wife was entitled to claim this. If his income was too low to use up the allowance, it could be transferred to his wife. From 6 April 1993, the allowance can be allocated either to the husband or the wife or split equally between them. If you wish to make this allocation for 1995/96, ask for a Form 18 from your Tax Inspector and return it before 6 April 1995.

There are higher levels of married couple allowance for those aged 65 or more during the tax year – see p. 135.

Finally, if the wife is totally incapacitated throughout the tax year and unable to look after herself *and* there is a child living with you, you may be able to claim additional personal allowance – see p. 101.

GETTING MARRIED

You claim the married couple's allowance for the part of the year you are married. For each month of the year (or part of the month) of marriage, you can claim one-twelfth of the married couple's allowance.

DATE OF MARRIAGE	AMOUNT OF ALLOWANCE
before	£
6 May	1,720
6 June	1,577
6 July	1,434
6 August	1,290
6 September	1,147
6 October	1,004
6 November	860
6 December	717
6 January	574
6 February	430
6 March	287
6 April	144

As long as you marry before 6 May 1994, you can claim the full allowance; if you marry before 6 June 1994 you can claim eleven-twelfths, and so on. The amount of the allowance is the same in 1994/95 as in 1993/94, although you will only receive 20 per cent of the amount after 6 April 1994.

If the man has a child living with him when he marries, he can carry on claiming the full additional personal allowance (also £1,720 for 1994/95, but again only 20 per cent) instead of the married couple's allowance (the full allowance is paid only if he marries before 6 May). He can't claim additional personal allowance after the year he marries.

EXAMPLE

Simon Halliday is divorced; his son Patrick aged eight lives with him. On 30 June 1994 he marries. Should he claim married couple's allowance or additional personal allowance for 1994/95? He can claim the full additional personal allowance of £1,720, but only a reduced married couple's allowance. Looking at the table on the left, he sees it would be £1,434. He should claim additional personal allowance.

If the woman has been claiming additional personal allowance, she can claim it for the year she marries but not after.

A LOW INCOME

If one of you has an income which is too low to use up all your allowances you may be able to transfer the unused part of some allowances:

● the husband can transfer all or half of the married couple's allowance to the wife

● the wife can claim all or half of the married couple's allowance

● either of you can transfer the unused part of a blind person's allowance to the other (even if the recipient is not blind)

● either of you have a right to half the married couple's allowance, but you can't transfer any of the extra allowance you get because of your age.

If you are entitled to transfer your allowances, write and tell your Tax Inspector. If you don't have a tax office, write to your wife's office giving both your names and NI numbers. If you ask for your personal allowance to be transferred (see p.108 for very few occasions this can be done), your tax office will automatically assume that you want the other allowances transferred too. If you ask to have your blind person's allowance transferred, it will be automatically assumed that you also want the married couple's allowance transferred. If you are the wife and want to transfer part of your blind person's allowance but you don't have a tax office, write to your husband's.

The exact amount of your income won't be known until after the end of the tax year, but an estimate of the amount of the allowances which can be transferred can be made at the start of, or during, the year. This can be included in the wife's PAYE code, for example. So you can get the benefit of the transferred allowances during the year. At the end of the year, the sums will be checked and you may find that too much or too little tax has been paid and a refund or extra bill is due. If you think it likely that you will have a low income in 1995/6 (for example, because you are a student), write and tell your Tax Inspector and ask to transfer the allowances. The normal six-year rule (see p. 50) for claiming allowances applies to the transfer of surplus allowances.

Once you have passed over your allowances for a tax year, you can't change your mind and ask for them back. But your Tax Inspector will allow you the benefit of your allowances if your income rises during the year (and your PAYE code will be adjusted).

TRANSFERRING MARRIED COUPLE'S ALLOWANCE

A husband or wife can transfer all or part of the married couple's allowance for 1993/94 if he or she has no income or his 'total income' (see p. 135) is less than the amount of his allowances.

EXAMPLE 1:TRANSFER OF MARRIED COUPLE'S ALLOWANCE

John Symes is a student with an income of £3,300 in 1993/94. His wife Penny works and has an income of £12,000.

John's tax bill	
Personal allowance	£3,445
Married couple's allowance	£1,720
	£5,165
less income	£3,300
Unused allowances	£1,865

The unused allowances of £1,865 are more than the married couple's allowance, £1,720, so the married couple's allowance can be transferred to Penny.

Penny's tax bill

Income	£12,000
less personal allowance	£3,445
Taxable income	£8,555

Tax due: 20% on £3,000	£600.00	
25% o£5,555	£1,388.75	
		£1,988.75
less married couple's allowance		
restricted to 20% of £1,720		£344.00
TOTAL TAX		£1,644.75

If John hadn't transferred the married couple's allowance, Penny's tax bill would be £1,988.75. So they have saved tax of £1,988.75 – £1,644.75 = £344.

TRANSFERRING THE HUSBAND'S PERSONAL ALLOWANCE

You can transfer the husband's personal allowance in 1993/94 only if you have transferred part of it in 1991/92 and 1992/93. And you can transfer the husband's personal allowance in 1994/95, only if you transferred part of it in 1993/94. You must also remain married to, and living with, your wife. The amount you can transfer is the smaller of:

A. the amount you deducted from your wife's income in the previous year

or

B. personal allowance *less* the husband's income for the current year.

INCOME

The type of income you have makes no difference to the allowances you can claim. But you may be able to transfer income from one to the other (by giving away your assets) and thus reduce the tax bill of one of you:

● a taxpayer could give investments to a non-taxpayer

● a higher-rate taxpayer could give investments to a basic-rate taxpayer

● a basic-rate taxpayer could give investments to a lower-rate taxpayer.

EXAMPLE

Jimmy Joplin has earnings of £25,000. His wife Petra is occupied full-time looking after their children, but has a small income (before tax £1,500) from an investment in unit trusts.

Jimmy's tax bill		
Earnings		£25,000
less personal allowance		£3,445
Taxable income		£21,555
Tax due: 20% on £3,000	£600.00	
25% on £18,555	£4,638.75	
		£5,238.75
less married couple's allowance		
restricted to 20% of £1,720		£344.00
TOTAL TAX		£4,894.75
Petra's tax bill		
Investment income		£1,500
less personal allowance		
(part of £3,445)		£1,500
Taxable income		nil

Petra cannot use up all her personal allowance. If Jimmy had some investments, such as shares or unit trusts, he could give them to Petra to enable her to use up the whole of her allowance and thus cut the tax bills paid by the two of them.

If you have investments which are jointly owned, your Tax Inspector will assume the income is split equally between you. If the investments are not owned in equal proportions, tell the Tax Inspector. You must make a joint declaration in writing on Form 17 and send it to the Inspector within 60 days (see p. 263). The allocation will start from the date your Form is received by the Tax Inspector.

HOME AND MARRIAGE

As a married couple you are entitled to claim tax relief for interest paid on a loan of £30,000 or less to buy or improve your only or main home; the tax relief will be split between you, any way you like. Unless you tell your Tax Inspector otherwise, the tax relief will be given to the partner who has the mortgage; with a joint mortgage, it will be split equally between the two of you. You are only allowed to claim 20 per cent of this interest paid from 6 April 1994 and 15 per cent from 6 April 1995.

If you choose to reallocate your tax relief on mortgage interest between you, you need to make an interest election (see p. 236 for when this might be sensible). For 1993/94 make this choice before 5 April 1995 on Form 15; and for 1994/95, before 5 April 1996.

If you each have a mortgage to buy a house before you marry, you can carry on getting the tax relief on both of them for up to twelve months. And if you are deciding to buy another home for you both to live in, you can also claim tax relief on a mortgage of £30,000 or less to do so. In all, you could be claiming tax relief on three homes when you first marry.

CAPITAL GAINS

You are each allowed to make £5,800-worth of net capital gains free of tax in 1993/94 and 1994/95 (see p.301). You can give an asset to your wife or husband and there will normally be no CGT bill. But from 6 April 1994 you are not able to use indexation relief to make a loss from a gain (see p. 307).

WHAT TO PUT IN YOUR TAX RETURN

You don't need to claim the personal allowance if you are under 65. If you are a husband, you claim married couple's allowance on page 11 of Forms 11P and 11 and page 3 of Form P1 under *Allowances to be claimed by married men*. If you are living with your wife, tick the box and give your wife's full name. And if you married after 6 April 1993, give the date of the marriage. But if you separated before 6 April 1990, are still married and wholly maintaining your wife, tick the second box.

Form 11P

You can only claim if you can tick in one of these two boxes.

See note 56.

Allowances to be claimed by married men

Married couple's allowance
Tick the relevant box to claim

You are living with your wife.

Give your wife's full name

You separated from your wife before 6 April 1990 but are still married to her and have wholly maintained her since the separation with voluntary payments for which you are not entitled to tax any relief.

If you married after 5 April 1993, give the date of marriage

/ /19

You can ask jointly to have the married couple's allowance allocated equally between the two of you or all to the wife. Or if you are the wife you can ask to have half the allowance allocated to you and it will be divided equally between husband and wife. Tick the box on page 11 of Forms 11 and 11P or page 4 of Form P1.

Form 11P

See note 57.

Married couples

Allocation of Married couple's allowance
A husband is responsible for claiming the married couple's allowance, but if you are living with your husband you may choose how the allowance is allocated between you.
For 1995-96 you can jointly ask for the whole of the allowance to be given to one of you.
Or, either of you can ask for half the allowance and it will then be divided equally between you.

Tick here if you wish to do this and you will be sent a form. (You do not have to complete a form if you want the allocation for 1994-95 to continue in 1995-96).

If you or your wife or husband want to transfer surplus allowances to each other, put a cross in the box under *Transfer of surplus allowances*. Ask for Form 575 to complete. If you have been sent this form with the Tax Return, complete it even if you have already transferred allowances.

Form 11P

Ask your Tax Office for A Guide for Married Couples (leaflet IR80). See note 62 for blind person's allowance

Transfer of surplus allowances to your wife or husband
To transfer any surplus allowances you must have been married and living with your wife or husband at any time in 1994-95. If you did not have enough income tax liability to use all (or any) of your married couple's allowance then you may transfer the surplus to your wife or husband.

Tick here if you need a transfer notice form.

If you have insufficient income to use all (or any) blind person's allowance you are entitled to then you may transfer any surplus to your wife or husband. If you are a husband who does not have sufficient income to use his personal allowance in some circumstances your wife may receive transitional allowance.

Additional personal allowance can be claimed if the wife is totally incapacitated and there is a child living with you by claiming it on page 11 of Forms 11P and 11 under *If your wife is unable to look after herself* (on page 4 of Form P1).

112

Form 11P

See note 59.

if your wife is unable to look after herself
You may be able to claim the additional personal allowance if
- you are living with your wife who is totally incapacitated because of disability or illness
- and you have a child living with you.

Give your wife's illness or disability

Tick here if your wife is likely to be unable to look after herself throughout the tax year ending on 5 April 1995.

Give the name of the youngest child for whom you can claim

Give the child's date of birth   /   /19

Tick here if child lives with you

If the child was 16 or over on 6 April 1994 and in full-time education or training give the name of the university, college or school or the type of training.

TREASURE TROVE CLUE No. 4

The maximum gift that can be made free of inheritance tax to someone getting married by someone not related to the bride or groom (4 digits).

14 · SEPARATED AND DIVORCED

Divorce and separation can lead to financial hardship – two households to support instead of one. Although the scope for tax-saving has reduced over the last few years, it still makes sense to structure your financial parting to take advantage of what little help the tax system gives you.

This chapter tells you:

● what happens when you separate

● how maintenance is taxed

● what happens to your home

● how your capital gains are taxed

● how your gifts are taxed.

WHAT HAPPENS WHEN YOU SEPARATE

You could make it a legal separation by getting a deed of separation or a Court Order, but you do not have to.

However, you have to tell your tax office if you separate permanently. You will be asked to complete a form and provide evidence that you have separated. Equally you must tell your tax office if you reconcile with your husband or wife or remarry.

Each of you remains entitled to your personal allowance. The husband can claim married couple's allowance if you separated before 6 April 1990, you are not divorced and you are wholly maintaining your wife by voluntary payments. If you separated after 6 April 1990, you cannot claim the married couple's allowance, except in the tax year of separation. From 6 April 1993, in the year you separate, each of you will get the married couple's allowance you were receiving at the time you separated. You can claim additional personal allowance if you have a child living with you. Both these allowances are restricted to 20 per cent from 6 April 1994.

HOW IS MAINTENANCE TAXED?

Maintenance can consist of direct payments or payments of household bills. It can be:

either

● voluntary (you cannot be forced to pay it). You do not get any tax relief on this, and there is no tax to pay by your spouse or former spouse

or

● enforceable (you can be made to pay up). It can be enforceable because you have some formal agreement with your spouse or because there is a Court Order or separation deed which specifies the maintenance payments. You can get tax relief on most enforceable maintenance payments you make.

The tax rules applying to enforceable maintenance payments differ depending on whether the arrangements were made on or after particular dates.

The 'new' rules apply to:

● maintenance agreements made on or after 15 March 1988 (unless they alter or replace an arrangement to which the old rules apply)

● maintenance agreements made before 15 March 1988 (but which you did not inform your Tax Inspector about in writing by 30 June 1988)

● Court Orders applied for after 15 March 1988

● Court Orders made after 30 June 1988 (unless they alter or replace an arrangement to which the old rules apply)

● maintenance assessed by the Child Support Agency.

Other agreements and Court Orders are taxed under the old rules. You can ask to have your maintenance treated under the new rules, but be careful it doesn't mean less tax relief for you – see p. 119.

HOW ENFORCEABLE MAINTENANCE PAYMENTS ARE TAXED UNDER THE 'NEW' RULES

RECEIVING MAINTENANCE

The maintenance payments you receive are tax-free. So you can, for example, have a further income up to the amount of the personal allowance (£3,445 in 1992/93 and 1993/94) without paying any tax (see example overleaf). If you remarry, and continue receiving payments from your former spouse, for example for a child, what you receive will still be free of tax.

PAYING MAINTENANCE

You can get tax relief equal to the married couple's allowance (£1,720 in 1993/94 and 1994/95). But from 1994/95 this is restricted to 20 per cent of £1,720. If your payments are less than this, your tax relief is the amount of your payments. In the tax year you separate, this tax relief is in addition to any other allowances you claim (see example overleaf).

The amount of the tax relief is reduced by the amount of tax relief you get on some other maintenance payments under the old rules.

You won't get tax relief if:

- the payments are made direct to a child

- the payments are to an unmarried partner with whom you are living

- the payments are voluntary

- the payments already get tax relief (e.g. mortgage payments)

- the payments are made under a foreign Court Order or agreement

- the payments are lump sum

- the payments are to an ex-wife or ex-husband who has remarried.

You can't get more tax relief than £1,720 for 1993/94 and 1994/95, even if you are making payments to two former spouses.

You will get tax relief on your maintenance payments through your PAYE code or through an adjustment to your tax bill at the end of the year. You do not deduct any tax from your maintenance payments.

EXAMPLE

Victor Lewis and his wife Susan separate on 30 September 1994. They have two children who will live with Susan after the separation. Victor's salary is £35,000 and Susan has a part-time job, which pays £7,500. Victor agrees to make maintenance payments of £2,496 in a full year, £48 a week. For 1994/95, this will make payments of £1,300 in total.

Susan's tax bill		
Earnings		£7,500
less personal allowance		£3,445
Taxable income		£4,055
Tax due: 20% on £3,000	£600.00	
25% on £1,055	£233.75	
		£863.75
less additional personal allowance		
restricted to 20% of £1,720		£344.00
TOTAL TAX		£519.75

Susan's after-tax income is earnings of £7,500 less £519.75 tax plus maintenance of £1,300, on which she pays no income tax. In total, for the year of separation her income is £8,280.

Victor's tax bill		
Earnings		£35,000
less personal allowance		£3,445
Taxable income		£31,555
Tax due: 20 % on £3,000	£600	
25% on £20,700	£5,175	
40% on £7,855	£3,142	
		£8,917
less married couple's allowance		
restricted to 20% of £1,720	£344	
maintenance of £1,300		
restricted to 20%	£260	
		£604
TOTAL TAX		£8,313

In 1995/96 Victor would not be able to claim the married couple's allowance, but only his personal allowance. But he would get the full relief for maintenance payments (equal to the married couple's allowance), so in practice he gets the same deductions as a married man.

HOW ENFORCEABLE MAINTENANCE PAYMENTS ARE TAXED UNDER THE OLD RULES

RECEIVING MAINTENANCE

For an ex-wife or ex-husband, the first £1,720 of maintenance received is tax-free in 1993/94 and 1992/93. If what you receive in maintenance has increased since 1988/89, you pay no tax on this extra bit. If you remarry and you carry on receiving the maintenance you won't get the tax-free bit equal to the married couple's allowance. If your child receives maintenance paid direct to him or her, rather than to you for his or her benefit, there is no tax-free band. But he or she will pay tax on the same amount as in 1988/89.

Children aged 18 or more
The rules vary for children aged 18 or over: see Chapter 16, 'Children and Students', on p. 128 and leaflet IR93 *Separation, Divorce and Maintenance Payments*.

PAYING MAINTENANCE

You can get tax relief on maintenance you pay to an ex-wife, ex-husband or your children (although the rules vary for children aged 18 or more – see below). You can no longer get tax relief on maintenance you pay to an unmarried partner.

The amount of tax relief which you will get in 1994/95 and 1993/94 will be the lower of your payments during the year or the amount on which you received tax relief in 1988/89. However, you only get 20 per cent of the first £1,720 of these payments. If you pay more maintenance than in 1988/89, you will not get tax relief on the extra bit. So, for example, if you got tax relief on maintenance payments of £3,000 in 1988/89, this is the maximum amount of tax relief you will get from now on even if your payments increase, £1,720 of these at 20 per cent and £1,280 at your highest rate of tax.

You will get tax relief by asking your Tax Inspector to adjust your PAYE code or by adjusting your tax bill at the end of the year.

Children aged 18 or more
If your payments under the old rules are made under an agreement to a child aged 18 or more, you can get tax relief at the basic rate only

(but at the higher rate, if applicable, for payments made under a Court Order).

From 6 April 1994, once your child reaches 21 you can no longer get tax relief on payments made direct to him or her.

EXAMPLE

Jeremy White pays maintenance under the old rules. He pays £3,000 to his ex-wife Sheila and £2,000 direct to each of his two children aged eight and ten, payable under a Court Order. In 1988/89, he paid £2,500 to Sheila and £2,000 to each of the children. How will the two households be taxed in 1994/95?

Jeremy's income is £30,000, but Sheila has no other income apart from her maintenance payments. Sheila can claim the full personal allowance (£3,445) and the additional personal allowance (£1,720) at 20 per cent only.

Sheila's tax bill		
Income		£ 3,000
less		
tax-free amount of maintenance deduction equal to married couple's allowance	£1,720	
increase over payments in 1988/89	£500	
		£2,220
		£780
less personal allowance (part of £3,445)		£780
Taxable income		nil

Sheila cannot use the whole of her personal allowances. She could earn the following amount without paying any tax: excess personal allowance (£3,445 − £780 = £2,665) + additional personal allowance (£1,720 at 20 per cent is £344) = £4,385.

Her two children can each deduct the personal allowance (£3,445) from the maintenance paid direct to each of them. As the allowance is more than the maintenance, neither child pays any tax. Both children have unused allowances of £3,445 − £2,000 = £1,445. The children are not entitled to the tax-free bit of maintenance of £1,720 which Sheila has.

Jeremy's tax bill

Income		£30,000
less allowances (excluding first £1,720 of maintenance)		
maintenance 1988/89 level for Sheila	£780	
maintenance 1988/89 level for children	£4,000	
personal allowance	£3,445	
		£8,225
Taxable income		£21,775
Tax due: 20% on £3,000	£600.00	
25% on £18,775	£4,693.75	
		£5,293.75
less first £1,720 of maintenance restricted to 20%		£344.00
TOTAL TAX		£4,949.75

SWITCHING TO THE NEW RULES OR STAYING WITH THE OLD?

You can switch from the old to the new rules if you wish. The decision whether to switch or not depends on the size of your maintenance payments and to whom you make them:

● if you make payments to children, you would lose the tax relief if you switched to the new rules – as Example 1 (overleaf) shows

● if you make payments to your former wife or husband only, you may find that at some stage you get more relief under the new rules. If the married couple's allowance (the amount of tax relief you get for maintenance under the new rules) is more than the payments on which you got tax relief in 1988/89, you will be better off under the new rules (as Example 2, overleaf, shows).

If you want to switch you must choose to do so within a year of the end of the tax year in which you want the new tax rules to apply. Ask for Form 142. The rules would apply for the whole of that tax year. Once you have chosen to be taxed by the new rules, you cannot change your mind and revert to the old ones. Take care when considering this because tax relief for married couple's allowance is reducing to 20 per cent from 1994/95, and 15 per cent from 1995/96.

SUMMARY OF HOW ENFORCEABLE MAINTENANCE PAYMENTS ARE TAXED

	UNDER OLD RULES	UNDER NEW RULES
If you are receiving maintenance	If spouse (or ex-), an amount equal to married couple's allowance is tax-free. Plus any increase over what you received in 1988/89	All maintenance is tax-free
If you are paying maintenance	Tax relief on amount of maintenance due and paid in 1988/89 to spouse (or ex-) or children. First £1,720 only allowed at 20 per cent	Tax relief equal to married couple's allowance on maintenance to spouse (or ex-) at 20 per cent
How maintenance is paid	All maintenance paid without tax deducted (sometimes to a child aged 18 or more)	All maintenance paid without tax deducted

EXAMPLE 1

How would Jeremy's and Sheila's households (see p. 118) be taxed if they switched to the new rules?

Under the old rules Jeremy gets tax relief of £6,500. Under the new rules it would be equal to the married couple's allowance of £1,720. Clearly he is better off sticking with the old rules.

EXAMPLE 2

Darren makes enforceable maintenance payments of £1,900 under the old rules to his wife Carey for his child. But this is an increase of £300 over the amount of maintenance he paid in 1988/89, so his tax relief is pegged at £1,600. Under the new rules he would get tax relief equal to the married couple's allowance of £1,720 at 20 per cent = £344. Clearly he should switch to the new rules.

WHAT HAPPENS TO YOUR HOME

Once you are separated or divorced, you are likely to need two homes instead of one. You can each get tax relief on loans of up to £30,000 to buy a home. But if only one of you is paying the interest for your spouse for a home bought with a loan on or after 6 April 1988, there will be no tax relief. If the home was bought with a loan before 6 April 1988, you can get a maximum tax relief of interest on loans of £30,000 for the two homes (from 6 April 1994 tax relief at the lower rate only). So the best financial arrangement is for each of you to pay the mortgage for the home you are living in.

HOW YOUR CAPITAL GAINS ARE TAXED

You can carry on making gifts to your husband or wife free of CGT in the year of separation. After this, CGT may be payable.

If one of you moves out of the family home and gives it or sells it to the other, any gain you make will be free of CGT as long as the transfer happens within two years of the date of separation. Even if the transfer occurs after that, there may still be no CGT to pay as long as your ex-spouse is still living in the family home and you have not claimed that any other property is your main home.

If you buy a home for your spouse or ex-spouse on or after 6 April 1988, there could be capital gains tax to pay when you dispose of it. For a house bought before 6 April 1988, there may be no CGT to pay.

HOW YOUR GIFTS ARE TAXED

If you are separated, any gifts the one makes to the other are free of inheritance tax (see p. 328). But once you are divorced, inheritance tax may be payable, unless the gift is for the maintenance of an ex-spouse or any children.

WHAT TO PUT IN YOUR TAX RETURN

If you receive maintenance or alimony under the old rules, you will find the slot to put this information on the 1994/95 Forms 11P and 11 on page 7 under *Maintenance and alimony you receive* and on Form P1 at the bottom of page 2.

Form 11P

Notes	
Other maintenance or alimony payments made under the first order or agreement following divorce, separation etc are not taxable.	**Maintenance and alimony you receive** Complete this item if you receive maintenance or alimony payments under: • a legally enforceable agreement first made before 15 March 1988 and received by a Tax Office by 30 June 1988 or • a court order first made before 15 March 1988, or by 30 June 1988 if the application to the court was made before 16 March 1988 or • a court order or legal agreement or Child Support Assessment which replaces, varies or adds to such an order or agreement.
	Date the original order or agreement was first made / /19
If there is not enough space, attach a separate sheet of paper.	Date of any further order, agreement, or Child Support Assessment, if original order or agreement has been amended, or replaced or added to since 15 March 1988 / /19
Up to £1,720 may be exempt from tax. See note 36. Ask for "Separation, divorce and	Amount received in 1993-94 £
	Tick here if you wish to claim exemption from tax for maintenance or alimony received.

Give the date of the original agreement and whether it has changed since 15 March 1988. Enter the amount of maintenance you received in 1993/94. Put a tick in the box to claim your tax-free bit (£1,720).

If your former wife or husband pays you something on a voluntary basis, you do not need to pay tax on it and so you do not need to enter it in your Tax Return.

If you are paying the maintenance turn to page 9 of Forms 11P and 11 (*Maintenance or alimony payments*), or page 3 of Form P1 (*Deductions: legally binding maintenance or alimony payments*).

Form 11P

	Other deductions
Do not give details of maintenance or alimony payments which cannot be legally enforced.	**Maintenance or alimony payments** Fill in this item if you make payments to maintain your children or divorced or separated husband/wife under a court order, decree of the court, a legally binding agreement or Child Support Assessment.
The rules for tax relief depend on the date of the first order or agreement. Your Tax Office will work out the amount you can claim. See note 48.	Date of your current order, agreement or Child Support Assessment / /19 If your current order, agreement or Child Support Assessment. is dated on or after 15 March 1988 and varies, replaces or revives an earlier order or agreement which was in force on 15 March 1988 give the date of that earlier order. / /19
	Amount you were ordered to pay in 1994-94 £
	Amount you actually paid in 1993-94 (if this is different from the amount given above) £ Name(s) of person(s) you paid
	Tick here if the payments are to your ex-husband/wife and he/she has remarried. Give the date of remarriage if you know it / /19
Payments of this type may be partly tax deductible in 1993-94 and later years	If you made payments to the Department of Social Security to cover Income Support for your separated or divorced wife/husband or for the maintenance by her/him of children of the marriage under a Court Order or Child Support Assessment, show the amount you paid in 1993-94 £ Tick here if you will be making payments of this kind in 1994-95.

Enter the date of the original agreement and the amount you were ordered to pay. If the amount you actually paid was different give this figure, too. Give the name of the person you paid and tick in the box if the payments are to a former wife or husband who has remarried. Give the date of the remarriage if you know it.

If your current agreement was made on or after 15 March 1988, and it alters or replaces an earlier order, give the date of the earlier order.

You are also asked for information about any payments you make to the Department of Social Security to cover Income Support for a separated or divorced spouse or for the maintence of your children from that marriage under a Court Order or Child Support Assessment.

Remember you can't get tax relief for any voluntary payments you make, so do not enter them.

If you have a child or children living with you and you are either separated or divorced, you may be able to claim an additional personal allowance (p. 100).

15 • WIDOWED

Sorting out your finances may seem like the last thing you want to do when you are first widowed. But knowing what your tax position will be and how much income you are going to have is very important. So do not neglect to find out this essential information.

As far as the tax system is concerned, your marriage is ended once you are widowed, whether man or woman. But there is a special allowance which can be claimed by a widow to ease the financial burden.

WIDOWS

If you are widowed you can claim in the first year:

● the rest of your own personal allowance not already claimed

● the rest of the married couple's allowance not already claimed by your husband (see p. 104 for how much this would be), but from 6 April 1994 this will be restricted to 20 per cent

● the full additional personal allowance, if you have a child or children living with you

● widow's bereavement allowance of £1,720, again only at 20 per cent

And you may be able to claim the benefits listed opposite.

In the second tax year you are widowed, you can claim the widow's bereavement allowance (unless you have remarried before the end of the first tax year) as well as your personal allowance. In the third tax year, you are entitled simply to a personal allowance. You can carry on claiming additional personal allowance if you have a child or children living with you.

EXAMPLE

Rosalind Smith's husband, Simon, dies in September 1994 leaving two young children, aged seven and nine. Rosalind has a part-time job and had earned £1,300 and received investment income of £3,500 before his death. Tax relief on their mortgage interest was given through the MIRAS scheme.

After his death and before the start of the next tax year, Rosalind earned another £1,500 and received investment income of £4,000. She also received income of £2,000 from Simon's pension scheme.

Rosalind's income will be taxed as follows:

Earnings from job	£2,800	
Investment income	£7,500	
Pension	£2,000	
Total income		£12,300
less personal allowance		£3,445
Taxable income		£8,855
Tax due: 20% on £3,000	£600.00	
25% on £5,855	£1,463.75	
		£2,063.75
less credit for allowances:		
additional personal	£1,720	
widow's bereavement	£1,720	
part of married couple's	£1,004	
	£4,444	
Credit for allowances restricted to 20%		£888.80
TOTAL TAX		£1,174.95

BENEFITS YOU CAN CLAIM

So far this chapter has explained the tax treatment of your existing income, plus pension. However, there are some social security benefits which you may be able to get.

You may be entitled either to *widowed mother's allowance* or *widow's pension*, both of which are taxable. You may also be able to claim *widow's payment* (one-off tax-free payment of £1,000).

For more information, ask for leaflet NP45 *A guide to widow's benefits* from your social security office.

WIDOWERS

You can claim the full married couple's allowance in the tax year your wife dies as well as your personal allowance. And you can claim additional personal allowance in the tax year she dies and after if you have children living with you.

WHAT TO PUT IN YOUR TAX RETURN

You claim the widow's bereavement allowance on your Tax Return by ticking the box and giving the date of your husband's death. You can find this under *Allowance for widows* at the bottom of page 11 on Forms 11P and 11 and on page 4 of Form P1.

Form 11P

See note 58.

Allowance for widows
You may be able to claim this allowance for the tax year in which you husband died and also the following year.

Give the date of
your husband's death

/   /19

Tick here to
make your claim

If you receive widow's pension, you will have to enter this on Forms 11P and 11 in the *Pensions* section on page 3 under *State Pensions* and in the *Pensions and benefits for 1993/94* section of Form P1 on page 2 under *Amount of State pension you were entitled to*.

Form 11P

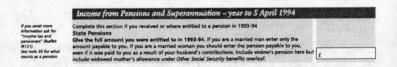

If you wnat more
information ask for
"Income tax and
pensioners" (leaflet
IR121).
See note 20 for what
counts as a pension.

Income from Pensions and Superannuation – year to 5 April 1994

Complete this section if you received or where entitled to a pension in 1993-94
State Pensions
Give the full amount you were entitled to in 1993-94. If you are a married man enter only the amount payable to you. If you are a married woman you should enter the pension payable to you, even if it was paid to you as a result of your husband's contributions. Include widow's pension here but include widowed mother's allowance under *Other Social Security benefits* overleaf.

£

Widowed mother's allowance is entered on page 4 of Forms 11 and 11P under *Other social security benefits* and on page 2 of Form P1 under *Widowed mother's allowance, invalid care allowance and industrial death benefit you were entitled to*.

Form 11P

	Other Social Security benefits		
If the benefit you are claiming is not listed here you do not have to give details	If you claimed any of these benefits, give the full amount you were entitled to in 1993-94.	Widowed mother's allowance	£
		Invalid care allowance	£
		Industrial death benefit	£

Do not put widow's payment or war widow's pension on your Tax Return as these are tax-free.

If you receive a pension from your husband or wife's former employer, enter details under *Other pensions* on page 3 of Forms 11P and 11 (*Other pensions received* near the top of page 2 of Form P1).

Form 11P

	Give the name(s) and address(es) of the payer(s) of the pension and the full amount of your pension(s) for 1993-94.	
If there is not enough space put the details on a separate sheet of paper		£

The Tax Return also asks for details of pensions you are currently receiving in the year 1994/95, to help ensure that the right amount of tax is deducted under PAYE. Enter the details requested on page 4 of Forms 11P and 11 under *Income from pensions – year to 5 April 1995*, and on page 2 of Form P1 under *Pensions you currently receive or expect to receive before 6 April 1995*.

Form 11P

Notes

This section asks for pension(s) information for the year ending on 5 April 1995. The pensions section on the previous page asked you for details about your pension(s) for the year which ended on 5 April 1994.

See note 20 for what counts as a state pension.

Income from pensions – year to 5 April 1995

If you currently receive a pension or expect to start receiving a pension before 6 April 1995, please give the details asked for below. In the column headed "Amount of pension you expect to receive or expect to receive", please show:

- for pensions you already receive – the amount you get at the time you fill the form in
- for pensions you expect to start receiving – the amount you will get (if you know it).

Starting date (if after 5 April 1994)	Amount of pension you receive or expect to receive	Say whether this is per week, every 4 weeks, each month, every 3 months or per year	Tick if this is after tax	Tick if a state pension
/ /19	£			
/ /19	£			
/ /19	£			
/ /19	£			
/ /19	£			
/ /19	£			

16 · CHILDREN AND STUDENTS

The idea that your newborn infant could be a taxpayer might strike you as laughable. Nevertheless, a child, no matter how young, is treated as a single person. Your child is entitled to personal allowances and may have to fill in a Tax Return. As far as the tax system is concerned, your offspring is a child until marriage or the 18th birthday intervenes, whichever is earlier.

This chapter looks at how children's income is taxed (see below), what allowances can be claimed (p. 129) and what happens to any capital gains (p. 130). The taxation of a student's income is described on p. 130.

A CHILD'S INCOME

INCOME FROM A JOB

Income your child earns from a job (for example as a paper-boy or girl) could be taxable. But the personal allowance can be deducted from it (see p. 129) and your child will probably not have to pay any tax on it.

If your child receives a grant or scholarship, it will not be income. However, if your employer gives your child a scholarship as one of your fringe benefits, you can be taxed on it.

INCOME FROM INVESTMENTS

Most children will be non-taxpayers, because their income is unlikely to be large and they can claim the personal allowance to deduct from it.

If your child is a non-taxpayer and has a bank or building society account, fill in Form R85 which means that the interest should be paid without tax deducted. Before 6 April 1991, tax deducted could not be claimed back by a non-taxpayer. If any interest has been paid since 6 April 1991 with tax deducted, you can claim back the amount of the tax (see p. 267).

For the income to be your child's, the money to make the investment should be, for example, a gift from a relative or earnings from a job. But an investment of money you give your child will produce income considered to be yours, apart from the first £100 each year. If your child's income from your gifts is coming up to £100 a year, your child should invest your gifts in investments which are treated as tax-free, such as National Savings Certificates.

INCOME FROM MAINTENANCE

If a child receives maintenance under the new rules (see p. 115), there is no tax to pay. If a parent or step-parent pays maintenance to a child under the old rules, your child can deduct a personal allowance from it, but can't claim the tax-free deduction (equal to the married couple's allowance) which an ex-wife or ex-husband can claim. However, if the amount of maintenance has increased over the level received by the child in 1988/89, the increase is tax-free income for your child.

Child aged 18 to 20

If your child is 18 but less than 21, maintenance payments under the old rules made under an agreement, rather than a Court Order, may be paid by the parent with basic-rate tax already deducted. Your child can claim a refund, if he or she should pay less tax. There is no higher-rate tax to pay on maintenance paid under an agreement, but could be if paid under a Court Order. If the amount of the maintenance has increased since 1988/89, the increase will be tax-free.

Child aged 21 or more

From 6 April 1994, there is no tax relief on maintenance paid to a child aged 21 or over.

ALLOWANCES FOR CHILDREN

Your child can claim the personal allowance (£3,445 in 1993/94 and 1994/95) to deduct from any income.

If you are divorced, separated, widowed or unmarried you can claim the additional personal allowance for a child who lives with you and is maintained by you. You may also be able to claim if you are a married couple and the wife is totally incapacitated during the whole of the tax year. Additional personal allowance is described in more detail on p. 100.

CAPITAL GAINS

If you give an asset to your child, any gain on the asset will be your child's (though any income from it will be yours). If your child (while under 18 and unmarried) sells the asset and invests it to produce an income, the income is still your income.

Note that your gift will be considered a disposal by you and capital gains tax might be payable.

STUDENTS

A STUDENT'S INCOME

A student's income is taxable and includes:

● earnings from a holiday job. If it is the student's only income and will not be more than the personal allowance, it can be paid without tax deducted. Ask for Form P38S from the tax office

● what is earned while at work, if the student is sponsored

● earnings from part-time jobs

● income from investments.

However, a student may also receive the following and these are normally not part of a student's taxable income:

● grants from a local education authority (although it can vary from area to area)

● if the student is sponsored, what is received from the sponsor while at college. To qualify as tax-free, the course must last an academic year and involve full-time attendance of at least 20 weeks. The amount of the payment from 6 April 1993 should be £7,000 or less or the amount which would be received as a grant, whichever is higher

● post-graduate grants from a research council

● other awards and scholarships may be tax-free.

A STUDENT'S ALLOWANCES

A student can claim the usual personal allowances to set against taxable income, that is, personal, married couple's or additional personal.

WHAT TO PUT IN YOUR TAX RETURN

You do not enter your child's income or claim your child's allowances in your Tax Return. These should be put in the child's own Tax Return. However, any income your child receives as a result of your gift should be put in your Return as it is treated as your income (unless £100 or less). Put this income under *Income and capital from settlements for which you have provided funds* on page 6 of Forms 11P and 11 and under *All other income* on page 2 of Form P1. Remember to show the split of income between husband and wife if it was a joint gift (see p. 263).

Form 11P

Income and capital from a settlement will be treated as yours if certain conditions apply. See note 34.

Income and capital from settlements for which you have provided funds
Complete this item the income, or payments of capital, should be treated as belonging to you for tax purposes.
Name and/or brief details of the settlement

Tick here if any income was taxed at 20% (or carried a 20% credit) £

Claim additional personal allowance (see p. 100) by entering the details asked for on the last page of the Tax Return under *If you have a child and are single, separated, divorced or widowed.*

TREASURE TROVE CLUE No. 5

The basic rate of income tax, as a percentage (2 digits).

17 • RETIRED OR NEAR RETIREMENT AGE

You will find that your finances will change when you get older. Your income will alter, the amount and its source. You are more likely to be receiving a state pension and a pension from your former employer or from your own personal pension scheme, rather than a salary from a job or income from your own business. You may also have investments which will pay interest and dividends, or even earnings from a part-time job. If you own your own home you could consider supplementing your income with a home income scheme.

Your taxation will also change, since you might have different forms to fill in and send to your Tax Inspector. You also will get higher tax allowances depending on your age. There are two levels at which your personal and married couple's allowances will increase, age 65 and age 75. However these increases will be scaled down if your income is over a certain level. You also get some tax relief on your private medical insurance premiums if you are aged 60 or over.

This chapter includes details on:

income

- pensions
- investments
- annuities
- Guaranteed Income Bond
- a job
- home income scheme
- 'total income'

allowances and deductions

- allowances in 1993/94 and 1994/95
- reduction of allowances
- outgoings

what to put in your Tax Return.

INCOME

PENSIONS

The following pensions are taxable:

- state retirement, including the amount relating to your past earnings
- old person's
- from your former employer
- from your own personal pension plan
- from a partnership of which you were a partner.

Even though the state retirement pension is taxable you will not have to pay any tax on it if it is your only income, because it will be less than your personal allowance. However if you have other income such as a pension from your former employer or income from investments, there will be tax to pay because the state retirement pension is paid without any tax being deducted. The tax on any other pensions will be collected through the PAYE system so it may seem that you are paying a lot of tax, because your state pension is being paid effectively 'tax-free' because it is less than your personal allowance. This means you have no personal allowance left to set against the other income.

A married woman can deduct her personal allowance from her pension, even if the pension is based on her husband's contributions, rather than her own (though not any dependency allowance her husband gets for her before she reaches 60).

Pensions from abroad are taxed slightly differently. Normally you pay tax on 90 per cent of the pension and it is taxed on a preceding-year basis. If you meet certain conditions, lump sum benefits paid by an overseas scheme will be free of tax. Ask your Tax Inspector for details of Extra-Statutory Concession A10.

If your extra income is from investments, then you will receive a Notice of Assessment on any extra tax that you may have to pay.

INVESTMENTS

If your total income reaches a certain level, then your higher allowances which you receive after 65 will gradually be reduced (although they will never be lower than the normal personal allowances which everyone gets).

Therefore if you have a high income and you have money to invest, it makes financial sense to go for investments which are tax free, such as National Savings Certificates.

If you are a non-taxpayer and have a bank or building society account, the interest can be paid without tax deducted if you fill in Form R85. And, from 6 April 1992, if you pay tax only at the lower rate (20 per cent), you can claim back part of the tax deducted from the interest (tax is deducted at the basic rate of 25 per cent). If you regularly have to claim tax back, ask for Tax Claim Form R40 rather than a Tax Return. Fill it in and you should get a rebate if you have paid too much tax. You can do this before the end of the tax year if you have already received all your income of this type and the refund is more than £50. If the refund is £50 or less you will have to wait until your tax bill is sorted out after the tax year.

ANNUITIES

One way of increasing your income if elderly could be to buy an annuity from a life insurance company. In return for a lump sum, the company will guarantee to pay you an income for the rest of your life, for example. There are many different variations on the theme and you should ask for advice on the best sort for you. You can get independent advice from businesses regulated by organizations such as FIMBRA. A company salesman can give you advice on one company's products.

With an annuity which you buy separately, not as part of a pension scheme, part of the income is thought to be a return of the money you have invested (and is tax-free) and part is interest. Only the interest part of the income you receive is taxed. The voucher you receive with your payment will show you the interest part to be taxed.

GUARANTEED INCOME BOND

There is a new National Savings bond which has been introduced for pensioners aged 65 or over. Interest will be paid monthly and gross which has advantages if you are a non-taxpayer. The bond will have a five-year fixed rate of interest.

A JOB

Once you reach retirement age, you do not have to pay National Insurance contributions any more, but if you are in a job your employer does.

HOME INCOME SCHEME

You can increase your income by using a home income scheme if you are aged 65 or more and own your own home (although it doesn't usually make financial sense unless you are 75 or 80). A life insurance company gives you a mortgage on your home and you use the lump sum raised to buy an annuity (see above). You get tax relief on the mortgage interest payments at the basic rate of 25 per cent (see p. 234).

(see p. 234)

'TOTAL INCOME'

To work out whether you are entitled to the higher level of personal and married couple's allowance for older people, you need to know your 'total income'. Broadly, to find your 'total income' you have to add up your income for the year and take away your deductions. Remember that your income is your gross income, which is that before any tax is deducted. Gross income includes gross interest. You also have to include in gross income any taxable gain you make on a life insurance policy, for example, a property bond. You don't have to include any income which is tax-free, such as the return from a National Savings Certificate. If you are married, your share of any income you receive jointly is included.

Your deductions include mortgage interest, pension contributions, premiums paid for insurance to cover private medical bills and half Class 4 National Insurance contributions (payable if under 65), but not investments in the Business Expansion Scheme.

ALLOWANCES AND DEDUCTIONS

ALLOWANCES

The allowances you can claim are:

● personal allowance

● married couple's allowance

There are two higher levels of personal and married couple's allowances: one for people aged 65 or more and a still higher level for those aged 75 or more. The allowances can be deducted from any kind of income you have – pension, earnings, investment income and so on.

You can claim the higher allowances if you are 65 or more (or 75 or more) during the tax year, although the higher married couple's allowance can be claimed if *either of you* is aged 65 or more (or 75 or more). So the amount of your married couple's allowance depends on the age of the older of you. As from 6 April 1994 the married couple's allowance is restricted to 20 per cent.

The allowances for 1993/94 and 1994/95 are:

	1993/94	1994/95
personal allowance (65–74)	£4,200	£4,200
personal allowance (75 plus)	£4,370	£4,370
married couple's (65–74)	£2,465	£2,665
married couple's (75 plus)	£2,505	£2,705

So, for example, for a married couple of 75, their joint allowances in 1994/95 would total £4,370 + £4,370 + £2,665 = £11,405 (a married couple under 65 would have total allowances of £8,610).

For the 1994/95 tax year, if you are under 65 you can choose to have the married couple's allowance of £1,720 deducted wholly from the wife's income or split between the two of you, rather than deducted wholly from the husband's income. But the extra age-related bit of the married couple's allowance (above £1,720) cannot be allocated differently – it will remain deducted from the husband's income.

REDUCTION OF ALLOWANCES

If your 'total income' (see p. 135) is above a certain level the amount of personal and married couple's allowances is gradually reduced until the allowances equal the level of the allowances for the under-65s.

For 1993/94 and 1994/95, if the husband's 'total income' is £14,200 or more, first the personal allowance is reduced until it reaches the level for the under-65s and subsequently the married couple's allowance is reduced, too. If a wife's 'total income' is £14,200 or more, only her personal allowance is reduced. The amount of the wife's 'total income' never affects the amount of the married couple's allowance – even if she is the older of the two and entitles you to a larger allowance than you would get based on the husband's age. It makes sense to take advantage of this when you are splitting your income from investments between the two of you.

The allowance is reduced by £1 for each extra £2 of income over the income limit. If part of your income includes income from investments, it makes sense to look at how you can avoid this trap and keep more of your age-related allowances. The main way you can do this is to look at tax-free investments, such as National Savings Certificates or TESSAs.

EXAMPLE 1

Joan Darby is 74. Her income comes from a variety of sources, including from investments and totals £14,500. This is £300 over the

£14,200 limit above which age-related allowance is reduced. The age-related allowance for someone of her age is £4,200 but this will be reduced by £1 for each £2 of income over the limit, that is by ½ of £300. Joan's allowance will therefore be £4,200 – £150 = £4,050.

EXAMPLE 2

Simon Potter is 70 and his wife Susan 76. Because of his age, Simon can claim the personal allowance for those aged 65 or more (£4,200). He can also claim the married couple's allowance for those aged 75 or more (£2,705) because Susan is over 75. Susan can claim the personal allowance for those aged 75 or more (£4,370).

However, while Susan's income is £10,200, Simon's income is £16,100. His income includes investment income, such as grossed-up building society interest and distributions from unit trusts. Simon's allowances will be reduced by £1 for every extra £2 of income he has over the limit. He has £16,100 – £14,200 = £1,900 income over the income limit. His allowances will be reduced by £1,900 ÷ 2 = £950. His personal allowance of £4,200 is reduced to £3,445 (a reduction of £755 to the level of the personal allowance for the under-65s). After this, the remaining £195 has to be deducted from the married couple's allowance so that is reduced from £2,705 to £2,510. This gives a total reduction in allowances of £950.

DEDUCTIONS: PRIVATE MEDICAL INSURANCE

If you pay the premiums for an insurance policy to provide private medical care, these can be deducted from your income under certain conditions. As from 6 April 1994, you can only get relief at 25 per cent. The policy must cover a person aged 60 or over during the tax year, but it can also cover a husband or wife under this age. No one else under 60 can be covered by the policy without losing tax relief. To keep the tax relief, the policy cannot include cash benefits of more than £5 a night, GP visits (apart from operations), dental treatment, eye tests, plastic surgery for cosmetic purposes or alternative medicine.

If you are paying the premiums for someone else you can get the tax relief, regardless of your age. But this doesn't normally apply if your employer pays.

You will get tax relief in the same way as you do for a mortgage – it will be deducted from what you pay for the insurance. This means non-taxpayers could benefit, too. And if you pay tax only at the lower rate of 20 per cent, the amount you pay will still include the full deduction for basic rate tax of 25 per cent.

138

WHAT TO PUT IN YOUR TAX RETURN

The Tax Return includes space to claim the higher levels of personal allowance and married couple's allowance. You can claim the higher level of personal allowance if you are 65 or more during the tax year by ticking the box on page 11 of Forms 11P and 11 or page 3 of Form P1.

Form 11P

See note 55.	**Allowances for those born before 6 April 1930**	
	You may be able to claim a higher amount of personal allowance if you were born before 6 April 1930. **Tick here to make your claim**	☐

If you are a married man, you can claim the higher level of married couple's allowance if you or your wife are 65 or more during the tax year. Claim it by ticking the box on page 11 of Forms 11P and 11 or page 3 of Form P1 and put your wife's date of birth.

Form 11P

See note 55.	**If you or your wife were born before 6 April 1930** If you are entitled to the married couple's allowance, you can claim a higher amount of allowance if you or your wife were born before 6 April 1930		
	Tick here to make your claim	☐	If your wife was born before 6 April 1930, give her date of birth / /19

Give the amount of state retirement or widow's pension you received in the last tax year under *State Pensions* on page 3 of Forms 11P and 11 and on page 2 of Form P1. Give details of other pensions received, whether from an employer's scheme, a personal pension, a service pension or an industrial disablement pension under *Other Pensions* on Forms 11P and 11 and under *Other pensions received* on Form P1.

Form 11P

	Income from Pensions and Superannuation – year to 5 April 1994	
If you want more information ask for "Income tax and pensioners" (leaflet IR121). See note 20 for what counts as a pension.	Complete this section if you received or where entitled to a pension in 1993-94 **State Pensions** Give the full amount you were entitled to in 1993-94. If you are a married man enter only the amount payable to you. If you are a married woman you should enter the pension payable to you, even if it was paid to you as a result of your husband's contributions. Include widow's pension here but include widowed mother's allowance under *Other Social Security benefits* overleaf.	£
If there is not enough space put the details on a separate sheet of paper	Give the name(s) and address(es) of the payer(s) of the pension and the full amount of your pension(s) for 1993-94.	£

The Tax Return also asks for details of pensions you are receiving, or expect to start receiving in the current tax year, to help ensure that the right amount of tax is deducted under PAYE (see p. 148). Enter the details requested on page 4 of Forms 11P and 11, page 2 of Form P1.

Form 11P

Notes

This section asks for pension(s) information for the year ending on 5 April 1995. The pensions section on the previous page asked you for details about your pension(s) for the year which ended on 5 April 1994.

See note 20 for what counts as a state pension.

Income from pensions – year to 5 April 1995

If you currently receive a pension or expect to start receiving a pension before 6 April 1995, please give the details asked for below. In the column headed "Amount of pension you expect to receive or expect to receive", please show:

- for pensions you already receive – the amount you get at the time you fill the form in

- for pensions you expect to start receiving – the amount you will get (if you know it).

Starting date (if after 5 April 1994)	Amount of pension you receive or expect to receive	Say whether this is per week, every 4 weeks, each month, every 3 months or per year	Tick if this is after tax	Tick if a state pension
/ /19	£			
/ /19	£			
/ /19	£			
/ /19	£			
/ /19	£			
/ /19	£			

If you have received a refund of contributions from a Free-standing Additional Voluntary Contributions scheme on retirement, give details at the bottom of page 3 on Forms 11P and 11. There is no space for this in Form P1, so attach a letter giving the details.

Form 11P

Surpluses repaid from a Free Standing Additional Voluntary Contributions scheme
Complete this item if, when you retired or left pensionable service, some of your contributions from a free-standing additional voluntary contributions (FSAVC) scheme were repaid to you. Give the gross amount shown on the certificate given to you by the scheme administrator.   £

If you get tax relief on private medical insurance premiums for yourself or someone else over 60, give the details requested in the *Other deductions* section on page 9 of Forms 11P and 11 under *Private medical insurance for people aged 60 or over*.

Form 11P

If you would like more details ask your Tax Office for "Tax Relief for Private Medical Insurance" (leaflet IR103).

See note 46. Basic rate relief is given at source: give the amount you actually paid

Private medical insurance for people aged 60 and over
Complete this if you paid private medical insurance premiums for someone aged 60 or over (including you and/or your husband/wife) under a contract that was eligible for tax relief. If you wish to claim tax relief at the higher rate, please ask your insurer for a certificate of premiums paid in 1993-94 and then send it to your Tax Office.
Name of insurer

Contract number   Net amount paid in 1993-94 £

18 · EMPLOYEES: EARNINGS AND EXPENSES

Employees may feel helpless when it comes to dealing with the tax system. A common view is that it is all handled by your employer and so there is nothing for you to do. And many of you may have little communication with your Tax Inspector and so feel divorced from the whole taxing process.

Whatever your view about the influence you can bring to bear on your tax bill, there is no need to pay more than you have to, even if it is only small sums that you can save. Both your Tax Inspector and your employer are fallible human beings and make mistakes. And so do you. You may have forgotten to claim some deduction against tax which would be allowed or to tell your Tax Inspector as quickly as you can about a change in circumstances which means less tax. To satisfy yourself that you are not paying too much tax, you have to follow up the information which you receive about the tax you are paying. This chapter should help you to do this.

As an employee, you need to know what is the income from your job (called earnings, or emoluments in tax jargon). You also need to know what expenses the tax system allows you to deduct from this earned income (p. 144). You may receive fringe benefits as part of your remuneration package; how these are taxed is explained in Chapter 19, 'Employees: Fringe Benefits', p. 161.

You can find the information you need to check the tax you pay on the earnings from your job in your:

● payslip (p. 153) which your employer gives you when you are paid

● Form P60 (p. 154) which your employer must give you at the end of the tax year

● Notice of Coding (p. 150), although you may not receive one every year. This will be sent to you by your Tax Inspector

● in some circumstances, your Tax Inspector will send you a Notice of Assessment (Form P70) when your tax bill is sorted out after the end of the tax year. This includes information about all your income, not just the income from your job. Chapter 9, 'The Forms', p. 64 tells you how to check this.

Income tax on your earnings is not the only tax you pay; you will also find that National Insurance contributions (p. 154) will be deducted from your wage or salary.

EARNINGS

Earnings are payments or rewards (e.g. money, fringe benefits, gifts) you receive for the work you do in your job. Not everything your employer pays you will be treated as earnings; genuine personal gifts (for example, wedding presents) are not taxable, although other gifts are. The deciding factor in determining whether a payment or a reward is part of your earnings is whether it is received because of your job. And payments received from someone else besides your employer can be earnings. But gifts costing less than £100 (including VAT) will be tax-free as long as it is not money (or vouchers or similar) and the gift isn't made to pay for a particular service.

Some of your earnings can be free of tax if your employer runs a registered profit-related pay scheme, in which part of your pay is linked to your employer's profits. There are quite a number of detailed rules and, broadly, these include:

● all the pay linked in this way will be free of tax for one-year periods, up to a maximum of pay linked of £4,000 a year or 20 per cent of your total pay for the period, whichever is less

● a scheme must include at least 80 per cent of employees

● generally, it must last for at least one year

● pay must go up and down with yearly adjusted profits.

TREASURE TROVE CLUE No. 6

The amount of the blind person's allowance for 1994/95 (4 digits).

WHAT ARE EARNINGS?

The following would all normally be treated as earnings by your Tax Inspector:

- wages and salaries
- bonuses, including Christmas ones
- commission
- profit shares
- fees
- overtime pay
- holiday pay
- cost-of-living allowances
- tips
- advances made on any of the above
- long-service awards (but tax-free if the award is not money, is paid after twenty years of service, costs £20 or less for each year of service and if you have not received a similar award within the last ten years)
- cash allowances, for example, meals or mileage allowance, over and above the amount of your allowable expenses (p. 145)
- pension from your former employer (p. 133)
- sick pay, including statutory sick pay
- maternity pay, including statutory maternity pay
- payments made under a permanent health insurance policy (but if you have been paying the premiums for the policy yourself and you are entitled to receive benefits before 6 April 1994, the payments received are tax-free until the end of a full tax year. If you become entitled to receive benefit on or after 6 April 1994, the income will be tax-free only for the first twelve months)
- the taxable value of fringe benefits (p. 161)
- payment made on becoming an employee ('golden hellos')
- payment made on leaving a job ('golden handshakes') or payment in lieu of notice (p. 177)
- payment made to compensate for giving up membership of a trade union
- the amount of any debts settled for you by your employer
- the amount of your share of National Insurance contributions paid for by your employer (that is, the employee's contributions, not the employer's)

- the amount of your council tax paid for you by your employer (even if you are required to work at home by your employer).

Earnings from a job are taxed under what's called Schedule E (p. 38). Other income which comes under Schedule E are the state retirement pension (p. 133) and other taxable social security benefits such as unemployment benefit or income support (p. 181).

WHAT ARE NOT EARNINGS

Gifts or payments made only for personal reasons are not earnings and normally not taxable. To be treated as not taxable, these items must be unexpected and non-recurring, for example:

- wedding presents
- prizes for passing external exams
- gifts by way of a testimonial.

Board, lodging, uniforms, etc., which are provided by your employer are not taxable as these cannot be turned into money. However, if you get a cash allowance for these items, what you do not spend on these expenses will be taxable. As an exception, miners who get cash allowances instead of free coal do not pay tax on the amount.

If you make a job-related house move on or after 6 April 1993 you will get tax relief on up to £8,000 of the costs of your move paid for by your employer. This applies whether or not you have sold your old home.

If you moved or agreed to move before 6 April 1993 and started your new job on or before 2 August 1993, you will be able to claim tax relief on most removal expenses and benefits paid for or reimbursed by an employer. And you move to a higher-cost housing area you will be able to receive tax-free payments to compensate you, up to a maximum of £13,440 a year (to be adjusted in line with changes in building society interet rates). The payments should reduce over a period of years.

WHEN YOU ARE SICK OR ON MATERNITY LEAVE

Nearly all employees are entitled to receive statutory sick pay for up to 28 weeks. This is paid through the PAYE system and both income tax and National Insurance contributions are deducted.

Once the period for claiming statutory sick pay has run out, you can claim sickness benefit and then invalidity allowance from the state. Both of these are tax-free.

Some employers operate their own sick pay scheme, which, for example, pays between two-thirds and three-quarters of your normal pay after an initial period. This will be taxed in the same way as normal earnings. If you have paid the premiums yourself for an insurance policy to do a similar task, the income is taxed slightly differently. There is a 'tax-free holiday'. If you are entitled to benefits under the policy before 6 April 1994, the 'holiday' finishes at the end of the first full tax year after you start to receive it; otherwise it finishes at the end of the first twelve months.

If you are expecting a baby, you may be entitled to statutory maternity pay which would be paid for up to 18 weeks, but only if you have stopped work because of your pregnancy. Statutory maternity pay is taxable and would be added to your income for the year in working out how much tax and National Insurance contributions you pay. If you aren't entitled to statutory maternity pay, you may be able to claim maternity allowance, which is tax-free.

EXPENSES

The rules about what employees can claim for expenses are much more stringent than the rules for the self-employed. From your taxable earnings, you can deduct expenses *which are incurred wholly, exclusively and necessarily in the performance of your duties*. In practice, this means that there is relatively little which can be deducted. If an expense is not allowable, the amount is added to your earnings and taxed in the normal way.

Wholly and *exclusively* do not mean that you will not be able to claim an expense if it is not all used in your job. For example, if you need an office in your house to be able to do your job (that is, in the performance of your duties, see below), you can claim part of the house expenses.

Necessarily means that the expense must be necessary for any suitable holder of the job to be able to do it, not that it is necessary for you personally. You can't, for example, claim the cost of travelling from your home to the office. But you can claim the cost of travelling between offices if your job involves your working in two different locations.

Finally, the words *in the performance of your duties* do not mean that you can claim expenses which allow you to do the job in the first place (for example, private child-minding expenses cannot be claimed). Nor do the words mean that expenses which allow you to do your job better can be claimed.

These rules about expenses apply regardless of who paid the money.

So it makes no difference to what you can deduct from earnings if:

● you paid for the expenses, or

● you paid and your employer paid you back, or

● your employer paid for them in the first place.

The fact that your employer insists that certain expenses are made does not alter the rules about what you can claim.

There are, however, some expenses which the law allows, regardless of whether they meet the rules above in your particular case. These include:

● certain flat-rate deductions for tools and special clothing. The amounts are agreed between the Inland Revenue and the trade union. For example, if you are an agricultural worker, you can claim a flat-rate deduction of £60. If you would be entitled to a bigger deduction than the agreed amount, you can claim the larger. Ask for leaflet IR1

● subscriptions, but not entrance fees, to certain societies approved by the Inland Revenue.

EXPENSES WHICH ARE NORMALLY ALLOWED

These include:

● what you spend for meals and lodging while temporarily working away from home. In theory, it is supposed to be the extra amount, but in practice, you will not have to deduct your home expenses if you can show that you still have to pay these. If your job involves travelling all the time, for example, lorry driving, you can also claim the cost of meals. Keep all your receipts to back up your claim

● the cost of travel between two places of work for the same employer

● car expenses, or a proportion, if you have to use your car in the performance of your duties. If your employer has agreed with the Inland Revenue to operate a 'Fixed Profit Car Scheme', the amount of tax relief will depend on the mileage and the size of your car's engine. The relief is much higher for the first 4,000 miles. If your employer pays you an allowance which is higher than the figure worked out from the Scheme, you'll be taxed on the extra. Here are the figures for 1993/94:

ANNUAL MILEAGE	CARS UP TO 1000cc	CARS 1001– 1500cc	CARS 1501– 2000cc	CARS OVER 2000cc
Up to 4,000 miles	26p	32p	40p	54p
Over 4,000 miles	15p	18p	22p	30p

You may also be able to claim a capital allowance for buying the car (p. 199)

● cost of keeping your name on a register if it is condition of your job, for example, chemist, optician

● subscriptions (see p. 145)

● cost of maintaining and replacing tools which you have to provide in your job, see previous page for flat-rate expenses agreed. You may be able to claim a capital allowance (p. 199) for buying the tools in the first place

● if you have to work at home, you may be able to claim a proportion of the cost of heating, lighting, cleaning, telephone and insurance. If you own your home and part of the house is used exclusively for work, you may have capital gains tax worries (p. 244)

● the cost of special clothing which you have to have for work and which you have to provide, for example, helmet for safety reasons

● the cost of books which you have to provide as part of your employment, but these may only be special reference books

● fees paid for training. An employee can get tax relief for fees paid for training which would count towards the National Vocational Qualifications and Scottish Vocational Qualifications up to level four (from 1 January 1994, up to level five). Relief at the basic rate will generally be deducted from the payments you make. Higher-rate relief should be claimed from the Tax Inspector

● the interest on loans (but not overdrafts or credit card debts) which you need to buy capital equipment qualifying for a capital allowance (for example, tools, car). You can claim only the interest for the tax year in which the loan begins and the following three tax years. If you buy a vehicle which you use for work, even if you also use it privately, the interest on the loan will qualify for relief – or at least a proportion based on business use

● under very strict rules, the expenses of a wife or husband accompanying you on a business trip may be allowable. This would apply if he or she had special qualifications needed on the trip, or if your health was very poor and you needed to be accompanied.

EXPENSES NOT NORMALLY ALLOWED

These include:

● the cost of travel between your home and your work and the cost of travel between two different jobs (that is, two different employers)

● the cost of getting a job in the first place, for example, travel cost to go to an interview, payment to an employment agency

● books you buy to help you do your job better

● the cost of a housekeeper, nanny, childminder to enable you to do the job in the first place (but see p. 164 for work-place nurseries). A new social security benefit, child care allowance has been introduced, payable to single parents

● clothing you wear for work which you could also wear out of working hours

● entertaining expenses for customers. However, if your employer refunds what you have paid and does not claim the amount as an allowable expense of the business, you will generally not be taxed on the amount.

HOW YOUR TAX INSPECTOR FINDS OUT ABOUT EXPENSES

There are three ways your Tax Inspector receives information about expenses which have been reimbursed by your employer. First, your Tax Inspector may not know all the details because your employer arranges with your Tax Inspector to give what's called a *dispensation* for expenses. The Tax Inspector will agree to this only if the expenses are allowable for tax relief; they will not be added to your earnings and so will not be taxed. If there is a dispensation, your employer does not need to give details of the expenses paid and you do not have to put them in your Tax Return.

Second, if a dispensation has not been agreed, and your earnings are at a rate of £8,500 a year or more (p. 162), your employer will fill in Form P11D with the amount of expenses and fringe benefits. You need to give details of all your expenses (even the allowable ones) in the *Income from employment* section of your Tax Return and claim the amount of the allowable expenses in the same section. Make sure that what you put in your Tax Return agrees with what your employer has put in Form P11D. You will be taxed on expenses which have been reimbursed by your employer but which are not allowable, as your Tax Inspector will classify those as earnings.

Finally, if you are not earning at a rate of £8,500 a year (p. 162), your employer fills in Form P9D.

If your expenses have not been reimbursed, the only way your Tax Inspector finds out about any which are allowable (that is, you can deduct them from your earnings and so get tax relief) is if you give the information in your Tax Return. So don't forget to do so.

HOW YOUR EMPLOYER WORKS OUT YOUR TAX

Your employer operates the PAYE system for the government. This system is designed to deduct tax from your earnings on a regular basis, for example, monthly if you are paid once a month. The intention is that at the end of the tax year, you should have paid the right amount of tax on your taxable earnings for the year. It is only common sense to check that this is so.

There are two forms which your employer will give you which should tell you what tax has been deducted:

● your payslip. You should get a payslip with each wage or salary payment (see p. 153 for how to check this)

● Form P60. You will be given this at the end of each tax year (see p. 154.

THE PAYE SYSTEM

All employers operate this system including those employing people in the home (for example, as a nanny). Your employer will have:

● your tax code, which is sent by your Tax Inspector
● tax tables.

Using these two things together tells your employer how much tax should be deducted every time your wage or salary is paid.

Your tax code reflects the amount of allowances and outgoings it is estimated you can set against your earnings in the current tax year. This is the amount of pay which will be free of tax in the tax year. If your code, for example, is 516H, you are entitled to £5,169 free of tax.

Your employer is given two sets of tax tables. One set tells your employer how much of the free-of-tax pay you will get each time you are paid. If you are paid monthly, you should get $\frac{1}{12}$ of your yearly free-of-tax pay each month; if you are paid weekly, it is $\frac{1}{52}$. So, with a tax code of 516H, a weekly-paid employee would receive £99.40 pay each week free of tax, that is, £5,169 divided by 52. The second set of tables tells your employer how much tax should be deducted from the rest of your pay, less any contributions to approved pension schemes. If you are employed in the home, your employer will probably operate a simplified PAYE system and may have only one set of tax tables, but the final result should be the same.

The PAYE system is cumulative. This makes it easy for the tax you pay to be adjusted if you become entitled to more or less tax-free pay during the year. Suppose, for example, you get married at some stage in the tax year. If you tell your Tax Inspector, you should get a new Notice of Coding with a bigger number in the code. In your next pay packet you should find less tax deducted.

On the other hand, if you have been paying too little tax, your code will be adjusted so that you pay the right amount of tax from now on. But your Tax Inspector may allow you gradually to repay any tax owing during the next tax year rather than in one big lump now.

YOUR PAYE CODE

Your code is made up of a number and a letter. The number tells your employer how much pay you get free of tax – see above. The letters are as follows:

L: you have been given the personal allowance for those aged under 65

H: you have also been given the married couple's allowance for those aged under 65 or the additional personal allowance

P: you have been given the personal allowance for those aged 65 to 74

V: you have also been given the married couple's allowance for those aged 65 to 74

K: the amount of the taxable value of your fringe benefits is greater than the allowances and deductions which you can claim so an amount will be *added* to your pay to give a figure for taxable pay.

These letters mean that if these allowances change during the tax year the changes can be made automatically to your salary. However, if you have the letter **T** after your number, changes cannot be made automatically and you may have to wait longer for any rebate to come through. You may have the letter T if, for example, you have asked your Tax Inspector to give you it because you do not want your employer to know what allowances you have, if you are getting the personal allowance for those aged 75 or more or if you have a company car.

There are some special codes which don't have numbers or which have numbers which don't stand for allowances. They mean that all your pay is taxed at a single rate of tax. These are:

BR: your earnings are taxed at the basic rate

D: your earnings are taxed at the higher rate

F: the taxable state benefits you get come to more than the amount of your tax-free pay, so the tax due will be collected from your earnings or pension from a former employer

OT: you are not entitled to any tax-free pay but you get the benefit of the lower rate band

NT: your earnings should be paid without any tax deducted.

Note that you are likely to be given either code BR or D if you have a second job.

Once you have been given a code, this is what will be used to work out your after-tax pay unless your Tax Inspector issues a new one. Changes in allowances, for example, an increase in the personal allowance, which are made in the Budget, will be sent automatically to your employer. But if you have other changes, for example, if you get married during the tax year, you should let your Tax Inspector know so that you will be given a new PAYE code. Otherwise, at the end of the tax year you will have paid too much tax and will have to claim a rebate, which can take quite a time to be worked out.

YOUR NOTICE OF CODING

You may not receive a Notice of Coding each year. You may receive one only if you inform the Tax Inspector of some change. Otherwise, your employer will be told to carry on using last year's code.

Notices of Coding are now printed by computer, so each Notice could have quite different headings on it – only the items which affect your Code.

EXAMPLE

Sanjay Patel has received a Notice of Coding for 1994/95 (see overleaf) and decides he should check it. The column on the left-hand side is where items are entered which reduce the amount of tax Sanjay pays.

Professional subscriptions: Sanjay pays a £200 subscription for membership of a society which the Inland Revenue accepts as relevant for his job.

Personal and Married Couple's: Sanjay can claim the personal and married couple's allowance for those aged under 65. At the bottom is the figure for *Total Allowances*; in Sanjay's case this comes to £5,365.

The entries in the right-hand column are those which will reduce the size of Sanjay's code to give him less tax relief. Note that these will be based on the last information the Inspector has.

Benefits in Kind: The entry of £150 is the taxable value put on Sanjay's membership of a gym which is subsidised by his company.

Benefits (car): Sanjay has a company car, so the figure of £6,660 appears. This is the taxable value put on his Mercedes estate, now over four years old. This taxable value is based on the old system for taxing cars as a company benefit and will have to be adjusted when his Tax Inspector knows what the list price of the car was when originally purchased – £30,000. The taxable value is 35 per cent – £10,500. As Sanjay travels more than 2,500 miles, but less than 18,000 miles a year on business, this value is further reduced by a discount of one-third to £7,000. Finally, because the car is more than four years old, it is reduced by a further discount of one-third to £4,667.

Medical/health insurance: Sanjay and his family are covered by a private medical bills insurance scheme, and £1,215 is the taxable value of this benefit.

Allce restriction: This is how Sanjay's Tax Inspector is going to allow for the restriction to 20 per cent for the married couple's allowance. As Sanjay is a higher-rate taxpayer, the entry is £860; if he were a basic rate taxpayer the figure would be £344. If this figure was not put in the reduction column, Sanjay would be getting too much tax relief.

Unpaid tax £971.71: Sanjay underpaid tax £971.71 in the previous year. As he is a higher-rate taxpayer, tax at 40 per cent on £2,429 (the figure entered in the reduction column) gives unpaid tax of £971.71.

Higher rate adj: Sanjay received interest from a building society account in the previous year (which is paid with basic-rate tax deducted). As he is a higher-rate taxpayer, the figure of £144 in the reductions column will give the amount of extra tax due.

152

Form P2

Inland **Revenue**

Notice of your income tax code

Your employer or pension payer will use your tax code to ensure
you pay the right amount of tax under Pay As You Earn (PAYE)

From: H M Inspector of Taxes

LONDON PROVINCIAL 24
COMMERCIAL BUILDING
LESLEY AVENUE
GLASGOW   GL1 4PT
Tel : 031 453 5610

MR S PATEL
30 WENDOVER ROAD
LONDON

SW17 4LH

You should quote both numbers
below if you contact us.

976/S2425

YR   38   42   63   C

Date 09.01.94

The net allowances figure below shows how much of
your pay or occupational pension will not have tax
deducted from it. This figure is made up of your total
allowances less the total reductions shown below. This
notice of tax code replaces any previous notice for the year.

If you think the code is wrong, or if your personal
circumstances change, you should tell your Tax Office
immediately. The 'See note' column refers to notes in *PAYE:
Understanding Your Tax Code* (leaflet P3(T)).

See note	Allowances	£	See note	Less amounts taken away to cover items shown below	£
	PROFESSIONAL SUBS	200	25	BENEFITS IN KIND	150
17	PERSONAL ALLOWANCE	3445	25	BENEFITS (CAR)	6660
17	MARRIED ALLOWANCE	1720	25	MEDICAL/HEALTH INS	1215
			33	ALLCE RESTRICTION	860
			29	UNPAID TAX £971.71	2429
			31	HIGHER RATE ADJ	144

Less total reductions 11458

Total allowances   5365   Net allowances - the amount of your pay or   −6093
occupational pension from which tax will
not be deducted

Your tax code is worked out from your net
allowances. Your code for the year to 5 April 1995 is   **K608**   See note **A** overleaf

P2(T)

The Tax Inspector would also enter in this column any other fringe benefits, taxable social security benefits or a pension from a former employer, if Sanjay had any of these.

The total reductions for Sanjay come to £11,458, giving a negative figure for allowances to be deducted from his salary of – £6,093. This is because the taxable value of the fringe benefits which Sanjay receives from his employer come to more than his tax allowances. When working out his net salary for the month, Sanjay's employer will have to *add* a figure to his salary to allow for all the fringe benefits, before working out his net salary. His code for the year to 5 April 1995 is K608. This will be adjusted later on when the correct information about the taxable value of his car will be notified to his Tax Inspector.

YOUR PAYSLIP

Each time you are paid by your employer, by law you should receive a written statement (usually a payslip) which shows the amount of your pay and the amount of any deductions.

If you are a basic-rate taxpayer, you can easily check that your employer has deducted the right amount of tax during the 1994/95 tax year:

STEP 1: Work out how much gross pay you should get each month (if paid monthly) or each week (if paid weekly).

STEP 2: Find the amount of tax-free pay. Do this by taking the number in your code and adding 9 to the end. (For example, turn 385 into 3859). If you are paid monthly, divide this figure by 12; if weekly, divide by 52.

STEP 3: Add this figure of free-of-tax pay to the amount of any pension contributions to an approved scheme, profit-related pay or payroll-giving donations.

STEP 4: Deduct the figure in STEP 3 from the amount of gross pay you found in STEP 1.

STEP 5: Deduct £250 if paid monthly or £57.69 if paid weekly.

STEP 6: Find the amount of basic-rate tax by multiplying the figure from STEP 5 by 0.25.

STEP 7: Add £50 if paid monthly or £11.54 if paid weekly to the figure you found in STEP 6.

The figure this calculation gives you may differ by a few pence from the figure in your payslip. This will probably be caused by the rounding differences in working out free-of-tax pay.

FORM P60

This is a form (or its equivalent) which your employer has to give you at the end of each tax year. It shows your gross and net pay, tax and National Insurance contributions for the year. Sometimes the figure for gross pay is given as pay after any contributions to an employer's approved pension scheme.

You will need Form P60 to enable you to fill in your Tax Return.

NATIONAL INSURANCE CONTRIBUTIONS

Both employer and employee have to pay Class 1 National Insurance contributions. These are a percentage of your earnings, but not worked out in quite the same way as pay for income tax purposes. The differences are:

● NI contributions are worked out on earnings before deducting any pension contributions to an approved scheme

● payments and fringe benefits are not included in earnings for calculating NI if someone other than the employer decides how they are paid out (as, for example, tips)

● deductions and allowances are not subtracted before working out the amount of any contributions

● profit-related pay which will be free of income tax will *not* be excluded in working out the amount of NI contributions.

Employer's contributions will be based on earnings including the value of a company car and free petrol, where appropriate (see pp. 167, 169).

WHAT CONTRIBUTIONS DO YOU PAY?

Class 1 contributions are paid by employees and employers; the self-employed pay a different class. The regulations allow some people to be treated as employees for contribution purposes even if they are not employed under a contract of service. These include:

● office cleaners

● most agency workers, including temps but not outworkers

● wives employed in their husbands' businesses and vice versa

● certain part-time lecturers and teachers.

There are also some groups of employees who do not pay Class 1 contributions. These include:

● employees whose earnings are less than the weekly lower-earnings limit (£56.00 for 1994/95; £57.00 for 1994/95)

● people of under 16

● people over retirement age, that is, women over 60 and men over 65 (but employers still pay the normal contributions)

● people employed outside Great Britain and its continental shelf

● in some circumstances, married women or widows pay a reduced rate – see p. 156.

Employees who are 'contracted-out' still pay Class 1 contributions, but at a lower rate. You can be 'contracted out' if you contribute to your employer's approved pension scheme or if you take out an appropriate personal pension scheme (see chapter 25, 'Pensions', p. 219). If you are contracted out, when it comes to your retirement you will receive the basic state retirement pension, but not the additional pension from the state, which is known as SERPS (state earnings-related pension scheme).

HOW MUCH ARE THE CONTRIBUTIONS?

The two tables on p. 156 show both the employee's and the employer's contributions for 1994/95. If your earnings are less than the lower-earnings limit (£57 a week in 1994/95), neither you nor your employer pays any contributions. If your earnings are above this limit, contributions are payable on all your earnings, including the amount below the lower-earnings limit, not just on what you earn above it. However, since 5 October 1989, you pay a lower rate on the earnings below the lower-earnings limit than on the earnings above it. If you are not contracted out, and your earnings are above the lower earnings limit of £57, you will pay two per cent on the first £57 and ten per cent on earnings above that amount up to a maximum of £430 a week. If you have contracted out, you will pay two per cent on the first £57 and 8.2 per cent above up to a maximum of £430 a week. Although there is a maximum to the amount you can pay in NI contributions, there is no maximum for your employer.

TABLE 1: CONTRIBUTION RATES FOR EMPLOYEES FOR 1994/95 (%)

WEEKLY EARNINGS	IF YOU ARE NOT CONTRACTED OUT		IF YOU ARE CONTRACTED OUT*	
	on first £57	on remainder	on first £57	on remainder
less than £57.00	nil	—	nil	—
£57.00 – £430.00	2	10	2	8.2

TABLE 2: CONTRIBUTION RATES FOR EMPLOYERS FOR 1994/95(%)

WEEKLY EARNINGS	IF YOU ARE NOT CONTRACTED OUT	IF YOU ARE CONTRACTED OUT*
	on all pay	on all pay
less than £57.00	nil	nil
£57.00 – £99.99	3.6	0.6
£100.00 – £144.99	5.6	2.6
£145.00 – £199.99	7.6	4.6
£200.00 – £430.00	10.2	7.2
over £430.00	10.2	10.2

*The contracted-out rate applies only to that portion of earnings between the lower and upper earnings limit.

REDUCED RATE OF CONTRIBUTION

If you were a married woman or a widow on 6 April 1977, you had the right to choose on or before 11 May 1977 to pay Class 1 contributions at a reduced rate. For 1994/95 the rate is 3.85 per cent on earnings up to £430 a week. The rate is the same whether you are contracted out or not. If you are paying this rate, these contributions cannot be used towards entitlement to benefits like retirement pension. However, you can claim certain benefits, like retirement pension and widow's benefit on the contribution record of your husband.

There are three circumstances in which you lose the right to pay at this reduced rate:

● divorce

● non-payment of your Class 1 contributions at this reduced rate, or no earnings from self-employment, for two consecutive tax years

● being widowed and not being entitled to widow's benefit or industrial or war widow's pension.

TWO OR MORE JOBS

You pay Class 1 contributions for each job. But there is a maximum amount you can be required to pay each year – broadly, 53 payments at the highest standard rate on the weekly upper earnings limit (£420 a week in 1993/94). For 1993/94, this is £1,795.64 for all jobs. If you have one job which is contracted out and another which is not, the contracted-out contributions are converted to the non-contracted-out level to see if your contributions are over the maximum yearly level. Leaflet NP28 *More than one job?* explains how it works. Get a copy from your local DSS office.

If you have paid too much (must be at least £2.17 more than the maximum for 1993/94), you can claim a refund. Get Form CF28F from a DSS office. Send it, together with evidence of overpayment (for example, your P60 forms from your jobs), to Refunds Group, National Insurance Contributions Branch, Newcastle upon Tyne NE98 1YX (091–213 5000). Refunds of half the lower earnings limit (£28 in 1993/94) or more should be received automatically.

If you know you will be paying more than the maximum for 1994/95, you may be able to defer payment (rather than pay now and reclaim later). Ask for Form CF379(87/88) from the Class 4 Group at the address above. You must apply before 14 February 1995 if you want deferment for the 1994/95 year .

WHO IS AN EMPLOYEE?

You cannot just decide to call yourself employed or self-employed. It depends on what you do in your work and how you do it. You are probably an employee if some of the following apply to you:

● you have to carry out your work personally, that is, you cannot employ someone else to do it

● you can be told what, when and how to do your work

● you get a pension, holiday pay, sick pay or overtime pay from someone else

● you work a certain number of hours a day, a week or a month

● you work mainly or completely for one business

● you work at a place decided by the person you are working for.

WHAT TO PUT IN YOUR TAX RETURN

Under *Income from employment etc – year to 5 April 1994* on Form 11P (page 1) and Form 11(page 2) and under *Earnings etc 1993-94* in Form P1 (page 1), give details of what you earned from your job (or jobs) for the tax year.

Form 11P

See note 2.

Income from employment etc – year to 5 April 1994

Complete this section if you worked for an employer full-time, part time or on a casual basis or for an agency. Also fill it in if you received director's fees or payments or benefits from any office you held.

If you have been given a form P60 by your employee, it should contain the information you need. Give your income before tax. If you are a director see notes 2 and 3. If you are not a director see notes 2 and 4.

Wages, salary, fees, bonuses etc.
Your occupation and employer's name(s) and address(es)

£

Enter your total earnings from your job, including wages, salary, fees and bonuses, but after deducting any contributions to your employer's pension scheme, payroll-giving donations or profit-related pay relief. However, you should include any statutory sick or maternity pay. You will get the figure from Form P60, which your employer gives you at the end of each tax year. As well as the amount of your earnings from each of your jobs, you have to give the name and address of your employer or employers, plus what your job is.

Next on page 1 of Form P1, give details of any casual earnings, tips or expense allowances which you may receive in your job. With Forms 11P and 11 put casual earnings and tips under *Other payments received* on page 2.

Form 11P

Notes
Include cash-in-hand payments, casual earnings, tips and any other payments.

Other payments received
Give the amount and type of work you did and the name(s) and address(es) of any employer(s) (if as overleaf, write 'As overleaf').

£

On page 2 of Form 11P and page 3 of Form 11, you also have to give information about expenses which were reimbursed to you or paid for in advance under *Other benefits in kind and expenses allowances*.

Form 11P

For examples of the most common benefits see note 6.

Other benefits in kind and expense allowances
List the benefits and give their values if you know them. List also the types of expenses allowances made to you and give the total amounts. You can leave out altogether (in this item and in the next item) all amounts where the Inland Revenue has agreed with your employer through what is known as a 'dispensation' that the expenses are allowable and no tax will be payable.

£

If you do not earn at a rate of £8,500 a year or more (p. 162), and you have been given a fixed expense allowance to cover expenses, say £25 a day if you are away from home on business, enter what you *have not* spent as allowable expenses. If you earn at a rate of £8,500 or more a year, you have to put the total amount of any expenses your employer gave you, unless your employer has a dispensation for all your expenses (p. 147) in which case you shouldn't enter the expense allowance or expenses at all. On Form P1, give information about expense allowances under *Casual earnings, tips, expenses allowances* on the first page.

Now claim for your expenses under *Expenses for which you wish to claim a deduction* on Forms 11P and 11 and *Employment expenses for which you wish to claim* on Form P1. Remember if your employer has a dispensation, don't enter what you received or paid out in expenses. Enter only what is not covered by the dispensation. Put here the amount of the expenses you are claiming for your employment. Give the details of what the expenses are for (see p. 145 for what you can claim).

Form 11P

See note 7.

Expense for which you wish to claim a deduction
List here the types of expenses and give the amounts

£

Claim for tax relief on your vocational training (see p. 146) on page 10 of Forms 11P and 11 (no place for this on Form P1, so attach a note for your Tax Inspector).

Form 11P

Notes
See note 45.

Vocational training

Name of training organisation

Net amount paid in 1993-94 for training that qualifies for tax relief.

£

With Forms 11P and 11, if you are in a profit-related pay scheme you need to give the number of the scheme in the box on the front page of Form 11P, page 2 of Form 11. There is no box to mark on Form P1, so give details in a letter.

Form 11P

Profit-related pay and profit sharing

Give the number of profit-related pay schemes to which you belong

Tick here if you received a taxed sum from the trustees of an approved profit-sharing scheme.

Tick here if this sum is included under *Wages, salary, fees, bonuses* etc above.

19 • EMPLOYEES: FRINGE BENEFITS

While employees may cast an envious eye over what the self-employed can charge up in expenses, the reverse happens, too. The self-employed may look longingly at fringe benefits which employees may receive as part of their pay package. Typical examples are company cars, luncheon vouchers or interest-free loans to buy your season ticket for the railway.

Fringe benefits can sometimes be a tax-efficient way of being paid. The value of fringe benefits is part of your taxable earnings, but sometimes the value placed on them can be relatively low, less than it would cost you to pay for the benefit yourself. And some fringe benefits are tax-free. So a fringe benefit from your employer can be more valuable to you than an increase in wages.

Fringe benefits are usually paid for by your employer, but if anyone gives you a benefit because of your work, it may be taxable, although probably not if it costs £100 or less (including VAT).

HOW FRINGE BENEFITS ARE TAXED

To find out how any benefit will be valued by your Tax Inspector (and hence how much tax you will pay on it), you have to look at both yourself as a taxpayer and the nature of the benefit. These simple rules should help you sort out how you will be taxed:

RULE 1: As far as fringe benefits go, taxpayers are divided into two categories: the first category is those earning at a rate of below £8,500 a year and the second category is those earning at a rate of £8,500 or above or directors (see overleaf).

RULE 2: Some fringe benefits are tax-free, regardless of what you earn (p. 163).

RULE 3: There is a general rule for valuing benefits paid to those earning below the £8,500 limit (p. 165) and another general rule for valuing benefits paid to those earning at the limit or above, or directors (p. 166).

RULE 4: Some fringe benefits are valued in special ways:

- cars and petrol (p. 167, 169)

- mobile telephones (p. 170)

- cash vouchers, credit tokens, credit cards and charge cards (p. 170)

- cheap loans (p. 170)

- living accommodation (p. 172)

- employee share schemes (p. 173)

- property, other than cars, which you are lent or have now been given (p. 173).

RULE 5: The taxable value of the fringe benefit is added to your earnings figure and taxed in the normal way.

BELOW THE £8,500 LIMIT, ABOVE THE LIMIT AND DIRECTORS

A crucial distinction in the taxation of fringe benefits is whether you are above or below the earnings limit. For 1993/94 and 1994/95, the watershed between the two categories is earning at the rate of £8,500 or more a year, which by today's standards is not a very high income at all. If you are at or above the limit, the tax rules for fringe benefits are harsher than if you are below it. Note that the limit is applied *pro rata* for someone working part-time: you would be above the limit, for example, if you earned £5,000 a year for working twenty hours a week.

The figure of £8,500 includes all your earnings from your job, together with the taxable value of any fringe benefits you receive (valued as if you are above the limit), but after deducting the yearly contributions to an approved pension scheme. You also have to include the amount of any expenses you paid for but which are reimbursed by your boss, although you will not have to include those for which there is a dispensation. You have to include the amount of these reimbursed expenses *even if* these are allowable.

EXAMPLE

Toby Townsley earns £8,200. He also has the use of a company car for his private mileage. Is Toby above or below the limit?

To check how he will be taxed he has to add the taxable value of the company car, valued as if he is above the limit, to his salary. For 1994/95, the list price of his car is £10,500. The cash equivalent of this is 35 per cent, ie £3,675. He drives around 10,000 miles a year on business, so gets a reduction of one-third giving a taxable value of £3,675 less one-third of £3,675 = £3,675 - £1,225 = £2,450. Adding this to £8,200 gives an income of £10,650 which takes Toby above the limit.

The rules for taxing fringe benefits if you are earning at the rate of £8,500 a year or more normally also apply if you are a director. If you are a director, you will escape the harsher tax treatment only if:

● you earn less than £8,500

and

● you own or control 5 per cent or less of the shares and either work full-time for the company or are employed by a non-profit-making organization or a charity.

BENEFITS WHICH ARE TAX-FREE

These benefits are generally tax-free regardless of whether you are above or below the limit:

● facilities provided by your employer while doing your job, for example, a carpet in your office, more secretarial help

● luncheon vouchers of up to 15p each working day

● contributions to an approved or statutory pension scheme, including life insurance if provided

● meals, if provided for all employees on your employer's premises, even if in different canteens

● tea or coffee

● up to £8,000 for reasonable removal expenses, if you have to move for your job on or after 6 April 1993. If you were committed to a job move before 6 April 1993 and started it on or before 2 August 1993, you may be able to claim more than this (see p. 143)

● Christmas party provided for all staff, provided the cost is no more than £50 a head

● medical insurance for treatment needed while abroad in your job

● medical check-ups

● the cost of an insurance policy to pay you an income while sick

● the provision of a nursery for your child, or after-school care or care during school holidays by your employer, but cash allowances, paying bills or vouchers for child care are not tax-free

● long-service awards (but not of money) in certain circumstances. The award will be tax-free if given after 20 years of service, the cost is £20 or less for each year of service and you have not received a similar award within the last ten years

● special clothes needed for work

● cheap or interest-free loans, but if you are above the £8,500 limit, from 6 April 1994 these loans are tax-free only if they total £5,000 or less or if, excluding loans which qualify for tax relief, they total £5,000 or less. Loans to buy a home are not free of all tax if you are a higher-rate taxpayer

● shares in your employer's company obtained through an approved employee share scheme (but there may be capital gains tax to pay when you sell the shares)

● subscriptions paid to professional societies, if approved by the Inland Revenue

● goods and services your employer lets you have cheaply, provided it does not cost your employer anything, for example, because you pay the marginal or additional cost of the goods. If you don't pay the additional cost, it is added as the taxable value to your earnings

● the cost of essential course books and fees (and possibly the expense of living away from home and additional travelling) incurred while attending educational courses, if the course is full-time or substantially full-time and you have been employed for two years full-time by your employer before starting the course

● entertainment or a gift costing £100 or less in a tax year provided by someone other than your employer, for example, a supplier or customer – but only if it wasn't organized by your employer or given to you as an inducement

● the cost of a taxi or hired car to take you home if you have occasionally been working late and public transport has ended (or it would be unreasonable to expect you to use it)

● a car parking space at or near your work

● cost of security services, for example, a bodyguard provided because of a special security threat in your job

● the provision of in-house sports facilities.

Note that if you are below the £8,500 limit, there will be other fringe benefits which are tax-free for you.

THE GENERAL RULES: HOW FRINGE BENEFITS ARE TAXED

These general rules do not apply to all benefits or perks; some of them have special rules for calculating the *taxable value* to be added to your earnings (p. 167). Nor will these rules apply if you give up part of your pay in exchange for a fringe benefit, for example, a car. Your Tax Inspector will tax you on the amount of pay you have given up if it is more than the taxable value which would normally be put on the benefit. And even if you don't swap cash for a fringe benefit, you could still be taxed on the amount of pay which another employee accepts in exchange for the perk.

BELOW THE £8,500 LIMIT

The general rule for working out the value to be added to your earnings is:

the taxable value of a benefit is its second-hand value.

The consequence of this rule is that many benefits are tax-free, or very lightly taxed, if you earn at a rate of less than £8,500 because a lot of perks have no, or very low, second-hand values. As the following have no second-hand value, these benefits are tax-free for you (but not if you earn at the rate of £8,500 or more including the taxable values of benefits as if you are earning more than £8,500):

- insurance to pay the cost of going for private medical treatment
- the use of a company car
- board and lodging, but not if you are paid cash
- any fees or subscriptions paid for membership of a society
- hairdressing service provided at work
- the use of property lent to you by your employer
- educational scholarships given to your children by your employer.

The second-hand value of other items can be low. For example, a suit which costs £200 might have a second-hand value of only a third of that, say £70. If your earnings were below the limit, your employer could give you a suit costing that amount and you would pay tax at the lower rate, say, on only £70. For the 1994/95 tax year, this would be tax of 20 per cent of £70, that is, £14. But if your employer had given you a pay rise of £200, you would have paid tax of 20 per cent of £200, that is, £40. A fringe benefit can leave you much better off than an equivalent salary rise.

ABOVE THE £8,500 LIMIT

The general rule for putting a taxable value on fringe benefits, if your earnings are at the rate of £8,500 a year or you are a director (p. 163), is:

what it costs your employer less what you pay towards the cost.

In the example of the suit above, you would pay tax on the £200 it cost your employer to buy the suit, that is, for a lower-rate taxpayer in the 1994/95 tax year, 20 per cent of £200, or £40. In this case, there is no advantage if you earn £8,500 or more to be given a fringe benefit rather than an equivalent rise in salary.

EXAMPLE

Rita Bernard earns £13,000 (that is, above the £8,500 limit). She checks what will be the taxable value added to her earnings for the year 1994/95. She gets the following perks:

- a company car with a list price of £15,000. The car is less than four years old and her mileage is around 10,000 a year
- a pension scheme including life insurance of four times her salary
- six suits costing her employer a total of £750 (but she has paid back £50)
- luncheon vouchers of £1 a day
- free tea and coffee.

First, Rita sees which of the benefits will be tax-free: the pension scheme, life insurance, the first 15p a day of her luncheon vouchers and the free tea and coffee.

Second, she looks at the taxable benefits:

company car (see below)	£3,500
suits (£750 *less* £50)	£700
luncheon vouchers (£1 *less* 15p for each working day)	£221
Total	£4,421

So £4,421 will be added to Rita's earnings of £13,000 to cover the taxable value of her fringe benefits.

THE SPECIAL RULES FOR VALUING BENEFITS

Some fringe benefits are valued in special ways. These include:

- cars
- petrol
- mobile phones
- cash vouchers, credit tokens, credit cards and charge cards
- cheap loans
- living accommodation
- property, other than cars, which you are lent (or have now been given)
- employee share schemes.

CARS

From 6 April 1994, the taxable value of a company car which is used privately will be 35 per cent of the list price. However, if you do more than 18,000 miles a year on business, this value will be reduced by two-thirds and by one-third if you travel more than 2,500 miles a year on business, but less than 18,000.

If the car is more than four years old at the end of the tax year, the taxable value is reduced by a further one-third. And if the car is not available to you for part of the year, the value is adjusted pro-rata. If you pay anything for private use, the taxable value is reduced by the amount you pay.

The list price of a car is the price published by the manufacturer or distributor on the day before the car was first registered. If includes charges such as delivery charges or taxes and any accessories you have fitted at the time you just had the car. You would also have to include any accessories costing £100 or more (including VAT, fitting and delivery) which were fitted later (after 31 July 1993). There is a maximum of £80,000 put on the list price.

If you contribute to the cost of buying the car, the price taken to work out the taxable value is reduced by the amount of your contribution or £5,000, whichever is less.

If your car is a 'classic car', market value is used instead of list price to work out taxable value. A classic car is taken to be one with a market value of £15,000 or more and which is 15 years old or more.

Using a pool car is not a fringe benefit and there will be no tax bill. To be a pool car, a car must:

● be included in the pool for the year and be used by more than one employee

● not usually be kept overnight near an employee's house

● be used privately only in an incidental way, for example, as part of a business trip.

From 6 April 1993, if you can make private use of a company van, you will pay tax on a value of £500 a year (£350 if the van is four or more years old). If more than one employee shares use of the van the taxable value will be apportioned between the employees.

Before 6 April 1994, the taxable value of a car for an employee earning £8,500 or more was set by the government, which increased it each year in the Budget – see Table for 1993/94 on the right. If you paid your employer anything for using the car, you deducted the amount from the value in the Table. And if you didn't have the car for the whole tax year, the taxable value put on your use is a proportion of the figure in the Table.

TABLE 1: TAXABLE VALUES FOR 1993/94

ORIGINAL MARKET VALUE	AGE OF CAR AT END OF YEAR	
	under 4 years £	*4 years or more* £
Up to £19,250		
Size of engine:		
up to 1,400 cc	2,310	1,580
1,401–2,000 cc	2,990	2,030
2,001 cc or more	4,800	3,220
£19,251 to £29,000	6,210	4,180
£29,001 or more	10,040	6,660

Note there were some exceptions to these figures. These included:

● you paid 1½ times the figure for the car, if you used the car for your job for 2,500 miles or less

● for 1993/94 you pay half the figure for the car if you used the car for your job for 18,000 miles or more

● if you had two company cars, you paid 1½ times the above figure for the car which you don't drive so much on business.

The taxable values in the Table included the cost of business petrol, (but not any private petrol), repairs or insurance. If you paid for these and your employer reimbursed you, you make two entries in your Tax Return in the *Income from employment etc* section, one for the expenses paid to you and one for the expenses you wished to claim.

Original market value meant its value at the time the car was new – so even if you bought a car second-hand for less than its original value, the taxable value is based on the latter. For example, if you bought a two-year-old car for £25,000, but its value two years ago when it was new was £32,000, its taxable value was based on the £32,000, not the £25,000. And market value meant the value in the UK: if the car was imported from the Continent at a cheaper price it didn't affect the taxable value, it was the UK price which counted.

The age of the car was taken from the date it was first registered. So, for example, if the car was first registered in March, it was taxed at the rate for cars which are four years or more when it is three years and one month old.

PETROL

The taxable value for free fuel provided by your employer and used for private mileage is set by the government and based on engine size.

	1993/94 £	1994/95 £
Petrol		
Up to 1,400cc	600	640
1,401cc to 2,000cc	760	810
2001cc or more	1,130	1,200
Diesel		
Up to 2,000cc	550	580
2,001 cc or more	710	750

These are the figures you are taxed on regardless of the number of miles you drive and whether you have one or two company cars.

MOBILE TELEPHONES

The taxable value for a mobile telephone is £200. This also applies to car telephones. There will be no tax to pay only if:

● you don't use the phone for private use, *or*

● you pay the full cost of any private use.

CASH VOUCHERS, CREDIT TOKENS, CREDIT CARDS AND CHARGE CARDS

All employees, whatever they earn, are taxed on the value of cash vouchers which they receive and which they could exchange for goods. This also applies to credit tokens, credit cards and charge cards. The value is what it costs your employer less anything you contribute towards it less any allowable expenses.

CHEAP LOANS

You may have a cheap or interest-free loan from your employer to help you buy:

● your railway season ticket
● your home
● some other item.

If you earn at a rate of less than £8,500, any of these loans would be a tax-free fringe benefit. If you are at the limit or above the limit, the loan could still be tax-free. From 6 April 1994, it is tax-free if it is £5,000 or less or all your loans together total no more than £5,000. This would not include a loan, for instance, to buy a house, because you get tax relief on it already. The taxable value of the loan is worked out by taking the difference between the interest (if any) which you pay and the interest you would pay at the 'official rate' of interest (7¾ per cent from 6 March 1993). This is added to your income to work out your tax bill.

If your loan is to buy your home, you can get mortgage interest relief within the £30,000 limit. This relief will be on the interest you actually pay and the interest you save paying.

EXAMPLE

William Bland has a loan of £25,000 from his employer to help him buy his home. He pays interest at the rate of 2 per cent. The official rate of interest is 7¾ per cent. He is a basic rate taxpayer.

The taxable value of his loan is the difference between the interest he pays and what he would pay at the official rate of interest:

Interest at the official rate = 7¾% of £25,000 = £1,937.50
The interest he pays = 2% of £25,000 = £500
Taxable value of the loan is £1,937.50 − £500 = £1,437.50.

The tax he should pay is 25 per cent of £1,437.50 = £359.38. However he is entitled to tax relief on this loan at 20 per cent, because it is to buy his home. The amount of tax relief he is due is 20 per cent of the interest he would have paid at the official rate − £1,937.50.

Tax relief due = 20% of £1,937.50 = £387.50

He will be charged tax of £359, but get relief of £387, so he will end up with a refund of £387 − £59 = £28.

Before 6 April 1994, these loans were treated differently. If the loan is for something which would entitle you to claim tax relief, the loan from your employer was a tax-free fringe benefit. For 1990/91, this applied to a loan of £30,000 or less to buy a home. However, from 6 April 1991, you were no longer entitled to higher-rate tax relief on mortgage interest. So, if you are a higher-rate taxpayer, and your employer gave you a cheap loan of £30,000 to buy a home you pay tax at the rate of 15 per cent on the value of the loan. But for a basic-rate taxpayer, a loan of £30,000 or less to buy a home remains tax-free until 6 April 1994.

If the loan was more than £30,000, the extra over £30,000 was taxable. If you had a loan from another source to buy a house, for example, from a bank or building society, and an interest-free loan from your employer took you over the £30,000 limit, that part of your employer's loan was a taxable fringe benefit. This applied even if you had your employer's loan before you took out the other one.

If the loan was not eligible for tax relief, or only at the basic rate, your Tax Inspector valued it as a benefit, using the following calculation. The value was the difference between the amount of interest you paid your employer and the amount of interest at the *official rate*, 7¾ per cent from 6 March 1993. You paid tax on the value if it was more than £300; if it was £301, you paid tax on £301, not just the £1 which was over £300. Before 6 April 1991, the limit for tax-free loans was a taxable value of £200.

LIVING ACCOMMODATION

Whatever your earnings, if your employer provides you with living accommodation, you will normally pay tax; the bill will be based on the 'annual value' (the gross value of the property for rating purposes) less any rent you pay. Note that there are special calculations for new property and property which has been materially altered since valuation – the abolition of domestic rates means that there are no up-to-date rateable values for these.

There are some special circumstances in which living accommodation could be a tax-free benefit (*job-related accommodation*). This applies if:

● it is necessary for you to do your job properly,

or

● it is customary for your sort of job to be provided with living accommodation to help you do your job better,

or

● it is necessary for security reasons.

Unless the living accommodation is for security reasons, it will not be tax-free for a director who owns more than 5 per cent of the share capital or who does not work full-time for the company or for a company which is a non-profit-making or charitable body.

If the accommodation is not a tax-free benefit and costs more than

£75,000, the tax bill will be higher than one based on the gross rateable value. It is worked out as:

cost of living accommodation *less* £75,000 × official rate of interest (p. 171)
less any rent you pay on the 'annual value' (above)

If you earn at a rate of £8,500 or more, you will always have to pay tax on what your employer pays for heating, lighting, cleaning, decorating or furnishing, even if the living accommodation is tax-free. There is, however, a limit put on the value of these, that is, 10 per cent of your earnings without including these benefits.

PROPERTY, OTHER THAN CARS, WHICH YOU ARE LENT (OR HAVE NOW BEEN GIVEN)

If your employer lends you something, like furniture or a painting, you have to pay tax each year on 20 per cent of its market value at the time it was first loaned to you (less anything you pay to your employer for using it).

If your employer gives you the item you have been borrowing, you are taxed on the greater of:

● the market value at the time you were given the item, less anything you have paid,

or

● the market value at the time you were lent the item, less what you have paid less the amount you have already paid tax on.

EMPLOYEE SHARE SCHEMES

There are several different sorts of employee share schemes. Some of them are 'approved' by the Inland Revenue, which means that they receive favourable tax treatment. Mainly, but not always, this means that you could pay capital gains tax rather than income tax. Although the two rates of tax are currently the same, this is a major advantage if you can use the yearly tax-free allowance for capital gains tax to reduce the bill (see p. 310). The approved ones are:

● share option schemes
● savings-related share option schemes
● profit-sharing schemes
● employee share ownership plans (ESOPs).

Share option schemes

A share option scheme is a way of buying into your employer's company. You have the right to purchase shares at some future date. The price you pay is fixed at the time of the option. The Inland Revenue approves schemes which meet certain conditions (among others):

● the option must be for a maximum of £100,000, or four times this or last year's earnings, if greater

● the price you pay to buy the shares should at least be the market value at the time of the option

● the option to buy should be for at least three, but not more than ten, years from the date of the option. You will be able to exercise the option once every three years

● you can be in the scheme only if you work at least 20 hours a week for your employer (and if you are a director, this should be 25 hours).

If the scheme is approved, you pay capital gains tax on the profit you make when you sell your shares. Provided the conditions about the price to pay are kept, there is no income tax to pay when you are granted the option nor when you exercise it. From 1 January 1992, the company is able to grant options to selected employees to buy shares at a discount of up to 15 per cent on the market value.

Savings-related share option schemes

With this type of approved scheme, you buy the shares using what you have saved in a special Save-As-You-Earn scheme, which runs for five or seven years. To be approved, the scheme must meet these conditions, among others:

● the most you can save in the SAYE scheme is £250 a month. The minimum saving required by the scheme cannot be less than £10 a month

● the scheme must be open to all employees who have been employed full-time by the company for five years

● the price fixed to buy the shares in the future cannot be less than 80 per cent of the market value at the time the option was given by your employer.

If the scheme is approved, there will normally be no income tax to pay but there could be capital gains tax when you sell the shares. Note that at the end of the saving period, you do not have to buy the shares, you can simply take the proceeds of your saving.

Profit-sharing schemes

If it is an approved scheme in which your employer provides money to trustees to buy shares, there will be no income tax to pay, except on dividends, unless you take out the shares before five years are up. The following conditions, among others, should be met:

● you are allocated shares of up to £3,000 or, if more, 10 per cent of salary with a maximum of £8,000 a year

● you do not withdraw your shares from the trust within five years of getting them

● the scheme must be open to all employees who have been employed full-time by the company for five years.

After the five-year period, if you sell or give away the shares, there could be capital gains tax to pay.

Employee share ownership plans (ESOPs)

Employers who set up an ESOP trust can get tax relief if it meets certain conditions. For example, shares which are bought by the trust must be distributed to employees within seven years.

If you receive shares from an ESOP trust, you get no special tax relief and you may have to pay income tax if you pay less than the market value for the shares.

WHAT TO PUT IN YOUR TAX RETURN

You have to enter what's called the *taxable value* (p. 165) of the fringe benefits you get from your employer. In the 1994 Tax Return you are asked to give this information on page 2 of Form 11P. There is a section on *Cars and car fuel* and another section *Other benefits in kind and expenses allowances*. On Form 11, these two sections are at the bottom of page 2 and the top of page 3. On Form P1 it goes on the first page under *Benefits in kind*. Give the details requested about cars on Forms 11P and 11. List your other benefits and give the taxable values if you know them.

Form 11P

<table>
<tr><td>Business mileage is mileage necessarily travelled in the course of your work. It does not usually include mileage between home and work. See note 6.</td><td>

Cars and car fuel

Tick here if you or a member of your family or household were provided with a car during the year because of your job and it was available for private use. ☐

Tick the box corresponding with your business mileage in the car.

2,500 or less ☐   2,501 to 17,999 ☐   18,000 or over ☐

If you received car fuel for private travel in the car provided for you (or for a member of your family or household) tick the appropriate box.

petrol ☐   diesel ☐
</td></tr>
</table>

<table>
<tr><td>For examples of the most common benefits see note 6.</td><td colspan="2">

Other benefits in kind and expense allowances

List the benefits and give their values if you know them. List also the types of expenses allowances made to you and give the total amounts. You can leave out altogether (in this item and in the next item) all amounts where the Inland Revenue has agreed with your employer through what is known as a 'dispensation' that the expenses are allowable and no tax will be payable.
</td></tr>
<tr><td></td><td></td><td>£</td></tr>
</table>

You also have to tell your Tax Inspector if you have received a taxed sum from an approved profit-sharing scheme. You do not have to enter the amount. With Forms 11P and 11, simply put a cross in the appropriate box and put a cross in the box below if the sum received is included in the earnings figure. With Form P1, there is a space for you to put the name of the scheme on page 1; again you don't need to put the amount.

Form 11P

Profit-related pay and profit sharing

Give the number of profit-related pay schemes to which you belong ☐

Tick here if you received a taxed sum from the trustees of an approved profit-sharing scheme. ☐

Tick here if this sum is included under *Wages, salary, fees, bonuses etc* above. ☐

20 · EMPLOYEES: STARTING AND LEAVING JOBS

Starting work, changing jobs and being sacked are all difficult and stressful periods of your life. The stress is magnified by the necessity to keep an eye on the tax side of these changes. You may need to fill in forms; you certainly need to check the forms you are given. Failure to do so may mean paying too much tax and having to claim a tax refund later.

LEAVING A JOB

When you leave a job, your boss should fill in Form P45; you should get two copies and your Tax Inspector a third. This should show your PAYE code, your total pay and the total tax you have paid so far in the tax year. When you start your new job, you hand over the P45 to your new employer.

If you do not have another job to go to and will be claiming unemployment benefit, you should give your Form P45 to the benefit office.

If you aren't going to another job and aren't going to claim benefit, you may be able to claim a tax refund. After a month, ask your tax office for Form P50. When you have filled it in, return P50 and P45 to your tax office.

WHAT HAPPENS IF YOU GET A LUMP SUM FROM YOUR BOSS?

It depends on what the lump sum is. If it is wages or salary owed to you, holiday or overtime pay, commission or bonus, these are taxed as earnings in the normal way under the PAYE system. However, if your employer gives you compensation for loss of office or any additional payment over and above the earnings due to you, it will be tax-free if the payment:

- is not specified in your contract of employment or service agreement
- is unexpected and is not for services rendered
- totals £30,000 or less.

These rules apply to lump sums you get from your employer whether you are being made redundant or being sacked, for example. Ex-gratia payments made in other circumstances, such as retirement, are likely to be interpreted by your Tax Inspector as payment for services rendered.

There are some special payments which could be made which would normally be tax-free (you do not need to include them in the tax-free £30,000 above). For example:

● certain lump sum benefits from your employer's pension scheme

● a lump sum payment to compensate you for an injury or disability which meant you could no longer do the job

● normally compensation for losing a job done outside the UK

● gratuities from the armed forces (but not for early retirement).

When you leave a job before retirement in which you have made contributions to an employer's pension scheme and these are refunded, any tax due will have already been deducted before you receive the refund.

From 16 March 1993, outplacement services, such as counselling, provided to employees who are made redundant are tax-free and not included in the tax-free £30,000.

WHAT HAPPENS IF YOU ARE MADE REDUNDANT?

Any money which is paid to you as part of the government's redundancy payments scheme or as part of an employer's scheme, approved by the Inland Revenue, is included in the first £30,000 of tax-free leaving payment. Any *ex gratia* payment by your employer will be added to these payments to work out what tax (if any) is payable (see above).

WHAT HAPPENS IF YOU HAVE BEEN UNFAIRLY DISMISSED?

If you take your case to an Industrial Tribunal, any compensation is tax-free. But any money paid for loss of wages is taxable as earnings. It will be paid to you after basic-rate tax has been deducted. You can claim a rebate if the tax deducted is more than the amount which would have been deducted if the money was a normal wage. Ask your Tax Inspector.

WHAT HAPPENS IF YOUR EMPLOYER GOES BUST?

Pay in lieu of notice from a liquidator or administrator (for a company) or trustee (for an individual who is bankrupt) is not tax-free. It is paid after tax at the basic rate has been deducted. You can claim a rebate if the tax deducted is more than the amount which would have been deducted if the money was a normal wage. Ask your local Redundancy Payments Office.

WHAT HAPPENS IF YOU BECOME SELF-EMPLOYED?

If you leave your job in the middle of a tax year and start up on your own, send your P45 to your Tax Inspector and ask for a rebate. If your Tax Inspector agrees (because it is assumed that your income from self-employment may not start until the next tax year) it will help your cash flow. It does not mean less tax to pay, as in the end you will pay tax on all your earnings for that year.

STARTING A JOB

You should hand your new employer the Form P45 you were given by your old employer. This shows what your tax code is, how much you have been paid and how much tax you have paid so far in this tax year. This information allows your new employer to carry on deducting tax in the same way as your old one.

If, for some reason, you cannot produce a Form P45 (for example, because you have not had a job in this tax year), your new employer will fill in Form P46 and send it to the tax office, after asking you to sign it. If you are starting work for the first time, your employer should also give you Form P15 to fill in which should enable you to get a PAYE code.

Until your employer has been told by the taxman what your PAYE code is, you will be taxed on an emergency code using what's known as a *Week 1* (or *Month 1*) basis. This assumes that you are entitled only to a personal allowance for those aged under 65 and that you have been earning at your current wage rate for the rest of the tax year. If you are entitled to more allowances or if you have not been earning so much, an emergency code means you will be paying too much tax. Once your employer has your proper code, you will get a tax refund in your wage packet.

If you have been unemployed before starting this job and claiming

unemployment benefit, the DSS should have given you the P45 to hand
to your new employer.

WHAT TO PUT IN YOUR TAX RETURN

There is a section called *Lump sum and compensation payments* on the
first page of Forms 11P and P1 and the second page of Form 11. Put
the amount of any payments and compensation you have received,
either on leaving or starting a job. Put the amount before any deduction.
Note that this does not include any earnings your employer owes you.

Form 11P

Some of these are not liable to tax. See note 5	**Lump sum and compensation payments** Give the amount of any lump sum or compensation payment you received during 1993-94, if this has not already been included in Wages, salary, fees, bonuses etc above.	£

TREASURE TROVE CLUE No. 7

The minimum age of a person for whom tax relief is available on
private medical insurance premiums (2 digits).

21 • UNEMPLOYMENT AND OTHER BENEFITS

It may seem a paradox that you should need to worry about your tax position when you are unemployed, but unemployment benefit is taxable, and so are some other benefits which you get from the state. The fact that they are taxable does not automatically mean that you will pay tax on them; but it does mean that you need to keep an eye on whether you have paid too much or too little tax during the tax year while you are unemployed, on strike or laid off.

There is, however, a wide range of benefits which are tax-free whatever the size of your income and which do not have to be entered in your Tax Return. There are more details of these on p. 185.

UNEMPLOYMENT

WHAT SHOULD YOU DO WHEN YOU ARE UNEMPLOYED?

You must give your Form P45 from your old job to the unemployment benefit office when you first sign on. If you have not had regular employment since leaving school or college and do not have a Form P45, ask to fill in Form P187. The unemployment benefit office will give you Form P187 and ask you to consider and sign the declaration in it, if it is applicable. You cannot claim a refund of tax paid while you were working, if you are entitled to one, until the end of the tax year or until you get a new job. The refund should be paid automatically.

WHAT MONEY DO YOU GET WHILE UNEMPLOYED?

You may be able to claim unemployment benefit while unemployed. And you may be able to claim income support in addition to unemployment benefit or instead of it, if you are not entitled to it. You can claim for yourself and one adult dependant. The benefit is normally taxable, just like a wage *but* no tax is deducted from it when paid. Instead what tax you pay or can claim back will be worked out at the end of the tax year (or when you get a new job, if this is earlier).

If, however, you are unemployed and not claiming benefit, you can claim a tax rebate once you have been out of work for four weeks. Claim on Form P50; ask your tax office for one.

WHAT HAPPENS WHEN YOU GET A JOB?

Fill in card UB40/UBL18 (which you were given when you first claimed benefit) and return it to your benefit office. The office will normally work out your tax position, if they have all the information, taking account of the benefit you have had. They will send you any refund due. The refund will be made by your new employer if it is over £100 and the Inland Revenue has not given authority to the benefit office to pay it. If you have paid too little tax, the extra you should pay will probably be included by your Tax Inspector in your PAYE code and collected in the next tax year.

The benefit office will give you two documents:

● a Form P45 which you give to your new boss

● a statement of taxable benefits which must be kept safe as it cannot be replaced. Check this at once, and if you disagree with it get in touch with the benefit office immediately and ask them to explain it. If you still think it is wrong, you have 60 days from the date the statement was issued to write to your Tax Inspector saying why it is wrong. If your disagreement cannot be sorted out with your benefit office, your tax office will work out your tax bill after the tax year has ended. If you still disagree, you can appeal (see p.92). Leaflet IR37 *Income tax and capital gains tax – appeals* tells you how to appeal and what is involved.

You must object in writing within 60 days or you will miss the opportunity to query the taxable amount of benefit. This is so even if you get a tax assessment later. The 60-day time-limit can be extended, but only if you have a good reason and your objection is made without further delay.

WHAT HAPPENS AT THE END OF A TAX YEAR IF YOU DO NOT HAVE A JOB?

Your benefit office will send you a Form P60U, which includes a statement of taxable benefit (see above for what to do if it is wrong).

If you have paid too much tax, the benefit office will normally give you a refund.

IS ALL THE BENEFIT TAXABLE?

Unemployment benefit is taxable. But you may receive income support while unemployed. This could also be taxable, although there are some people for whom income support is tax-free. You will not have to pay tax on the income support you receive if you are:

- aged 60 or over
- a single parent with a child aged under 16
- staying at home to look after a severely disabled person.

If you are not in one of the above categories, some income support received while unemployed could still be tax-free. The tax-free bit is what you receive, if any, over the standard weekly amount of unemployment benefit for a couple or for a single person.

Even if you receive unemployment benefit or income support for an adult dependant (e.g. your wife or husband), what you receive is all treated as your earned income – it cannot be split between the two of you.

EXAMPLE

Richard Parkes loses his job at the end of 1993 and signs on for unemployment benefit at the beginning of January 1994. He's received £12,000 in wages so far this tax year; tax deducted is £2,014. Unemployment benefit of £72.20 a week is paid to him, and no tax is deducted, although it is taxable. Richard is still unemployed at the end of the tax year.

The benefit office gives him a statement of taxable benefits showing that he has received taxable benefits of £1,011 in the tax year. His income, allowances and tax due for the year are as follows:

Earnings	£12,000	
Benefits	£1,011	
Total		£13,011
less allowances		
personal allowance	£3,445	
married couple's allowance	£1,720	
Total allowances		£5,165
Taxable income		£7,846

The tax due is £1,836 (£500 tax at the lower rate and £1,336 on the basic rate). But Richard has had tax deducted under PAYE of £2,014 and so is due a refund of £178.

ON STRIKE

You cannot get any benefit for yourself while on strike or considered to be directly interested in a strike. But under the income support scheme, a spouse (or an unmarried partner living with you) may be able to get income support for him- or herself and any dependent children. Any strike pay received will be taken into account and even if none is received a sum of £22.50 is assumed.

Income support is not payable for the first seven days of the dispute. It is taxable only if the claimant is the striker and his or her partner, who is *not* a striker, were to receive half the normal personal allowance for couples. The benefit is recoverable from the person making the claim by the DSS. The tax is not deducted from your benefit when paid; instead it is included in your taxable income for the year (see p. 182 for how this will be collected). If you have paid too much tax you will get the refund only when you return to work (and *not* at the end of the tax year if this should be earlier).

When the strike is over, or at the end of the tax year, the local social security office will give you a statement of taxable benefits (see p. 182 for what to do).

LAID OFF OR ON SHORT-TIME WORKING

Any benefit you receive for yourself and one adult dependant is taxable, but the benefit office pays it without tax deducted. The part of the benefit which is taxable is the same as for unemployment, see p. 182. The benefit is treated as the income of the person making the claim.

When work returns to normal, the benefit office will send you a statement of taxable benefits. Any tax due will be collected in the same way as if you were unemployed.

Sometimes your employer pays any benefit along with your wages. Normally in this case, tax will be deducted from your benefit (if it is due) under the PAYE system. If your employer does not deduct tax, the benefit office will send you a statement of taxable benefit and tax due will be collected at a later date.

CHECKLIST OF MAIN BENEFITS

Benefits which are taxable are treated as earned income under Schedule E, the same schedule as earnings from a job or a pension from your employer.

FOR CHILDREN

Tax-free:
- family credit and childcare allowance
- maternity allowance
- social fund maternity payments
- student grants
- child benefit
- child dependency additions paid with widow's benefit, invalidity benefit, severe disablement allowance, retirement pension, invalid care allowance, unemployment benefit, the premiums paid for children with income support, unemployability supplement, higher rate industrial death benefit
- child's special allowance (only payable to those already claiming before 6 April 1987)
- one parent benefit
- war orphan's pension
- guardian's allowance.

Taxable:
- statutory maternity pay.

FOR WIDOWS

Tax-free:
- war widow's pension
- widow's payment

Taxable:
- widowed mother's allowance
- widow's pension
- industrial death benefit for a widow (only payable if death occurred before 11 April 1988).

FOR THE SICK AND DISABLED.

Tax-free:

- severe disablement allowance
- sickness benefit
- war disablement benefits
- industrial disablement benefit (including disablement benefit, constant attendance allowance, exceptionally severe disablement allowance, unemployability supplement and reduced earnings allowance)
- invalidity allowance when paid with invalidity benefit
- invalidity benefit (but only if claimed before April 1995)
- disability living allowance
- disability working allowance
- attendance allowance.

Taxable:

- statutory sick pay
- invalid care allowance
- invalidity allowance, when paid with retirement pension.
- new incapacity benefit (from April 1995).

OTHER BENEFITS

Tax-free:

- housing benefit (rent rebates and allowances)
- council tax benefit
- most income support, but see p. 183
- payments from the social fund
- YT training allowance, employment rehabilitation allowance and employment training allowances
- similar benefits paid by foreign governments.

Taxable:

- some income support paid to the unemployed, those on strike and short-time working
- unemployment benefit (p. 183)
- Enterprise Allowance (or its equivalent)
- retirement pension (see p. 133) and old person's pension.

CHANGES IN SOCIAL SECURITY BENEFITS

A new benefit, incapacity benefit, will replace invalidity benefit and sickness benefit in April 1995. Incapacity benefit will be taxable (invalidity benefit and sickness benefit are tax-free payments).

From 1996, unemployment benefit will be replaced by Job Seeker's allowance; this will be taxable and paid for only six months, compared to twelve months for unemployment benefit.

WHAT TO PUT IN YOUR TAX RETURN

Do not enter any of the benefits which are tax-free. But you will have to enter details of taxable benefits (see p. 138 for what to enter if you receive state pensions).

If you claimed unemployment benefit or income support because you were unemployed during the last tax year, give the name of your benefit office under *Income from National Insurance and social security benefits – year to 5 April 1994* on page 4 of Forms 11P and 11. In Form P1 the information goes under *Unemployment benefit or income support claimed because you were unemployed* in the *Pensions and benefits for 1993-94* section on page 2.

Form 11P

For information about benefits see note 21 or ask your Tax Office for "Income Tax and the Unemployed" (leaflet IR41).

Income from National Insurance and Social Security benefits – year to 5 April 1994

If you claimed unemployment benefit or income support because you were unemployed during 1993-94 give the name of your benefit office

If you claimed widowed mother's allowance, invalid care allowance or industrial death benefit, enter the amount you were entitled to in the same sections.

Form 11P

If the benefit you are claiming is not listed here you do not have to give details

Other Social Security benefits

If you claimed any of these benefits, give the full amount you were entitled to in 1993-94.

Widowed mother's allowance	£
Invalid care allowance	£
Industrial death benefit	£

22 • WORKING ABROAD

There is one group of individuals who can receive their earnings free of tax. To include yourself in this select band you need to meet certain conditions which would radically alter your lifestyle, that is, work abroad for a period of 365 days. The exact rules are explained in this chapter.

You can qualify for this special treatment even if you are resident and ordinarily resident in the UK, although in general the UK tax system seeks to tax *all* the earnings of people who fall into that category, whether earned in the UK or abroad. What *resident* and *ordinarily resident* mean is explained below.

The tax laws actually aim to spread the net wider still by taxing the income of people who live abroad and are paid income from the UK, as well as those who live here but receive income from abroad. But the tax treatment of those who live abroad is beyond the scope of this Guide and you should take professional advice, for example from your bank or an accountant.

What happens to income from investments abroad if you live in the UK is explained in Chapter 28, 'Investments', p. 262.

RESIDENT AND ORDINARILY RESIDENT

If you are both of these, according to your Tax Inspector, all your earnings are subject to the UK tax laws. You can be resident and ordinarily resident for one tax year, and not necessarily for the next; a fresh decision is taken each year.

You are *resident* for a tax year if:

either

● you are in the UK for at least six months (in practice taken to be 183 days, ignoring the day you arrive and the day you leave)

or

● you visit the UK yearly and stay for a long period. Your Tax

Inspector would take a visit of three months to be a long period and you would be regarded as resident if you had been doing this for the last four years, say

or

● you are a British or Irish subject, ordinarily resident in the UK (see below) who is occasionally resident abroad

or

● up to 5 April 1993, if you have a home in the UK, whether owned or rented does not matter, and you come to the UK in that tax year for a visit, no matter how short. This rule could be ignored if you work full-time abroad, either in a job or running your own business. This rule has now been relaxed so you could own a house here now even if you do work abroad.

You are *ordinarily resident* if you intend to be in the UK on a more permanent basis, although this is rather ill-defined. You can be resident but not ordinarily resident, for example. But if you have been resident for a number of years, or plan to be when you first arrive in the UK, your Tax Inspector will probably classify you as ordinarily resident. Normally, ordinary residence will apply from the beginning of the tax year after the third anniversary of your arrival here.

GETTING TAX RELIEF ON ALL YOUR EARNINGS

Your Tax Inspector will try to tax all your worldwide earnings if you are resident and ordinarily resident. However, if you can qualify for the 100 per cent deduction on earnings from abroad, it means that all your earnings from abroad will be free of UK tax. The basic rule is that you must be working abroad for a qualifying period of 365 days or more; this period can straddle two tax years. You can meet this basic rule in two ways:

● *either* you are abroad for the whole of the qualifying period

● *or* you can return for short visits to the UK. No intervening period in the UK can be longer than 62 days *and* the total number of days in the UK cannot be more than one-sixth of the total number of days in the new qualifying period. The new qualifying period consists of the days in the continuous period so far (abroad and in the UK), plus the number of days you now spend abroad until your next return to the UK.

You can have a succession of periods in the UK and periods abroad and still qualify for the 100 per cent deduction, as long as the above conditions are met for each absence.

A day of absence from the UK means one where you are not in the UK at the end of the day, so your travelling days to the UK will not count as part of the qualifying period. However, the travelling days from the UK are days of absence.

Seafarers have different limits for intervening periods. From 6 April 1991, the limits are intervening periods of no longer than 183 consecutive days and the proportion of days in the UK can be no longer than one-half. Before 6 April 1991, the limits were 90 consecutive days and one-quarter.

EXAMPLE

Christine Barber gets a job working abroad for her employer. Her trips to the UK and the number of days working abroad are as follows:

abroad	95 days
UK	60 days
abroad	120 days
UK	30 days
abroad	180 days

None of the trips to the UK breaks the 62-day rule, but what about the one-sixth rule? At the end of her second trip abroad of 120 days, Christine has spent 60 days in the UK out of a period of $95 + 60 + 120 = 275$ days. This is more than one-sixth of the total and so can't count towards the continuous period for the 100 per cent deduction.

The counting can start again from the beginning of Christine's second trip abroad. At the end of her third trip abroad, Christine has spent 30 days in the UK out of a total of 330 days $(120 + 30 + 180)$ in this period. This is less than one-sixth of the total and would count towards the continuous period; but it is not long enough. It needs to be a continuous period of 365 days. If Christine now returns to work in the UK, she will not be able to claim the 100 per cent deduction on any of her earnings.

However, if she returns abroad for a fourth trip of 90 days after spending 20 days in the UK, and starting from the beginning of her second trip abroad, she has spent:

$$30 + 20 \text{ days} = 50 \text{ days in the UK, and}$$
$$120 + 180 + 90 = 390 \text{ days abroad}$$

– that is, 440 days in total in the continuous period.

This period now meets all the conditions for getting the relief on her earnings, starting with her second trip abroad, the 120 days. None of the trips in the UK is longer than 62 days, the continuous period is more than 365 days and the trips to the UK come to less than one-sixth of the continuous period.

Residents in the UK can claim the usual personal allowances. So, if you are entitled to the 100 per cent deduction on your earnings for work abroad, you can set the allowances off against any other income, for example, investment income.

Note that from 6 April 1992, there has been a change for non-residents returning from abroad to establish that they are resident and ordinarily resident – and so claim the 100 per cent deduction. They will no longer be able to claim their absence abroad as part of the 'qualifying period'. Ask your Tax Inspector for more details.

WHAT TO PUT IN YOUR TAX RETURN

If you have worked abroad during the year, you have to give details in your Tax Return. On Forms 11P and 11, for employees, there is space under the heading *Earnings from work abroad* (page 2 on Form 11P and page 3 on Form 11). Give your occupation abroad, your employer's name and overseas address, the date of periods spent abroad and the earnings for which you are claiming a deduction. On Form P1 tick the box under *Work abroad* on page 1 if you want to claim a foreign earnings deduction.

Form 11P

If you were abroad for all, or nearly all, of a 365-day period, you may be able to claim a foreign earnings deduction of 100% (unless you were employed by the Crown). Ask for "Going to Work Abroad" (leaflet IR58). If you have paid foreign tax on your foreign earnings, you may be able to claim double taxation relief. See note 8.

Earnings from work abroad
Only complete this item if you wish to claim a foreign earnings deduction.

Your occupation abroad and employer's name and overseas address

Dates of period(s) spent abroad

From   / /19   to   / /19   From   / /19   to   / /19

If there is not enough space put the details on a separate sheet of paper

From   / /19   to   / /19   From   / /19   to   / /19

Give the amount of your earnings in 1993-94 already included under one of the income items above which relate to the periods you have worked abroad.   £

23 • THE SELF-EMPLOYED

Being in business for yourself can be a fairly traumatic experience. One of the extra difficulties you face will be that you are responsible for much more work on your tax affairs than if you were employed, where quite a lot of the work is done by your employer. Just because you work for yourself does not mean that you have to do the tax work yourself; you can employ someone, like an accountant or bank, to do it for you. However, if you do this, you should certainly try to understand how your tax bill is worked out, so you can keep an eye on what your adviser does.

Getting your adviser to present your tax affairs to your Tax Inspector gives them an air of greater credibility. But even if you do this, your accounts are only as solid as the records on which they are based. If you do not keep accurate records, you or your adviser will have difficulty producing accurate accounts and tax calculations. And if your Tax Inspector is not happy with the figures you submit, you will not have the records to back them up.

Life is simpler for some small businesses (individuals or partnerships). If your sales are £15,000 or less a year, you don't need to present full-blown accounts to the Tax Inspector – three-line accounts showing sales, purchases and expenses and net profit will suffice. However, this does not reduce the amount of record-keeping you need in your business as you *must* be able to substantiate your accounts, just in case the Tax Inspector wishes to look at your accounts more closely.

Being self-employed has tax advantages. There are more expenses you can deduct from your income than if you are an employee. You will also find that you are not paying tax on your income as you earn it, as you do if you are an employee paying tax under the PAYE system; indeed, under the system for 1993/94 there can be a considerable delay between earning the money and paying tax on it.

However, this advantage will be diminished from the 1997/98 tax year. From that year, you will pay tax for the year in which you get the income, not the preceding year as in the current system. Under the new system, for the income in the 1997/98 tax year, you will pay half the estimated tax in January 1999 and half in July 1999.

There will be a transition between the systems which will mean that businesses which are already up and running will pay tax on half the profits for a two-year accounting period ending in 1996/97. If you start a business on or after 6 April 1994, the new system will apply at once i.e. you are taxed on a current year basis.

You can be in business for yourself in three ways:

● you can be self-employed. This chapter explains your tax treatment. Note that you cannot just 'go' self-employed; you have to convince your Tax Inspector that you are in business for yourself (p. 211). In tax jargon, as a self-employed person you are taxed under Schedule D Case I or Case II

● you can be in partnership with someone else. The tax treatment is explained briefly in Chapter 25, 'Partners', p. 214

● you can work for your own company as a director. You are treated as an employee.

If your earnings are only occasional and consist of the odd bit of freelance work, you may find that your Tax Inspector wants to tax you as a freelance, see p. 40.

HOW TO WORK OUT TAXABLE PROFIT

Your first step in working out your tax bill is to transform what you have got in your accounts into what your Tax Inspector needs. If you only had a magic wand it would be easy, but as you do not, instead you have to add on a bit here and take away a bit there to turn the figure you have for profits from your accounting records into taxable profits. Broadly:

1 *start* with accounting profit

2 *deduct* any expenses which are allowable for tax, but which are not in your accounts (p. 195)

3 *add* any expenses which you have claimed in your accounts which are not allowed for tax purposes (p. 198)

4 *deduct* money which you have received which is not income, such as proceeds from the sale of an asset. Chapter 4, 'Income', p. 28 explains in more detail what is and what is not income. You should also

deduct the amount of any Enterprise Allowance (or its equivalent received from a TEC) you have included

5 *add* any items taken from stock for own use and not in the accounting figure. Include them at your usual selling price

6 *gives* you business profits. The next stage is to:

7 *deduct* the amount of capital allowances you are claiming for capital expenditure (p. 199)

8 *deduct* losses on which you are claiming tax relief against profits from the same business (p. 203)

9 *deduct* half your Class 4 National Insurance contributions for the year (p. 206)

10 *add* any balancing charges or *deduct* any balancing allowances (p. 201)

11 *gives* you taxable income from self-employment.

There may well be other deductions and allowances you can subtract from this figure, such as your personal allowance or personal pension payments, before you arrive at the final figure for working out your tax bill. Chapter 10, 'Checking Your Income Tax Bill', p. 78 shows you how to do this.

EXAMPLE

Rupert Bainbridge calculates his taxable income for the 1994/95 tax year:

1 His accounting profit is £16,753, but he needs to work out how much he will pay tax on:

2 and 3 First, he scrutinizes expenses. Depreciation of £444 is not allowable and he adds that back. However, he has forgotten to claim anything for the cost of cleaning his office, and he deducts £120 for that.

4 and 5 He has not included anything but income in his accounts and he hasn't received any Enterprise Allowance (or its equivalent). Nor has he used anything from stock without paying for it.

6 His business profits are £17,077 that is, (£16,753 + £444 − £120).

7 He can claim capital allowances of £520 on the equipment he is buying.

8 There is no loss relief to claim.

9 His Class 4 National Insurance contributions come to £734, and he can claim relief on half this amount, that is, £367 (see p. 206 for how to work this out).

10 He has not sold any business asset on which he has claimed a capital allowance, and so there is no balancing charge or allowance.

11 Rupert's figure for taxable income from self-employment is £17,077 – £520 – £367 = £16,190.

EXPENSES

You can get tax relief on a business expense if it is incurred 'wholly and exclusively' for the business. Claiming business expenses, which are allowable for tax relief, reduces the amount of tax you have to pay. So this is an area of your accounts to which you should pay close attention.

It is worth noting that different expenses are allowable for different businesses; and different amounts of the same expense can be allowable for one but not another. There is no definitive ruling which applies to all businesses; you have to show that an expense is justified in your case.

Just because you use something in your private life does not also mean that it is not an allowable expense for the business. It may well be, and it is always worth claiming something just in case it is allowed. Common examples of items used for both private and business purposes are use of your car and use of your home as your office. As long as your car is sometimes used wholly for business purposes, you can claim a proportion of the car expenses, for example, a proportion based on a ratio of the number of business miles to total miles.

But you may have difficulty claiming as allowable an expense which happened jointly for business and private reasons. For example, a trip abroad to see a customer which you combine with a holiday means that none of the expenses of the trip are strictly allowable.

Part of the running costs of your home, such as part of your gas and electricity bill for heating and lighting, burglar alarm maintenance, insurance and telephone, will be allowable if it is also your office – and if you don't own your home you can claim part of the rent. Note that if a house is let out for more than 140 days a year, it will be liable for uniform business rate (rather than council tax), which will be an allowable expense.

There may be some situations where a property is used partly for business, partly domestic and the council tax, rather than business rates, is payable. You should normally be able to claim a deduction for the proportion of council tax which relates to your business. But beware, there may be capital gains tax implications (see p. 245).

If you cannot claim back VAT, for example, because you are not registered, the VAT included in the cost of an item is part of the allowable expense. If you can claim back VAT, it is not allowable and you will not get tax relief on that part of the cost.

CHECKLIST OF EXPENSES YOU CAN NORMALLY CLAIM

General business

You can claim the normal business expenses of running a business, such as:

● cost of goods you sell or use in your product

● selling costs, such as advertising, sales discounts, gifts costing up to £10 a year (if the gift advertises your business or product and is not food or drink)

● office or factory expenses, such as heating, lighting, cleaning, security, business rate, rent, telephone, postage, printing, stationery, normal repairs and maintenance

● cost of computer software, if bought separately from hardware

● proportion of home expenses, including council tax, if used for work (see pp. 195, 244)

● books, magazines, professional fees and subscriptions to professional and trade organizations which are of use to your business

● travel expenses (but not between home and work, or, usually, lunches), running costs of car (see p. 195), delivery charges, charge for hiring capital equipment, such as cars, leasing payments for cars (but only the full amount if the retail price of the car is £12,000 or less)

● replacing small tools

● accountancy and audit fees.

Staff expenses

● wages, salaries, bonuses, redundancy and leaving payments, gifts to employees, contributions to approved pension schemes, pensions to former employees and their dependants (but not your salary or your partner's salary), training costs, council tax paid on behalf of an employee (or an employee's family) if a genuine part of remuneration package subject to PAYE

● cost of employing your wife or husband (p. 211)

● employer's National Insurance contributions (but not all your own, see p. 205)

● staff entertainment, for example, Christmas party

● subscriptions and contributions for benefits for staff.

Financial expenses

● bank charges on business accounts

● interest on loans and overdrafts for business purposes, and cost of arranging them (but not interest on capital paid or credited to partners, or interest on overdue tax)

● the interest part of hire purchase payments (that is, the amount you pay less the cash price)

● premiums for insurance for the business (but not your own life insurance, or sickness insurance)

● specific bad debts (but not a general reserve for bad or doubtful debts). Part of a debt given up under a voluntary arrangement (from 30 November 1993)

● contributions made before 1 April 2000 to local enterprise agencies, if approved by the government, but not if you receive any benefit from the agency

● from 30 November 1993, contributions to Business Links made before 1 April 2000

● contributions and trade or professional subscriptions which secure benefits for your business or similar payments to societies which have arrangements with the Inland Revenue (sometimes only part of the payment will be allowed)

● additional accountancy expenses needed as a result of Inland Revenue 'in-depth' investigations, but *not* if the investigation reveals that profits have been understated, so for example interest or penalties are charged and there are additions to the assessments for previous years

● incidental cost of obtaining loan finance, but not stamp duty, foreign exchange losses, issue discounts or repayment premiums.

Legal expenses

● legal charges such as debt collection, preparing trading contracts, employee service contracts, settling trading disputes and renewing a short lease (that is, 50 years or less)

● premium for grant of lease, but limited to the amount assessed on the landlord as extra rent spread over the term as the lease is paid

● fees paid to register trade mark or design, or to obtain a patent.

EXPENSES WHICH ARE NOT NORMALLY ALLOWED

● your own income and living expenses

● most of your National Insurance contributions (p.205), income tax, capital gains tax, inheritance tax, fines and other penalties for breaking the law (but you could pay a parking fine for an employee), costs of fighting a tax case, VAT surcharge

● your council tax if your home is used only for domestic purposes. You may be able to deduct part of your council tax if you work from home (but watch out for capital gains tax – see p. 244)

● depreciation or initial cost of capital equipment, buying a patent, vehicles, fixed advertising signs, buildings and the cost of additions, alterations or improvements to them. Computer hardware (and software if bought at the same time), licences for software. However, you may be able to claim capital allowances for all these items (see rightow)

● legal expenses on forming a company, drawing up a partnership agreement, acquiring assets such as leases (but not short leases)

● business entertaining expenses, cost of partners' meals at regular lunch-time meetings, gifts to customers (but see p. 196), normal charitable subscriptions and donations, donations to political parties

● reserves or provisions for expected payments, such as repairs, general reserve for bad and doubtful debts (but see p. 197).

● wages to employees which remain unpaid 18 months after the accounting date.

CAPITAL ALLOWANCES

What you spend on plant, machinery and vehicles is not an allowable expense. But this does not mean that you are unable to get any tax relief for spending on capital equipment for your business. You can, but by claiming what's called a capital allowance. You deduct the amount of the allowance you claim from your profits and thus pay less tax. The normal allowance you will claim is called a writing-down allowance. But for the year ending 31 October 1993, bigger allowances can be claimed for machinery (but excluding most cars) and plant.

To be able to claim a capital allowance, the rule is the same as for allowable business expenses; the expenditure must be *wholly and exclusively* for your business. But, as with expenses, if you have bought something which you use in your business as well as privately, you can claim a proportion of the allowance.

WHAT ARE THE RATES OF ALLOWANCE?

You can claim writing-down allowances for plant and machinery, lorries and vans, patents and know-how; the maximum is 25 per cent. A writing-down allowance is worked out on the value as it is written-down over the years you own it (but if you claim a writing-down allowance in the first year it is worked out on the cost). For one year only, until 31 October 1993, you could claim a bigger allowance on what you spent on plant and machinery (but not cars) during that year; this was an initial allowance of 40 per cent.

In the November budget, the Chancellor introduced new rules to make clearer the definition of what is plant and machinery (for the purposes of claiming capital allowances). The new rules mean that expenditure on building, structures, alteration of land or interest in land can not be defined as plant or machinery.

For cars the maximum allowance from 11 March 1992 is the lower of 25 per cent or £3,000 each year (before 11 March 1992, was the lower of 25 per cent or £2,000).

There is an initial allowance of 20 per cent for the construction of new industrial and agricultural buildings which are contracted for in the year to 31 October 1993 and used by the end of 1994. Apart from this, the rate of allowances for industrial buildings, agricultural buildings, and hotels with ten or more bedrooms, the rate is worked out each year on the original cost at a rate of 4 per cent.

These rates of writing-down allowances are maximums. You do not have to claim the whole amount. If your profits were fairly low one year, and you had outgoings and personal allowances which you could claim and which would wipe out your tax bill, the effect of the allowance would be wasted, because there would be no extra tax saving. Instead, you can defer claiming an allowance (or part of it) and carry forward the value of the asset as it is to the next year. However, initial allowances have to be claimed in the first year and cannot be carried forward. Note that you can claim allowances of 100 per cent on buildings in enterprise zones.

IF YOU HAVE ONE BUSINESS ASSET

Capital allowances work something like this. If you have only one piece of capital equipment, in the first year you own it, you deduct the amount of the allowance you are claiming from the original cost of the asset. The amount you have deducted is used to reduce your taxable profits. The value of the asset which you carry forward to the next year is the initial cost less the allowance claimed.

EXAMPLE

Paula Barber has been in business in a small way for a number of years. She currently has only one item of capital equipment which cost £1,000, an electronic typewriter. She claims the initial allowance of 40 per cent; she bought it in the year before 31 October 1993. The amount of the allowance she deducts from profits is 40 per cent of £1,000, that is, £400. The value of the typewriter which she carries forward to the next year is £1,000 − £400 = £600. She will be able to claim a further allowance on the typewriter next year of 25 per cent of £600 = £150. And the value she would carry forward would be £600 − £150 = £450.

MORE THAN ONE ASSET

If you have more than one asset, capital allowances are not worked out on each individual piece of equipment you have. Instead, you put the values of all the assets (with a few exceptions, see right) in what is called a *pool of expenditure*. And each year you work out the writing-down allowances for the year on the value of your pool of expenditure at the end of the year. You deduct the amount of the allowance you are now claiming from the value of the pool and carry the new value of the pool forward to the next year.

However, for the year to 31 October 1993, you will need to claim your initial allowances on plant and machinery separately before adding the written-down value to the pool at the start of the next year.

EXAMPLE

David Simonsen has been in business for a number of years. At the start of the current accounting year, the value of his pool of expenditure is £33,658. During the year to 31 October 1993, he bought a new printing machine, costing £15,000. He works out how much he can claim in capital allowances. He can claim 40 per cent of £15,000 = £6,000 for the printing machine and 25 per cent of the pool, i.e. 25 per cent of £33,658 = £8,414. In total, he can claim capital allowances of £6,000 + £8,414 = £14,414. The value of the pool at the start of the next year is £33,658 − £8,414 + £15,000 − £6,000 = £34,244.

There are three categories of assets which have their own separate pool:

● cars *must* have their own pool, separate from the rest of your equipment. From 11 March 1992, for cars costing more than £12,000, you will have to create a separate pool for each car, with a writing-down allowance of no more than £3,000 each year. Before that date, the figures were a cost of £8,000 and a writing-down allowance of £2,000

● capital equipment which you use partly in your business, partly in your private life, must have its own pool

● any item of capital equipment (not cars, but it could be calculators, tools or computers, for example) which you expect to sell or scrap within five years can be put in a separate pool if you choose. These are known as short-life assets. Being in a separate pool can be an advantage when you sell one of these assets, see below.

WHAT HAPPENS WHEN YOU SELL ASSETS?

When you sell an asset, you have to deduct it from the pool of expenditure. You do this before you work out what capital allowances you can claim for that year. The amount you deduct from the pool is the smaller of either the original cost of the asset or the money you receive when you sell it. Occasionally, especially with assets in their own pool such as cars, the proceeds are greater than the value of the pool. The excess, the *balancing charge*, is added to your profit – see example overleaf.

If you sell or scrap an asset which you have put in a separate pool because you expect it to have a short life (see above), and the proceeds come to less than the value of the pool, you can deduct the difference, the *balancing allowance*, from your profit for the year.

EXAMPLE

Roderick Whittaker has a car he uses in his business. It forms its own pool and the value at the start of the current accounting year is £3,450. During the year, Roderick sells the car for £3,700. This is more than the value in the pool, so Roderick has to add the difference, known as the balancing charge, of £250 to his profit, increasing the size of his tax bill. If he is a basic-rate taxpayer in 1994/95, his tax bill goes up by 25 per cent of £250 = £62.50.

LEASING AND HIRE PURCHASE

With equipment which you lease rather than buy, you do not get a capital allowance. Instead, the leasing payment counts as an allowable expense. There are restrictions on the amount for cars – from 11 March 1992, you can claim the full amount of the leasing payment only if the retail price of the car is £12,000 or less (before that date £8,000 or less).

If the machinery is being bought using hire purchase, you can claim a capital allowance when you first use the equipment. The interest part of the hire purchase payment can be claimed as an allowable expense, not as a capital allowance.

WHEN YOU START IN BUSINESS

When you start up on your own, and you take into the business a piece of capital equipment which you already own, you can claim a capital allowance on the value. The Tax Inspector will accept market value as the original value for working out the capital allowance.

During the first years of a business started before 6 April 1994, it can be tricky working out when you are going to get the capital allowance on an asset. This is because in the opening stage the profits of one accounting year can be taxed twice, while the profits of another year are taxed not at all, see p. 208.

A capital allowance is claimed once. You can claim the allowance for the first year in which it is eligible for tax relief. If the same profits are taxed again, you cannot claim the allowance based on its original cost but on its value after being written down. For businesses started on or after 6 April 1994, this will not be a problem as profits will be taxed only once, in the tax year in which they occur. The same will apply when existing businesses have all switched to the new system starting in 1997/98. For 1996/97, the profits of two years will be averaged.

If your first period of business starts midway through a tax year, the writing-down allowance will be restricted to that proportion of the

25 per cent amount worked out on a time basis. For example, if you start business on 5 September, there is seven months until the end of the tax year. You are entitled to a writing-down allowance of $7/12$ of 25 per cent.

LOSSES

Businesses do not always make profits; you may face the situation one day when you have made a loss. The tax system allows you to set off the loss to reduce other tax bills. You can choose to deduct it from:

● your other income for the same tax year (this could include profits from the same business which you made in the *preceding* tax year or investment income) and a capital gain *or*

● your other income and a capital gain for the next tax year, as long as you are still carrying on the business in which you made the loss (a different business does not count) *or*

● future profits from the same business (but not a different one).

In the early years of the business, losses (which are calculated in the same way as profits) have to be split between tax years on a time basis. If the loss is an isolated one, occurring after your first four years of business, your Tax Inspector may accept a claim for a loss for an accounting year ending in the current tax year.

SETTING THE LOSS AGAINST OTHER INCOME AND A CAPITAL GAIN

If you have other income, it will improve your cash flow to set the loss against it rather than future profits (and, in any case, these may be uncertain). However, you must set the loss off before your personal allowance or deductions on which you can get tax relief, such as mortgage interest. As you cannot carry forward an unused personal allowance from one tax year to the next, making this choice may mean losing part of your allowance if the income is not big enough to cover both the loss and the allowance. If this is the case, consider setting the loss against your other income for the next tax year (but not any future ones), and future profits. To get this relief by setting losses against other income, claim within two years after the end of the year in which you make the loss.

You can also deduct a loss from a capital gain made in your business in the same year as you made the trading loss or in the next tax year, if you are still running the business which made the loss.

SETTING THE LOSS AGAINST FUTURE PROFITS

If you decide not to set the loss against other income for the same or the next tax year, you can choose instead to deduct it from future profits for as many years as you need to get tax relief on it all. It must be profits from the same self-employed activity, and not any other.

To get this relief, you must claim within six years of the year in which you want it; the amount of the loss must be claimed within six years of the year of the loss.

LOSSES IN A NEW BUSINESS

If you make a loss during the first four years of your business, you can carry it back and deduct it from other income in the previous three years, starting with the earliest year. You will be allowed this tax relief only if there is some prospect that the business could be profitable.

To get this relief, you must claim within two years after the end of the year in which you made the loss.

LOSSES IN A CLOSING BUSINESS

A loss made in the last twelve months of a business can be:

● deducted from other income

or

● deducted from the profits of the same business which you made in the three tax years before you close it, starting with the most recent year first.

NATIONAL INSURANCE CONTRIBUTIONS

You may have to pay two different lots of National Insurance contributions:

● for yourself, that is, Class 2 and perhaps Class 4 contributions
● for an employee, that is, employer's contributions.

CONTRIBUTIONS FOR YOURSELF: CLASS 2

Most self-employed people will pay Class 2 contributions. Some self-employed will also have to pay Class 4 contributions.

Class 2 contributions are flat-rate – £5.55 for 1993/94 and £5.65 for 1994/95. They used to be paid weekly by buying NI stamps from the post office and sticking them on a contribution card, but payment since 11 April 1993 must be either by quarterly bills or by monthly direct debit. Paying these contributions gives you access to most social security benefits, with some exceptions. You may be able to claim basic sickness benefit, basic invalidity benefit, basic maternity allowance, basic retirement pension and, if you are a married man, your Class 2 contributions would entitle your wife to the basic widow's benefits in the event of your death. Class 2 contributions don't entitle you to unemployment benefit but in certain limited circumstances you may be able to claim it (see leaflet FB30 *Self-employed?* available from the Department of Social Security). Nor do Class 2 contributions entitle you to industrial injuries benefit or additional earnings-related pension or widow's benefits.

You do not have to pay Class 2 contributions for the tax year if:

● you are aged 65 or over, if a man, or 60 or over, if a woman

● you are under 16

● you hold a certificate of exception because your earnings from self-employment are, or are expected to be, below the exception limit for Class 2 contributions. You may apply to be excepted from liability to pay if your earnings have been less than £3,140 during 1993/94, and there has been no real change in your earning power, or you expect to earn less than £3,200 in 1994/95. If you think that you should be excepted, apply straightaway as there is a time limit. The certificate will usually be effective from the date of your application, although it may be backdated for up to 13 weeks. If you want to know more about small earnings exception, or want to apply for it, get the leaflet NI27A from your Social Security office. There is an application form in the leaflet. Note, that if you don't pay Class 2 contributions, you lose some rights to benefits

● you are a married woman who had what's known as 'reduced liability' on 5 April 1978. You must hold a certificate of election CF383 – this entitles you to choose not to pay Class 2 contributions. Some married women who were self-employed before 6 April 1975 will not hold a CF383. They should contact their local DSS office who will arrange for the issue of the certificate. If you are not in this category and don't hold a certificate, you cannot now make this choice

● you are not 'ordinarily' self-employed, for example, you are an employee and your earnings from your part-time self-employment are not likely to be more than £800 in a tax year. See leaflet NI27A.

You do not have to pay Class 2 contributions for any particular week, if for a full week (Monday to Saturday):

● you are incapable of working, because you are ill (you will need a sick note to establish this) *or*

● you are receiving sickness, invalidity or industrial injury benefit or the maternity allowance *or*

● for any day in the week you are receiving the unemployability supplement to the industrial disablement benefit or to a war disablement pension or you are getting invalid care allowance *or*

● you are working outside the UK *or*

● you are in legal custody or in prison.

CONTRIBUTIONS FOR YOURSELF: CLASS 4

Class 4 contributions are earnings-related and paid, at the same time as your income tax bill, on profits you earn between an upper and lower limit:

1993/94 – 6.3% on profits or gains between £6,340 and £21,840

1994/95 – 7.3% on profits or gains beetween £6,490 and £22,360

This gives a maximum contribution of £976.50 for 1993/94 and £1,158.51 for 1994/95.

Profits for contribution purposes are worked out in much the same way as profits for income tax purposes, except that:

● losses can only be deducted from your future profits from the same self-employed activity (p. 204)

● any Enterprise Allowance or other financial support from a TEC are included (p. 210).

You can deduct one-half of your Class 4 contributions from your profits before working out your income tax bill. Class 4 contributions do not increase the amount or range of social security benefits you can claim.

You do not have to pay Class 4 contributions if, among other exceptions, you are:

- aged 65 or over, if a man, or 60 or over, if a woman
- not 'ordinarily' self-employed (see p. 206)
- non-resident (p. 188)
- not yet 16 during the tax year.

For more information, see leaflet NP18 *Class 4 National Insurance Contributions*.

EMPLOYER'S CONTRIBUTION

There is no limit on the amount of employer's contribution you have to pay for an employee. The amount of the contribution for 1994/95 is given in the Table on p. 156.

Note that if you employ someone over the normal retirement age, so they do not pay employee's contribution, you still have to pay employer's contribution.

If you give an employee a company car, from 6 April 1991, the taxable value is included in the earnings figure for working out employer's National Insurance contributions, but not the employee's.

PAYING YOUR TAX BILL

If you started your business before 6 April 1994, to know what your tax bill is going to be, you need to know which are the profits to be taxed in this tax year. Assuming your business has been going at least three years, you are normally taxed on what is known as a *preceding-year basis* (see p. 208 for what happens in first few years). So you will be taxed on the profits you earn in the accounting year ending in the previous tax year. For example, if your year-end is 30 June you will be taxed for the 1994/95 tax year on the profits you earned between 1 July 1992 and 30 June 1993.

Being taxed on a preceding-year basis means there can be quite a delay between earning the profits and paying the tax due on them. If your profits are rising year by year, you will be earning a higher income while paying tax on lower profits earned earlier. This delay is one of the major tax advantages of self-employment. However, this will be swept away for all businesses by the 1997/98 tax year (with a transitional arrangement for 1996/97) and replaced by a current year basis.

You can choose any year-end you like for your business. Just because you start your business on 1 November, say, does not mean your accounting year has to end on 31 October of the following year. Nor does your accounting year have to be a calendar year, that is, 1 January to 31 December. But with the change to the current year basis, there is no particular financial advantage to be gained by choosing one year-end rather than another.

You can change your year-end if you want, but think twice as it is a complicated procedure (see Inland Revenue leaflet IR26).

Whereas employees pay their income tax each month or each week, the self-employed have to pay in two equal instalments. The first half is due on 1 January and the second on 1 July.

STARTING AND CLOSING A BUSINESS

STARTING BEFORE 6 APRIL 1994

The rule about paying tax on the profits you earn in the accounting year ending in the previous tax year could not apply for a business started before 6 April 1994 for the obvious reason that there is no previous year. So there are special rules about how you are taxed. You have some freedom to choose which profit you are taxed on in the second and third tax years of your business; your Tax Inspector has the choice when it comes to closing the business. If you started a business in 1993/94, for example, you will be taxed as follows:

1993/94 Your tax bill is worked out using the profit you actually earned before 6 April 1994 (that is, in the first tax year). Finding out your actual profit may mean that you need to split profits between tax years – see opposite for how to do this.

1994/95 You can choose. You can make it the profit you earned in your first twelve months of business. Or, you can opt for the tax to be based on the profit you actually earned in the second tax year (1994/95).

1995/96 This is the transitional year. Your tax bill will be based on the average of the profits you earn in the two-year accounting period ending during 1995/96.

1996/97 Your tax bill will be based on the profits you earn in the accounting period ending in 1996/97.

STARTING A BUSINESS IN 1994/95

Your tax bill is based on the profits you make in 1994/95. So, if you start your business on 1 May 1994, you will be taxed in 1995/96 on the profits you earn to 30 April 1995.

CLOSING YOUR BUSINESS IN 1993/94

Your Tax Inspector in 1993/94 can make the choice. For 1991/92 which is two tax years before you close, your tax bill will be worked out on your profit in your accounting year ending in 1990/1991. Or, if your Tax Inspector chooses for both this and 1992/93, the profit you actually earned in 1991/92 (see below).

For 1992/93, your tax bill is based on your profit in your accounting year ending in 1991/92. Or, if your Tax Inspector chooses for both this and the previous tax year, the profit you actually earned in 1992/93.

Finally, in 1993/94, your tax bill is based on the profit you actually earned in 1993/94.

MAKING THE CHOICE

The opening rules which apply to a business started before 6 April 1994 mean that some profits may be taxed more than once. If you are claiming capital allowances in the opening years, however, you cannot claim the same allowance twice; for the second year the profits are taxed, the allowance will be worked out on the value after the writing-down allowance has been claimed for the first year (p. 199).

To make the choice of being taxed on actual profit in the second and the third tax years, you must tell your Tax Inspector within six years after the end of the third year of assessment.

The current closing rules mean that some profits may not be taxed at all. But if you have capital expenditure in those years, you will be able to claim your allowance. For what you spend on capital equipment in the period of profits which are not taxed, you can claim as if it was spent in the next period, unless that is the last tax year. In this case, you can claim as if it was spent in the previous period.

HOW TO SPLIT PROFITS (AND LOSSES) BETWEEN TAX YEARS

To check whether you should make the choice of being taxed on actual profit, you need to work out what profit figure this would give you. Actual profit is the proportion of profit earned during the tax year and is calculated on a time basis. Start with the profit figure for the accounting period and multiply by the number of months of the period in the tax year and divide by the number of months in the accounting period. Note that your Tax Inspector strictly could ask you to apportion profits on a day-by-day basis, not just monthly.

Losses are apportioned in the same way as profits.

EXAMPLE

Joshua Thwaites started his business on 1 January 1993 and his first accounting period ended on 30 April 1994. His first tax year is 1992/93 and three months and a few days of his first accounting period falls in that year. Profits for the first accounting period are £10,000. His actual profit for the tax year 1992/93 is likely to be accepted by his Tax Inspector as:

$$\frac{3 \text{ months}}{16 \text{ months}} \times £10,000 = £1,875$$

WHAT YOU SPEND BEFORE YOU START YOUR BUSINESS

You may find that you have to spend money before you start trading, for example for rent or printing letterheads. As long as it is a normal business expense, it is *pre-trading expenditure*. You can claim it as a loss in your first year of trading and claim loss relief; see p. 204 for how you can do this. For a business which you started before 1 April 1993 (but on or after 1 April 1989) you can go back five years. For a business which started on or after 1 April 1993, you can go back seven years and the type of expenditure covered is wider, for example, covering certain types of interest.

FINANCIAL SUPPORT ON STARTING A BUSINESS

This scheme used to be called the Enterprise Allowance scheme. It is paid to you to help you start a business. The scheme is now run by Training and Enterprise Councils (in Scotland Local Enterprise Companies) under a variety of different names and paying out different amounts.

The allowance is not taxed in the same way as your business profits if you started the business before 6 April 1994. You will pay tax only once on the allowance, if any tax is due, whereas with profits in the opening years, you may be taxed more than twice on them. The allowance will be taxed in the current year, in tax jargon under Schedule D Case VI (see p. 40), but still treated as earned income. Do not include it in the figure for business profits which you put in your Tax Return.

If you receive income from your self-employed business within six years of closing it (*post-cessation receipts*), you can choose to have it treated as income received on the last day of your business. Otherwise it will be treated as earned income when you receive it and taxed in the current year (in tax jargon, under Schedule D Case VI).

You must tell your Tax Inspector within two years of the end of the tax year in which you receive the income if you wish to make this choice.

WHO IS SELF-EMPLOYED?

Whether you are self-employed or an employee is not just a question of your convenience. You are probably self-employed if you can answer 'yes' to some of the following questions:

● can you determine what work you do, whether you or someone else does it, how you do it and when and where you do it?

● do you pay for the capital equipment of your business?

● have you put your own money into the business?

● if the business makes a loss, do you have to cover it?

● if work is unsatisfactory, do you have to put it right in your own time and out of your own pocket?

EMPLOYING YOUR FAMILY

You would need to establish that your family actually carry out the work you say and that they are paid the going rate for the job, if you wish to employ your wife or husband or your children in your business. You will also have to satisfy your Tax Inspector that they actually receive the money you say you pay them.

Your family members will be able to claim the personal allowance (£3,445 in 1994/95) to deduct from what you pay. However, if you pay more than the lower-earnings limit for National Insurance contributions, £57 a week for 1994/95, both of you will have to pay contributions (p. 204).

WHAT TO PUT IN YOUR TAX RETURN

If you are self-employed, the Tax Return you will probably be getting is Form 11, where you must enter details of your business under the heading *Income from self-employment – year to 5 April 1994* on the first page. If you are sent Form 11P, give the same information starting at the bottom of the second page.

You have to give details of what sort of self-employed work you do (for example, barrister, boat-builder and so on). You must also state your business address and the name you trade under.

Form 11

If your sales figure is less than £15,000, you don't need to send accounts but enter the figures for sales (turnover) and allowable business expenses in the spaces provided under *Businesses with a turnover of less than £15,000*.

Form 11

All businesses should put the amount of taxable profit at the bottom of page 1. If your sales are £15,000 or more you need to enclose your accounts and all businesses should state the accounting period.

Form 11

| See note 6 for expenses. See note 7 for losses | **All businesses: Profit for tax purposes** Your profit for tax purposes is your turnover less allowable business expenses. It does not include enterprise allowance received. Give your profit for the accounting period you specify below. If you have made a loss enter 'Nil'. | £ |

At the top of the second page of Form 11, give details of the year covered by your accounts.

Form 11

Period covered by your accounts or statement of turnover and expenses
Give the period covered by your accounts (or the partnership accounts), or by the statement of turnover and expenses above, which ended on a date between 6 April 1993 and 5 April 1994. If you stopped being self-employed, give the date you stopped

| See note 8. | Start of period | / /19 | End of period | / /19 |

Below this you need to give information about capital allowances, balancing charges, enterprise allowance and Class 4 National Insurance contributions.

Form 11

See note 9.	**Capital allowances** Give the amount you are claiming or tick here and give details on a separate sheet of paper if you want your Tax Office to help work out the figure.		£
See note 10.	**Balancing adjustments** Give the amount of the adjustments or tick here and give details on a separate sheet of paper if you want your Tax Office to help work out the figure.		£
See note 11.	Enterprise allowance received		£
To find out if you qualify see note 11.	Further relief on class 4 National Insurance		
	Type of relief		Amount. £

With Form P1, you need give only turnover, allowable expenses and profit on the first page.

24 • PARTNERS

A partnership can be a burden shared: the difficulties and the traumas of a business shouldered by two or more of you. But this sharing of obligations may prove to be illusory. What you must look for in a partnership is complete trust that your partner will fulfil your partnership agreement.

When it comes to income tax, this trust in each other is especially important. If your partner does not pay what is due, you will have to cough up for the whole of the partnership income tax bill. The moral is choose your partner carefully; you do not want to be left holding the tax bill (or any other bill).

This chapter outlines the basic tax rules which may be helpful to you if you are thinking of forming a partnership or if your partnership is very simple. If your affairs are at all complicated, you should consult your tax adviser.

Just as with the sole trader, major changes are afoot for the taxation of partnerships. More details are given on p.217.

BRIEF GUIDE TO TAX FOR PARTNERS UNDER THE CURRENT SYSTEM

1 The figure for taxable income for the partnership is worked out in the same way as if you were in business on your own (p. 193). So you can deduct expenses, capital allowances, losses and half the Class 4 National Insurance contributions which the partnership pays.

2 The tax bill on the partnership profits is worked out for the partnership as a whole and is in the partnership name. Although the bill will be shared between the partners (see 7), each partner is liable to pay all of the bill. So, if your partner does not pay up, you can be made to cover the whole amount of tax due.

3 If the partnership has any non-trading income (for example, income from investments) or any capital gains, you are not responsible

for the full amount of any tax due on it, as you are with the partnership profits. Instead you are responsible only for your share.

4 Profits are taxed on a preceding-year basis, that is, in the current tax year, you are paying tax on profits earned in the accounting year ending in the previous tax year. But as far as your Tax Inspector is concerned, the profits are divided as you are dividing them in the current tax year, regardless of what happened in the previous year. So your Tax Inspector can assume a quite different share-out of the profits from the one that actually happens. (But this will change from 1996/97 – see p. 217).

5 Once your Tax Inspector has divided up the profits for tax purposes, the tax bill for each partner is worked out. This takes account of the rate of tax each partner is paying, for example, one of you could be paying tax at the basic rate and the other at 40 per cent.

6 The Tax Inspector tots up the tax for each partner and sends the partnership one tax bill to be paid for the total amount, with a separate memorandum account showing how the tax bill should be split between partners.

7 You and your partner may decide to share out the tax bill in quite different proportions from those assumed by your Tax Inspector.

8 If a new partner joins you and you sign a *continuation election* (p. 216), your Tax Inspector will apportion your new partner part of the profits earned before joining. If you do not sign this election, it is assumed that the existing partnership has ceased and the closing rules apply (p. 209).

9 The partnership tax bill is due to be paid in two equal instalments on 1 January and 1 July.

EXAMPLE

Joe Johnson and David Lock have been partners for several years. In the accounting year ending 31 December 1993, they share profits of £24,000 equally between them. From 1 January 1994, they agree that Joe will take three-quarters of the profits and David a quarter.

For the tax year 1994/95, their tax bill will be based on the profits of £24,000 (profits of the accounting year ending in the preceding tax year), but their Tax Inspector will assume a profit split of 3:1. It will be assumed that:

● Joe has £18,000

● David has £6,000

What actually happened is that those £24,000 profits were shared equally between them, that is, £12,000 each.

When the Tax Inspector works out the partnership tax bill, it is done by looking at the tax rates paid by Joe and David. For 1994/95, Joe's highest rate of tax is the basic rate, that is 25 per cent, and David's the higher rate 40 per cent (he has other income as well as from the partnership). Both are entitled to a married couple's allowance as well as personal allowance giving total allowances of £5,165.

Joe's taxable income is £18,000 – £5,165 = £12,835

David's taxable income from the partnership is £6,000 – £5,165 = £835.

The tax due is:

20% of £3,000 (Joe)	=	£600.00
25% of £9,835 (Joe)	=	£2,458.75
40% of £835 (David)	=	£334.00
		£3,392.75

The partnership will pay tax of £3,392.75. How the bill is divided between the two partners depends upon what they have agreed.

A PARTNER JOINS OR LEAVES

Either a partner leaving or a partner joining means that for tax purposes the business has ceased and the closing rules apply (p. 209). However, if at least one partner before and after the change is the same, you can sign a *continuation election* which means that the partnership will carry on paying tax on the normal preceding-year basis. To make this choice, all partners before and after the change have to sign the election. It must be made within two years of the change.

If you could make a continuation election but choose not to do so, the tax bills for the first four years of the new partnership are based on the actual profits made (p. 209). You can choose for both years five and six that the tax due is worked out on the actual profits rather than the preceding-year basis. You must make this choice within six years of the end of the sixth year of assessment of the new partnership.

IF THE PARTNERSHIP MAKES A LOSS

You get tax relief for losses in the same way as if you were self-employed (p. 203). The loss is split among the partners in the same ratios as the profits would have been shared in the period covered by the accounts. Each of you can decide to treat your share of the loss in the way that suits you the best; you do not all have to make the same decision on how you will get tax relief for the loss.

PUTTING CAPITAL IN A PARTNERSHIP

You can get tax relief on a loan of any size which you use to buy a share in or make a loan to a partnership. But you can get the relief only if you are an active partner yourself; that is, if you are a limited partner you are not eligible.

THE NEW SYSTEM FOR TAXATION OF PARTNERS

Partnership taxation will be shaken up beginning with the tax year 1995/96. Here are the main changes:

1 Just as sole traders, your tax bill will be based on the accounting period ending in the current year not the preceding year. But the transitional year 1995/96 will consist of the average of the two year period.

2 Although the partnership will remain responsible for the tax bill, there will no longer be just one tax bill. Once the partnership return and accounts have been agreed, each partner will be responsible for his or her own tax bill.

3 The profits will be shared among the partners for the purpose of the tax bills in the same proportion as in the accounting period (no longer the tax year). But for the transitional year 1995/96, it will be based on the tax year and not the current accounting period until 1996/97.

4 Partners *must* make continuation elections.

WHAT TO PUT IN YOUR TAX RETURN

You give details of your partnership in the same space as if you were self-employed and on your own (see p. 212), except that you enter only your share of the partnership profits.

To claim tax relief on a loan, see p. 46, you enter the details in *Other qualifying loans* on page 8 of Forms 11P and 11 and in *Other loans qualifying for tax relief* on page 3 of Form P1. Put the lender's name , the purpose of the loan and enclose a certificate of loan interest paid which you can get from your lender.

218

Form 11P

Notes

For details of loans on which you can claim tax relief see note 40. For details on loans to buy or improve rental property see notes 24 and 25. If you have more than one qualifying loan, give details on a separate sheet of paper.

Other qualifying loans

Complete this form if you can claim tax relief on other loans. Only give details of loans not included elsewhere on this form. Enclose a certificate of interest paid from your lender. Do not include loans on your main home.

Name of lender

Purpose of loan

Give the address of the property if the loan is for the purchase or improvement of property used for letting

The number of weeks let

Amount of gross interest paid in the 1993-94 tax year £

In addition, the partnership will have to fill in another Tax Return.

25 • PENSIONS

It's hard when you're in the prime of life to start worrying about pensions and retirement. But there are two good reasons for even the youngest and most active to give some thought to that far-off day of retirement.

First, the earlier you start, the easier it is to provide for your old age. If you've neglected your pension in your 20s and 30s, you may still be able to catch up in your 40s and 50s. But the cost will be high and the later you leave it, the higher it gets.

Second, the government offers handsome tax incentives to encourage you to provide for your retirement. These mean that saving for the future through a pension will almost certainly provide a better return on your money than any other type of investment.

This chapter looks at the tax reliefs for pension schemes whether you belong to an employer's pension scheme or make your own personal pension arrangements. For details of how pensions are taxed once you start drawing them, see Chapter 17, 'Retired – or Near Retirement Age', p. 132.

EMPLOYERS' PENSIONS

Employers' pension schemes vary considerably, but usually provide you with an income on retirement, either linked to your earnings before retirement (a *final pay* scheme) or related to the amount of contributions paid in by you and your employer (a *money purchase* scheme). And most offer some or all of the following benefits: life insurance cover before you retire; a lump sum when you retire; and a widow's/widower's pension.

Employers' pensions and other retirement benefits are paid for out of a fund built up from contributions made by the employer and, except with non-contributory schemes, employees who belong to the scheme. There are valuable tax incentives to encourage saving through an approved pension scheme:

● there is tax relief on contributions to the pension scheme, both for the employer and employee (within limits)

● the employer's contributions made for you are not taxable as your income or as a fringe benefit

● the fund in which the money goes pays no income tax or capital gains tax, so that the investment return is tax-free (and certainly ought to be higher than if you invested the money yourself and paid tax on profits and income)

● you can take a substantial tax-free lump sum when you retire in lieu of some pension.

These tax incentives are available only for pension schemes which are approved by the Inland Revenue. Approved schemes must offer benefits within set limits:

● the maximum pension you can draw is two-thirds of final salary

● the maximum tax-free lump sum is 1½ times final salary

● the maximum lump sum payment which can be made on death in service (i.e. life insurance cover) is four times your salary.

There are also limits on the benefits which can be paid to widows and widowers. For example, the maximum widow's or widower's pension is two-thirds the pension the spouse would have got if still alive.

THE PENSION SCHEME EARNINGS CAP

There are restrictions on the pension benefits you can draw from an approved scheme set up on or after 14 March 1989, or if you joined an older scheme on or after 1 June 1989. The amount of salary which can be taken into account is limited by the *pension scheme earnings cap* which is £76,800 for the 1994/95 tax year (it was £75,000 for the 1993/94 tax year). This means the following limits in cash terms on the pension benefits you can begin to draw in 1994/95 if the cap applies to you:

● a maximum pension of £51,200 (two-thirds of £76,800)

● a maximum lump sum of £115,200 (1½ times £76,800)

● a maximum payment for death in service of £307,200 (four times £76,800).

Other benefits are also subject to the pension scheme earnings cap (for example, widow's and widower's pensions).

Note that the pension scheme earnings cap should be considered if you are thinking of joining a new pension scheme or altering your membership of an old scheme. Most people earn well below £76,800 a year and will find the cap does not affect them. But if you're likely to be affected by the cap, think carefully before throwing away your rights to higher benefits.

CONTRIBUTIONS

The amount you are required to contribute to an employer's pension scheme is decided by your employer, but cannot exceed 15 per cent of your earnings (this can include the value of fringe benefits). Provided the pension scheme is approved by the Inland Revenue, you can get tax relief at your highest rate of tax on these contributions. Your contributions will be deducted from your income before working out how much tax has to be paid under PAYE (though your National Insurance contributions are worked out on your full pay, that is, before deduction of pension contributions).

However, if the scheme was set up on or after 14 March 1989, or you joined it on or after 1 June 1989, contributions are restricted to 15 per cent of earnings up to the pension scheme earnings cap mentioned above. For the 1994/95 tax year, the pension scheme earnings cap is £76,800 – so you can get tax relief on maximum contributions of £11,520 for the year.

Pension contributions can be repaid to you before retirement from an approved scheme only if you leave the scheme within two years of joining. In this event, tax is deducted from the repayments at a flat rate of 20 per cent, to recover the tax relief you have had.

ADDITIONAL VOLUNTARY CONTRIBUTIONS

If you are going to qualify for less than the maximum permitted amount of an employer's pension and want to improve the benefits you will get, you can get tax relief on extra pension contributions known as Additional Voluntary Contributions (AVCs). AVCs can be used to increase the pension you will get, the widow's/widower's pension and your life cover. But you cannot normally increase the tax-free lump sum you will get unless the AVCs began on or before 7 April 1987.

AVCs enjoy the same tax benefits as an approved pension scheme, so should grow faster than if you invested the money yourself. You can choose between two different ways of investing your AVCs:

● through your employer's pension scheme (*in-scheme AVCs*). With some schemes (in the health service and local authorities, for example), AVCs can be used to buy 'added years': this means making up contributions for years of service when you did not belong to the scheme so as to get a higher percentage of final pay as a pension. More usually, your AVCs will be invested in an insurance company pension policy or building society deposit account fixed up by your employer (these still qualify for the tax benefits of the full pension fund)

● by making your own arrangements with an insurance company, bank, building society or unit trust manager (*free-standing AVCs*). Although this involves more hassle, a free-standing AVC can easily move with you when you change jobs.

You can get full tax relief on AVCs, provided that the amount you contribute, when added to any contributions to your employer's pension scheme, does not exceed the 15 per cent contribution limits set out above. So if your pension contributions are 6 per cent, you can pay up to $15 - 6 = 9$ per cent in AVCs.

A further condition is that your contributions do not buy you pension benefits greater than the maximum limits set by the Inland Revenue for approved schemes. If you inadvertently contribute so much in AVCs that the benefits would exceed the Inland Revenue limits, the excess will be paid back to you at retirement, with a deduction to cover the tax relief the contributions have enjoyed.

PERSONAL PENSIONS

A personal pension scheme provides you with an income for retirement from a fund which you have saved up with an insurance company, bank, building society or other pension provider. The fund is used to buy an annuity when you start drawing the pension: this can be at any time between your 50th and 75th birthdays (even earlier if you are a sportsman or in other occupations where early retirement is the norm). The annuity provides an income for the rest of your life, the amount depending on interest rates at the time the annuity is bought.

You can take some of the fund you have accumulated as a lump sum in return for a lower pension. And you may be able to trade in some pension in order to provide a widow's/widower's pension. If you die before drawing the pension, you'll normally get back the premiums you've paid, usually with interest. But this is unlikely to be enough to provide for your dependants, so many personal pension providers also offer some sort of optional life insurance cover.

The personal pension fund you accumulate is personal to you. So if you change jobs or become self-employed, you can go on building up your personal pension. You decide your own level of contributions to the fund (within limits); an enlightened employer can also contribute to it. And the government will even make a contribution to an *appropriate personal pension scheme* if you contract out of the state earnings-related pension scheme (SERPS) – see below.

As with employers' pensions schemes, there are tax incentives to save through personal pensions:

● there is tax relief on your contributions (within limits)

● any employer's contributions made to your scheme are not taxable as your income or as a fringe benefit

● the fund your contributions are invested in pays no income tax or capital gains tax

● you can take a substantial tax-free lump sum when you retire in lieu of some pension.

There's no Inland Revenue restriction on the amount of pension you can take – this depends on the size of the fund you have saved up and the level of annuity rates when you draw the pension. But there are limits on the amount you can contribute (see p. 224). And the lump sum must not come to more than a quarter of the fund you have accumulated (with a cash limit of £150,000 if you took out the personal pension scheme on or before 26 July 1989).

Note that personal pensions taken out before 1 July 1988 are known as *retirement annuities,* with somewhat different rules – see p. 229.

APPROPRIATE PERSONAL PENSION SCHEMES

The government will pay into your personal pension scheme if you use it to contract out of the state earnings-related pension scheme (SERPS). To leave SERPS and qualify for the government's contribution, you must take out an *appropriate personal pension scheme,* which includes the following features:

● a pension starting at the state pension age (60 for women, 65 for men)

● a pension which continues for life, increasing yearly by 3 per cent or the rate of inflation if less

● in most cases, a widow's or widower's pension at 50 per cent of the full rate

● benefits for your dependants if you die before drawing the pension.

Although you have to contract out of SERPS to get the government payments, you and your employer go on paying the higher rate of National Insurance contributions for people in SERPS (the contracted-in rate – see p. 156). The extra you and your employer pay at this rate is what the government contributes to your personal pension, adding in the equivalent of basic-rate tax relief on your portion. The government contributions are known as the National Insurance rebate, or 'minimum contributions', and none of the pension fund built up by the NI rebate can be traded in for a tax-free lump sum.

For people aged 30 and over contracting out of SERPS for the first time, there is a further incentive from the government. From 6 April 1993 onwards, the NI rebate is increased by 1 per cent of your earnings between the National Insurance earnings limits.

If your employer has a contracted-in pension scheme (that is, one which is on top of SERPS instead of a substitute for it), you can contract out of SERPS *and* remain in the employer's scheme. But you will be restricted to a special type of appropriate personal pension scheme which can only receive the government's NI rebate on your behalf. With this special type of personal pension, neither you nor your employer can contribute.

CONTRIBUTIONS

The maximum contribution you can make to a personal pension scheme is a percentage of your *net relevant earnings* (see opposite). The percentage depends on your age at the beginning of the tax year, ranging from 17½ per cent for people under 36 to 40 per cent for those aged 61 and over. But the pension scheme earnings cap (see p. 220) sets an overall limit on the amount of net relevant earnings which can be taken into account. For the 1994/95 tax year, the pension scheme earnings cap is £76,800 – so if you are entitled to contribute 17½ per cent of your net relevant earnings, the maximum cash sum for the year is 17½ per cent of £76,800 – i.e. £13,440. For the 1993/94 tax year, the pension scheme earnings cap was £75,000. The Table gives the details of the limits on contributions for both tax years:

AGE ON 6 APRIL	% OF NET RELEVANT EARNINGS	MAXIMUM CONTRIBUTION 1993/94	1994/95
35 or under	17½	£13,125	£13,440
36 – 45	20	£15,000	£15,360
46 – 50	25	£18,750	£19,200
51 – 55	30	£22,500	£23,040
56 – 60	35	£26,250	£26,880
61 and over	40	£30,000	£30,720

These limits apply to the total of your personal pension contributions. If your employer makes a contribution towards your personal pension scheme, the maximum you are entitled to contribute is reduced by the amount your employer contributes. But contributions by the government towards an appropriate personal pension scheme (including the bonus) do not count towards the limit.

If the personal pension scheme includes a lump sum life insurance benefit, the cost of providing this, up to a maximum of 5 per cent of your net relevant earnings, is deducted from the amount you can contribute to the personal pension. Suppose, for example, you are entitled to tax relief on personal pension contributions of 17½ per cent of your net relevant earnings, and these come to £20,000 in a tax year. You can get tax relief on those earnings for personal pension contributions of £3,500 (17½ per cent of £20,000); but of this £3,500 no more than £1,000 (5 per cent of £20,000) must go towards life insurance benefits.

NET RELEVANT EARNINGS

Net relevant earnings are defined as follows:

● if you're an employee, your earnings from non-pensionable jobs, including the taxable value of fringe benefits (p. 165) but after deduction of allowable expenses (p. 144)

● if you're self-employed, your taxable profits (p. 193), less certain payments made by your business after deduction of tax (for example, patent royalties, covenant payments).

A husband and wife each have their own net relevant earnings and thus their own allowance for tax relief on personal pension contributions.

Lydia Naismith earns £33,000 a year from a job which has no pension scheme. She is 44 and is therefore entitled to tax relief at her top rate of tax on personal pension contributions of up to 20 per cent of her net relevant earnings.

To work out her net relevant earnings, Lydia adds the £33,000 salary to the £2,180 value of her fringe benefits and deducts the £180 of allowable expenses she can claim. Thus her net relevant earnings are £33,000 + £2,180 − £180 = £35,000.

So Lydia can get tax relief on personal pension contributions of 20 per cent of £35,000, that is, on contributions of up to £7,000. If her top rate of tax is 40 per cent, her tax bill will be reduced by 40 per cent of £7,000, that is, £2,800. So £7,000 of contributions will cost Lydia only £4,200 after allowing for the tax relief.

BACKDATING PERSONAL PENSION CONTRIBUTIONS

If you make contributions to a personal pension scheme in one tax year and you paid less than the maximum you were entitled to in the previous year, you can opt to have some or all of the contributions treated as if they were made in that preceding year. If you had no net relevant earnings in the immediately preceding tax year you can backdate the contributions one further tax year.

Suppose, for example, that you were entitled to make personal pension contributions of up to £4,000 in 1993/94, but made contributions of only £2,000. That leaves £2,000 of unused relief, and you could backdate up to £2,000 of contributions made during the next tax year (i.e. 1994/95) to the 1993/94 tax year. You might want to do this because your top rate of tax in 1993/94 was higher than in 1994/95.

To claim backdating, fill in Form PP43 (available from tax offices). You must make the claim on or before 5 July following the end of the tax year in which you make the contributions. In the example above, the payments to be backdated are made in 1994/95, and the taxman would have to be notified by 5 July following the end of the 1994/95 tax year, that is, 5 July 1995.

UNUSED RELIEF FROM THE LAST SIX YEARS

If you've used up all your contribution allowance for the tax year, you can still get tax relief on further contributions in that year if you haven't used all the contribution allowances you were entitled to in the previous six tax years. This can be used in one of two ways:

● to make a one-off bigger-than-normal contribution in one tax year, drawing on previous years' unused allowances to make a contribution over the allowance for that year

● to continue making regular contributions in years in which your non-pensionable income fluctuates below the level required to permit such a contribution.

Unused relief from the earliest years is used first, as the following example shows.

EXAMPLE

Linton Johnson's net relevant earnings over the past six complete tax years are as set out in the second column of the Table below. He is 32, so is entitled to tax relief on personal pension contributions of 17½ per cent of his net relevant earnings in each of those years (the amounts this would be are given in the third column of the table).

TAX YEAR	NET RELEVANT EARNINGS	MAXIMUM PREMIUMS	PREMIUMS PAID	UNUSED RELIEF
	£	£	£	£
1988/89	10,000	1,750	1,200	550
1989/90	8,000	1,400	1,200	200
1990/91	10,000	1,750	1,200	550
1991/92	12,000	2,100	1,200	900
1992/93	14,000	2,450	1,800	650
1993/94	13,000	2,275	1,800	475

The fourth column of the Table shows the pension contributions Linton made during those six years: for four of the years, he paid £100 a month (£1,200 a year); emboldened by improving results, he increased that to £150 a month in 1992/93 (£1,800 a year). In none of the six years have his premiums been greater than the amount on which he is entitled to tax relief, and so there is a total of £3,325 in unused tax relief for the past six complete tax years. This provides a useful cushion for 1994/95:

● if Linton's net relevant earnings fell below £10,000, he could continue to make personal pension contributions of £1,800 a year. Even though the maximum contribution allowance for that year would be less than £1,800, he could use some or all of the unused £550 from 1988/89 (and if that were insufficient, unused relief from 1989/90 and later years)

● even if Linton's net relevant earnings were over £10,000 (i.e. more than enough to qualify for tax relief on £1,800 of premiums), he could draw on the unused relief from the previous six years to make a once-for-all lump sum contribution in 1994/95 – of as much as £3,325, plus any unused relief for the 1994/95 tax year. However, the full current year's entitlement must be paid before any unused relief is taken up.

Note that unlike the backdating procedure outlined earlier, where the surplus premium is set off against tax at the top rate paid in the previous year, claiming unused relief for the past six years brings the allowance forward to the current tax year and gives tax relief at that year's top rate.

The contribution limits for 1993/94 are on p. 225. The same limits also applied to 1989/90 (pension scheme earnings cap of £60,000), 1990/91 (cap of £64,800), 1991/92 (cap of £71,400) and 1992/93 (cap of £75,000). The maximum contributions for the 1988/89 tax year were as follows:

AGE ON 6 APRIL	PERCENTAGE OF NET RELEVANT EARNINGS
50 or under	17½
51 – 55	20
56 – 60	22½
61 – 74	27½

To carry forward unused relief from earlier years, fill in Form PP42 (available from tax offices and scheme administrators).

CLAIMING THE TAX RELIEF

If you work for an employer, you will get tax relief on your personal pension contributions by paying them net of basic-rate tax. So if the basic rate of tax is 25 per cent and you contribute £1,000 to a personal pension scheme, you would hand over £750 (i.e. £1,000 less 25 per cent of £1,000). The pension provider would reclaim the £250 tax relief from the Inland Revenue.

If you are entitled to higher-rate tax relief, you will have to claim it from your Tax Inspector. You can do this when you take out the personal pension by sending your Tax Inspector the PPCC certificate the pension provider will give you.

If you are self-employed, you pay personal pension contributions in full and claim the tax relief when your tax bill is worked out.

RETIREMENT ANNUITIES

Personal pension schemes taken out before 1 July 1988 are known as retirement annuities (or *Section 226 policies* after the clause of the Taxes Act that established them). Although similar in many ways to personal pension policies, retirement annuities are covered by different rules on matters such as the maximum lump sum and the limits on contributions (see below). Your employer can't get tax relief on contributions to your retirement annuity. And you can't draw the pension as early as with a new-style personal pension scheme: the normal age for drawing the pension must be between 60 and 75.

You can convert a retirement annuity into one of the new personal pension schemes at any time, simply by telling the insurance company. You might want to do this so that your employer can contribute to your personal pension, or to draw your pension at 50 rather than 60.

LIMITS ON THE LUMP SUM

The maximum tax-free lump sum for retirement annuities is three times the pension the remainder of the fund will buy. In practice, this is about 30 per cent of the total fund – more than you would be able to get with a new-style personal pension scheme.

For retirement annuities taken out after 17 March 1987, there is a further cash limit of £150,000 on the amount that can be taken in a tax-free lump sum.

CONTRIBUTIONS

The maximum contributions to a retirement annuity you can get tax relief on in any tax year is a percentage of your net relevant earnings (see p. 225) for the year. The percentage depends on your age at the beginning of the tax year, and is as follows:

AGE ON 6 APRIL	PERCENTAGE OF NET RELEVANT EARNINGS
50 or under	17½
51 – 55	20
56 – 60	22½
61 – 74	27½

The rules for backdating contributions to earlier tax years and claiming unused relief from earlier years are the same as for personal pension schemes – see p. 226.

If you take out life insurance cover with a retirement annuity (known as a *Section 226A policy*), the cost of this, up to a maximum of 5 per cent of your net relevant earnings, is deducted from the amount of contributions you can get tax relief on. Suppose, for example, you are entitled to tax relief on retirement annuity contributions of 17½ per cent of your net relevant earnings, and these come to £20,000 in a tax year. You can get tax relief on those earnings for up to £3,500 of retirement annuity contributions (17½ per cent of £20,000); but of this £3,500, no more than £1,000 (5 per cent of £20,000) must go in life insurance premiums.

CLAIMING THE TAX RELIEF

With retirement annuities, you pay the contributions in full and claim tax relief from the taxman, whether you are self-employed or work for an employer.

If you pay tax under PAYE, your PAYE code can be adjusted to give you the tax relief through lower tax deductions from your earnings (see p. 149).

If you work for an employer and convert a retirement annuity into a personal pension scheme, you will also switch to paying the contributions net of basic-rate tax (see p. 228).

To backdate contributions to an earlier tax year, you must complete Form 43 (available from tax offices). To claim unused relief from earlier years, complete Form 42.

WHAT TO PUT IN YOUR TAX RETURN

There is no need to enter details on your Tax Return of contributions you make to an employer's pension scheme or in-scheme AVCs. The figures you enter from your P60 for earnings from full-time employment are normally your before-tax earnings after deduction of pension contributions and in-scheme AVCs (p. 158).

There is a large section of Forms 11P and 11 devoted to *Pension contributions etc* (pages 8 and 9). Fill this in if you made payments to a personal pension, retirement annuity or free-standing AVC scheme.

The first part of this section is for retirement annuity payments and personal pension contributions. Enter the name of the insurance company or pension provider and the contract number or membership number you have in the scheme. Give details of the payments you handed over in the last tax year and the amount you expect to hand over in the current tax year. If you are an employee and your employer contributes to your personal pension, enter the amounts paid by your employer in the last tax year and to be paid in the next tax year.

Form 11P

Pension contributions etc

You may be able to claim certain payments as a deduction from your earned income. See notes 41, 43 and 44. If you only pay into your employer's occupational pension and/or AVC scheme, you do not need to fill in this section.

Complete this section if you made payments to retirement annuities, personal pension contracts, free-standing additional voluntary contribution schemes (FSAVC), or trade union or friendly society death benefit and superannuation schemes.

Retirement annuity payments
Name of retirement annuity provider

Contract or membership number

Amount paid in 1993-94   £

If your payments altered during 1993-94 enclose the original payment receipts or statement of revised payments from your retirement annuity provider.

Tick here if you want to deduct all or part of the payments you made in 1992-93 from your profits or earnings from an earlier tax year. You will be sent a separate form to make your claim.

See note 42.   Amount you expect to pay in 1994-95   £

Basic rate tax relief on personal pension contributions made by employees is given at source.

Personal pension contributions
Name of personal pension provider

Contract or membership number

Amount paid in 1993-94   £

See note 42.
You cannot deduct employer's contributions from earnings from an earlier tax year.

Tick here if you want to deduct all or part of the pension contributions you made in 1993-94 from your profits or earnings from an earlier tax year. You will be sent a separate form to make your claim.

Amount contributed by your employer in 1994-95   £

If this is your first claim, enclose the original contributions certificate (PPCC) from your pension provider. If your payments have altered during 1993-94, enclose original payment receipts or any original supplementary form PPCC.

Amount you expect to pay in 1993-94 (if you know it)   £

Amount your employer expects to contribute in the 1994-95 tax year (if you know it)   £

You may run out of space if there is more than one scheme involved: give the full details on a separate sheet of paper and attach it to the Tax Return. Enclose any PPCC certificates given to you by the pension provider if you haven't already sent them off. Remember that if you want to backdate contributions, you need a claim form from the tax office. There's a special box to tick for retirement annuities and for personal pensions.

There's space at the top of page 9 of both forms to give similar details of free-standing additional voluntary contributions you make. You should send off the voluntary contributions certificate (VCC) with your first claim for tax relief on these. If you vary the payments, enclose the payment receipts you get from the AVC provider.

232

Form 11P

Notes

Basic rate tax relief on FSAVCs is given at source. See note 44.

FSAVC schemes
Complete this item if you pay into a free-standing additional voluntary contribution (FSAVC) and you wish to claim higher rate tax relief. Give the amount you paid this year before your FSAVC scheme claimed any tax refund.

Name of FSAVC provider

Contract or membership number

Amount paid in 1993-94 £

If this is your first claim, enclose the original contribution certificate (VCC) which your FSAVC provider should have sent you. If your payments have altered during 1993-94, enclose original payment receipts from your FSAVC provider.

Amount you expect to pay in 1994-95 (if you know it) £

With Form P1, there's no space to enter details about personal pension contributions, retirement annuities or free-standing AVCs. If you make these, send back details on a separate sheet of paper.

Part of some contributions to a trade union or friendly society for pension-type benefits may also qualify for tax relief:

● the part of your trade union subscription which provides pension, life insurance or funeral benefits.

● the death benefit part of certain payments to friendly societies for sickness and death benefits

Provided you have not already had the tax relief by paying lower premiums, claim this at the bottom of page 8 on Forms 11P and 11.

Form 11P

See note 43.

Trade union or friendly society death benefit and superannuation schemes
Name of the trade union or friendly society or scheme

Total amount paid in 1993-94 £

Amount relating to death or superannuation benefits £

Give the name of the scheme and the total paid in the tax year. On Form P1, give these details at the bottom of the front page, under *Earnings etc.*

TREASURE TROVE CLUE No. 8

The lower rate of tax, as a percentage (2 digits).

26 • HOME

When it comes to spending money, buying a home is probably the biggest purchase you make. Your mortgage payments will almost certainly be the largest outgoing in your monthly budget. It is important, therefore, to make sure you get all the tax relief you are entitled to on the interest you pay – especially if you move home. Mortgage interest tax relief looks to be on the way out, but until it disappears completely, this chapter tells you how to get the most from it.

Over the longer term, your home is likely to be a worthwhile investment – hard though that might be to believe in the current property market. But unlike most other investments, you won't have to pay capital gains tax on the profit you make on selling your only or main home. This chapter explains the rules and how to get the most from them even if you have not lived in the home throughout the time you owned it.

For details of what happens if you let out property or even just a room in your home, see the next chapter, 'Property', p. 248.

MORTGAGE INTEREST TAX RELIEF

You can get tax relief on interest you pay on loans of £30,000 or less to buy your only or main home (or to improve it if the loans were taken out on or before 5 April 1988). Your only or main home is normally the one you live in for most of the time, though there are occasions when you can get tax relief on loans for homes you're not currently living in – see p. 239.

The rate of tax relief is being gradually reduced:

● for the 1993/94 tax year, you got tax relief at the basic rate of tax of 25 per cent. So every £1 of interest you paid within the £30,000 limit was reduced by 25p tax relief to 75p. A gross interest rate of 8 per cent was 6 per cent after the tax relief

● for the 1994/95 tax year, the rate will be at the lower rate of tax of 20 per cent. So every £1 of interest you pay within the £30,000 limit will be reduced by 20p tax relief to 80p. A gross interest rate of 8 per cent will then be 6.4 per cent after the tax relief

● for the 1995/96 tax year, the rate of tax relief will fall to 15 per cent. So every £1 of interest you pay within the £30,000 limit will be reduced by 15p tax relief to 85p. A gross interest rate of 8 per cent will then be 6.8 per cent after the tax relief.

HOME INCOME PLANS

People over 65 who have taken out a mortgage to buy an annuity under a home income plan get tax relief at the basic rate of tax of 25 per cent. For more about home income plans, see p. 134.

WHICH LOANS CAN YOU GET TAX RELIEF ON?

The relief is available on loans to buy a house or flat, leasehold or freehold, located in the UK or Republic of Ireland. Loans for a houseboat designed to be used as a home are also eligible. So, too, are loans for a caravan (or mobile home) used as your only or main home.

You can still get tax relief if part of the loan is used to pay the costs of buying the home, such as stamp duty, valuation and survey fees, legal costs and insurance premiums (for example, for a mortgage indemnity policy). And if the loan is increased to cover buildings insurance premiums or unpaid interest, you can get tax relief on the extra interest paid on up to £1,000 added to the original loan (or 12 months' arrears, if greater).

The loan doesn't have to be a mortgage secured on your home for you to get tax relief on the interest. Interest on personal loans from banks and other lenders qualifies as long as the loans are used to buy your only or main home. But you won't get tax relief for interest on a bank overdraft or credit card debts – even if incurred on your home. And there's no tax relief if the loan has to be repaid within a year of being taken out (unless it is from a bank, stockbroker or discount house).

Normally when buying a new home, you have to take out a new loan to get mortgage interest tax relief on the interest. However, if you carry a loan over from one home to another on or after 16 March 1993, you can go on getting the tax relief as if you had taken out a new loan. This concession was introduced to help people who want to move but cannot afford to pay off the mortgage because their homes are worth less than the loan outstanding (that is, people with what is known as *negative equity*). If the lender agrees that they can switch the loan to another home, they can go on getting tax relief on the interest.

HOW BIG A LOAN?

If you are a married couple or single person living on your own, you can get tax relief on interest you pay for loans of £30,000 or less which qualify for tax relief. Single in this case includes widowed, divorced and separated people. There are special rules for sharers (single people who share a home, or married couples who share a home with another couple or single person) – see p. 237.

If you borrow more than £30,000, you get the tax relief only on a proportion of the interest you pay. With a single loan over £30,000, you get tax relief on the following proportion of the interest:

$$\frac{£30,000}{\text{Amount of loan}}$$

For example, if your loan is £40,000, the proportion of interest on which you get tax relief is:

$$\frac{£30,000}{£40,000} = \frac{3}{4}$$

If you miss some interest payments (or don't increase your payments when the mortgage rate goes up), your loan could creep up above £30,000. You will continue to get tax relief on all the interest you pay so long as no more than £1,000 of interest is added to the loan.

HOW YOU WILL GET THE TAX RELIEF

Most people get their tax relief on mortgage interest automatically by making reduced payments to the lender. This system is known as mortgage interest relief at source (MIRAS), and means that if £100 interest is due on your mortgage, you pay £100 minus the tax relief. So if the tax relief is 20 per cent, you pay a net amount of £100 – £20 = £80. The Inland Revenue pays the £20 of tax relief direct to the lender. You get this tax relief even if you don't pay tax, or you pay less than the tax relief you get – you won't have to hand back any of the relief you've had through MIRAS.

Most building societies, banks, local authorities, insurance companies and other lenders operate the MIRAS system, though it doesn't apply to interest on loans which are only partly for qualifying purposes. If the loans exceed £30,000 MIRAS gives you tax relief for interest on £30,000 of the loans. But if the loans over £30,000 were

236

taken out before 6 April 1987, they come into MIRAS only if you ask the lender to operate the scheme on your loans *and* the lender agrees.

If you aren't getting basic-rate tax relief through the MIRAS scheme, you will have to claim it direct from the taxman – you'll need a certificate of interest from the lender.

MARRIED COUPLES

A married couple get tax relief on interest they pay for loans of £30,000 or less in total. If the loan is in one of their names only, that person gets all the tax relief. With a mortgage in their joint names, the mortgage interest tax relief will be divided 50:50 between them. But it could pay in some circumstances to allocate the tax relief in different proportions, or even all to one partner:

● if one or both partners is over 65, mortgage interest tax relief could reduce 'total income' below the level at which the higher allowances for the over-65s are reduced (see p. 135), cutting the couple's tax bill by more than just the mortgage interest tax relief

● if the loan is outside the MIRAS system and one partner pays no tax at all, allocate all the interest to the partner who pays tax – otherwise there'll be no tax relief at all on half the interest.

You can allocate the tax relief between husband and wife in any way you choose: you both have to sign Form 15. You have up to a year after the end of the tax year to make the choice. So for the 1993/94 tax year, you have until 5 April 1995 to send in Form 15. The allocation can be varied from year to year, simply by filling in a new Form 15. To revert to a 50:50 split, you should withdraw the allocation on Form 15-1.

MORE THAN ONE LOAN

You can get tax relief on several different qualifying loans, provided they add up to £30,000 or less. If they add up to more than £30,000, you get the tax relief on the earliest loans first, up to the £30,000 limit. Thus, if you are getting two or more loans from different lenders to buy a home (for example, a mortgage plus a top-up loan) and they take you over the £30,000 limit, make sure that you arrange to get the loan with the higher interest rate at least a day before the less expensive one.

Note that there is an exception to this general rule for interest-free loans which you get from your employer as a fringe benefit. Even if you get such a loan first, later loans for things which would entitle you to claim tax relief are counted first towards the £30,000 limit. There's an example of how this works in Chapter 19, 'Employees: Fringe Benefits', p. 161.

EXAMPLE

Fiona Quin bought a house with two loans: £25,000 from a building society and £10,000 from an insurance company.

Fiona gets tax relief on all the interest she pays on the first loan, because it is less than the £30,000 limit. But the second loan takes her total over £30,000, so she will get tax relief on only part of the interest on it. The proportion on which she will get tax relief is worked out as follows.

Since Fiona is already getting tax relief on the £25,000 first loan, that leaves £30,000 − £25,000 = £5,000 of the second loan which qualifies for tax relief on the interest paid. The proportion of interest paid on the second loan on which she gets tax relief is

$$\frac{£5,000}{£10,000} = \frac{1}{2}$$

Fiona will get tax relief on only half the interest paid on the second loan.

TAX RELIEF FOR SHARERS

If two or more single people buy a home together, or a married couple buy with another couple or single person, the tax relief is restricted to interest on £30,000 of loans *per home* – irrespective of the number of people sharing it. For example, two single people would share between them the tax relief on the interest paid for £30,000 or less of loans (that is on £15,000 of loans each). Where a married couple shares with a single person, the couple would get tax relief on interest they pay on two-thirds of the £30,000 limit (£20,000) with one-third (£10,000) for a single person. If a sharer has a loan smaller than his or her entitlement, the unused part can be transferred to the other sharers, as the example below shows.

EXAMPLE

David Cave, Bernie Pilgrim and Ellen Giorghiou share a flat bought in early 1990. David has a mortgage of £12,000, Bernie a mortgage of £7,000 and Ellen a mortgage of £14,000.

David, Bernie and Ellen are entitled to tax relief on interest they pay on loans of £30,000 or less in total. The tax relief is divided equally between them, so each is entitled to tax relief on interest they pay on loans up to one-third of £30,000 = £10,000.

Bernie's £7,000 loan is less than his £10,000 entitlement, so he gets tax relief on all the interest he pays – and £3,000 of his entitlement is unused. David and Ellen both have loans over £10,000, but can take advantage of Bernie's unused £3,000 entitlement to get tax relief on the interest on more than £10,000 of loans.

Bernie's unused £3,000 entitlement will be divided between David and Ellen in proportion to the amount by which their mortgages exceed £10,000:

● David's loan is £12,000, so his excess is £2,000 (£12,000 – £10,000)

● Ellen's loan is £14,000, so her excess is £4,000 (£14,000 – £10,000).

The total amount of the two excesses is £2,000 + £4,000 = £6,000.

The proportion of Bernie's unused £3,000 allowance which David is allocated is:

$$\frac{£2,000}{£6,000} = \frac{1}{3}$$

One-third of £3,000 is £1,000, so David can get tax relief on interest paid on an extra £1,000 over the £10,000 limit, that is, on £11,000 of loans. Thus David will get tax relief on the following proportion of the interest he pays on his £12,000 mortgage:

$$\frac{£11,000}{£12,000} = \frac{11}{12}$$

Ellen's proportion of Bernie's unused £3,000 allowance is as follows:

$$\frac{£4,000}{£6,000} = \frac{2}{3}$$

Two-thirds of £3,000 is £2,000, so Ellen gets tax relief on the interest paid on £10,000 + £2,000 = £12,000 of loans. That means she will get tax relief on the following proportion of the interest she pays on her £14,000 mortgage:

$$\frac{£12,000}{£14,000} = \frac{6}{7}$$

SHARERS BEFORE 1 AUGUST 1988

Sharers who bought a home before 1 August 1988 and still live in it will each be entitled to tax relief on the interest on £30,000 of loans.

So two single people who have shared a home since before 1 August 1988 each get tax relief on the interest paid on up to £30,000 of loans taken out before that date (that is, on £60,000 in all). These rules continue to apply until the loan is paid off, replaced with a new loan or switched to a new home.

HOME-IMPROVEMENT LOANS

If you took out a loan before 6 April 1988 to improve your only or main home, you can also get tax relief on the interest you pay on it, so long as your total qualifying loans add up to £30,000 or less. Loans for permanent improvements to the building or land around it qualified, including extensions and loft conversions, insulation of walls or roof, double-glazing, rewiring, installing a fitted kitchen, making up an adjoining road and building a swimming pool.

If you pay off a home-improvement loan taken out on or before 5 April 1988 and replace it with a new loan (at a lower rate of interest, say), you won't get tax relief on interest paid on the new loan.

A HOME FOR AN EX-SPOUSE OR DEPENDENT RELATIVE

You can get tax relief on a loan taken out on or before 5 April 1988 to buy or improve a home for one of the following:

● your former husband or wife, or one from whom you are separated (whether by Court Order, deed of separation or in any other way which seems likely to be permanent)

● your mother or mother-in-law if widowed, separated or divorced

● any relative of yours or your husband or wife who is unable to look after him or herself because of permanent illness, disablement or old age (over 64 at the start of the tax year), and who lives in the home rent-free.

The tax relief continues only for so long as the ex-spouse or dependent relative continues to live in the home as their only or main residence. If you pay off such a loan after 5 April 1988 and replace it with a new loan (at a lower rate of interest, say), you won't get tax relief on interest paid on the new loan.

MOVING HOME

You can normally get tax relief on just one loan at a time, to buy your only or main home. However, you can get tax relief on a loan to buy a new home at the same time as getting it on your previous home. You can also go on getting tax relief on a mortgage loan on a home for some time after you have moved out of it.

BRIDGING LOANS

If you take out a *bridging loan* to buy a new home before you have sold your old one, you can get tax relief on the interest for up to £30,000 of the bridging loan, as well as on £30,000 of loans on your old home. This second lot of tax relief is available for up to twelve months (longer if your Tax Inspector thinks that the delay is not unreasonable). It doesn't matter which of the homes you live in during the transitional period, but the second lot of relief will be taken back if you do not move into the new home at the end of the bridging period.

Newly-weds can get tax relief on three loans if they are moving into a joint home and selling the two homes they lived in when single (p. 110).

MORE THAN ONE HOME

You can get tax relief on interest paid on loans for a home which you aren't living in as your main home if any of the following applies:

● you have put the home up for sale and moved out – even if you haven't taken out a loan on your next home. For interest paid on your old home on or after 16 March 1993, you can go on claiming the tax relief for up to a year after moving out (longer if you can persuade your Tax Inspector that selling the home is difficult)

● you have temporarily moved out of the home for a period of up to a year

● you have moved out because your employer requires you to be away from home. You can go on claiming the tax relief provided the absence is expected to last no more than four years. If the absence lasts longer, you lose the tax relief from then on only (and if you move back in for at least three months, further such absence of up to four years is allowed)

● you live in *job-related accommodation* (that is, a home you must live in by the nature of your job – see p. 172). You can go on getting the tax relief indefinitely on your own home, provided you intend to live in it eventually

- you are self-employed and have to live in work-related accommodation (for example, over the shop or at the club). Again, you can go on getting the tax relief on your own home provided you intend to live in it eventually.

You can also get tax relief on a second home in the year in which you get married (p. 110).

CAPITAL GAINS TAX ON HOMES

If you sell most types of investment (including property) for more than you paid for them, there may be capital gains tax to pay (see Chapter 31, 'Capital Gains Tax', p. 301). But if you sell your only or main home, there is normally no capital gains tax to pay.

However, there may be capital gains tax to pay on your home in certain circumstances, for example, if you use it for business or leave it for prolonged periods. And if you own more than one home, only one of them can be free of capital gains tax. If you do have to pay CGT on selling a home, it can mean a hefty tax bill, given the growth in house prices over the years.

WHAT KIND OF HOME IS FREE OF CGT?

Your only or main home is free of capital gains tax, provided the garden isn't excessively large (see p. 244). This applies whether it's a house or flat, freehold or leasehold, and wherever in the world it is situated.

You must occupy the home exclusively as your residence if it is to be free of capital gains tax. If part of the home is used for work or business, you may have to pay tax on part of the gain (p. 244). And letting out some or all of your home can mean a capital gains tax bill. For details, see the next chapter, 'Property', p. 248.

A home which an ex-spouse or dependent relative lives in rent-free is also free of capital gains tax provided it fell into this category on or before 5 April 1988 and for so long as the ex-spouse or dependent relative continues to live in it after that date. The relatives who qualify for this relief are the same as for relief on mortgage interest (see p. 239).

If you live in a caravan or houseboat, there's normally no capital gains tax to pay on it, even if it is not your only or main home. Caravans and boats are free of CGT as wasting assets with a useful life of 50 years or less (p. 302). But if you own the land on which a caravan stands, you might have to pay CGT if you sell it, unless the caravan was your only or main home.

Note that if you regularly buy and sell houses for profit (for example, doing up unmodernized homes for resale), you might have to pay CGT on the gain, even though you live in the home while you own it. If you do it on such a scale that you are classified as a dealer in land, you will be liable to income tax on the profits.

IF YOU OWN MORE THAN ONE HOME

If you own more than one home, your main home will be free of capital gains tax and there'll be capital gains tax to pay on any other home you own when you come to sell it. But you can choose which of your homes is to be free of CGT as your main home: it doesn't have to be the one you live in most of the time, or the one on which you get mortgage interest tax relief.

So you should work out which home is likely to make the largest gain and nominate it as your main home for CGT purposes. You must make your choice within two years of buying the second home: tell your Tax Inspector in writing. If you want to change your mind, you can do this at any time, backdating the change up to two years. Again, write and tell the taxman both that you wish to change your choice and when you want the change to operate from.

If you haven't nominated which is your main home, the Inspector of Taxes will decide, probably on the basis of which home you spend the most time at. You can appeal against this decision in the normal way (p. 92), but you will have to prove that the Inspector's decision was wrong, that is, that the other home really was your main one.

So if you get married and keep the two homes you owned before the wedding, make sure that you nominate which is to be your main home within the two-year limit. And if you live in a home which you do not own because of your job, nominate the home that you own as your main one if you want to avoid paying CGT on it.

AWAY FROM HOME

If you don't live in your home for some or all of the time that you own it, you might have to pay CGT when you sell it, even though it is the only home you own or you have nominated it as your main home. Normally, you will have to pay tax on a proportion of the taxable gain, found by time apportionment as follows:

$$\frac{\text{Number of complete months of absence}}{\text{Number of complete months of ownership}}$$

Only months of ownership or absence since 31 March 1982 count in working out the proportion of the gain which is taxable (see p. 305).

But you won't have to pay capital gains tax for periods of absence if you are away for any of the following reasons (even if you let the home out while you are away):

● you or your spouse live in *job-related accommodation* (p. 172). Provided you intend to live in your home in the future, you won't have to pay CGT, even if you never get round to living in the home (if you sell it while still living in the job-related accommodation, say)

● you or your spouse are required to work away from home by your employer. There is no CGT to pay for periods of absence, however long, working entirely abroad and absences totalling up to four years while working elsewhere in the UK. But you must have lived in the home before the job took you away and return to it afterwards (unless prevented by the job)

● you have just bought the home and haven't moved in because either it needs modernizing or rebuilding or you can't sell your old home. There is no CGT to pay for the first year of ownership (longer if you can persuade the Tax Inspector that it is necessary), so long as you eventually move in

● you intend to sell the home and have moved out of it for whatever reason (including having a new home which you have nominated as your main one). You have up to three years to sell the home after moving out of it without paying CGT

● any other absences totalling up to three years, provided you live in the home both before the first absence and after the last.

You can add together some or all of these reasons to make longer periods of absence which are free of capital gains tax.

EXAMPLE

Martin O'Grady bought a house in July 1986. In February 1987 his employer sent him on an overseas posting lasting until February 1990. On Martin's return to the UK, his employer sent him to work away from home until February 1993. He lived in the home until October 1993, when he bought a new home, eventually selling his old home in February 1994.

There are three absences from the home totalling six years and four months during the seven years and seven months Martin has owned the home. But none of these absences will be taken into account in deciding whether CGT will be due on the gain made when the home was sold:

● February 1987 to February 1990 – these three years are tax-free as a period of employment entirely abroad

● February 1990 to February 1993 – these three years are tax-free as a period of employment elsewhere in the UK

● October 1993 to February 1994 – these four months are tax-free as part of the last three years of ownership.

YOUR GARDEN

Freedom from capital gains tax applies to both your home and garden. But there are rules to stop people taking advantage of this to avoid capital gains tax on dealing in land.

For a start, if the area of your home and garden exceeds half a hectare, there may be tax to pay on the gain you make on the excess. The gain on any excess will be free of CGT only if you can convince the Inspector of Taxes that a garden of that size is appropriate for the home (for example, if it is a Capability Brown garden designed for the house).

If the area of the home and garden is less than half a hectare, you can sell part of the garden without having to pay capital gains tax. But if you divide the garden to build a second home which you sell off, there could be tax to pay on the gain. And if you sell the home and keep some of the land, there may be capital gains tax to pay when you eventually sell the land.

WORKING FROM HOME

If any part of your home is used exclusively for work, there may be a capital gains tax bill when you sell the home. This applies to both work for your own business (that is, if you are self-employed) or work for an employer.

So if you use one or more rooms entirely for business (as an office or workshop, for example), there will be tax to pay on a proportion of the gain when you come to sell the home. You will have to agree the proportion with the Tax Inspector, who may use one of the following yardsticks:

● the number of rooms used

● the floor area used

- the rateable value of the part used exclusively for business

- the market value of the part used exclusively.

If you claim a proportion of the rent and council tax as business expenses (p. 195) or as expenses of employment (p. 144), the same proportion of the gain is likely to be taxable. But in modest cases you may be able to persuade your Inspector of Taxes to allow you the expenses without a CGT bill.

Even when tax has to be paid on a proportion of the gain from selling a home which has been partly used for work, the taxable gain will be reduced by indexation allowance (p. 306). Only the gain made since 31 March 1982 is taxable (see p. 305). And no tax is due on gains under the tax-free limit (£5,800 for 1993/94 and 1994/95 – see p. 309). If there is a tax bill, it can be deferred if you buy another home also partly used for business (see *roll-over relief* on p. 320). And you may be able to claim *retirement relief* (p. 320).

WHAT TO PUT IN YOUR TAX RETURN

You have to give details of your mortgage under *Mortgage or loan for main home* on page 7 of Forms 11P and 11. On Form P1, look for *Deductions: mortgage or loan for main home* on page 3.

If you have a joint mortgage with someone who is not your husband or wife, tick the first box on Forms 11P and 11 (not on Form P1). There's a reminder to give details only of your share of the mortgage.

Form 11P

| See note 39. | **Joint mortgages with someone who is not your husband/wife**
Tick here and give details below only for your share of the mortgage. | ☐ |

The next box on Forms 11P and 11 is for married couples with a mortgage who wish to alter the way that the tax relief is split between them (see p. 236). If you tick this, you will be sent Form 15 to fill in to reallocate the tax relief. There's a similar box on Form P1.

Form 11P

| If you had more than one loan during the year, for example if you moved and paid off a loan give details | **Husband and wife: change in interest relief split**
If you are married and you and your husband/wife want to change the way mortgage interest relief is split between you, tick here and you will be sent a form on which you can do | ☐ |

Now give details of the loan: the name of the lender, the loan account number you'll find on mortgage statements and the date of the loan. Tick the box if the loan is *not* in MIRAS (most mortages are in MIRAS – and you get tax relief by paying a lower rate of interest). Information on loans to buy or improve your only or main home (including bridging loans) and on homes for dependent relatives should also be given here.

Form 11P

Building societies and other lenders operating the MIRAS system automatically send details of mortgage interest tax relief to the Inland Revenue. For other loans, you'll need to send a form MIRAS 5 or other certificate of interest paid (ask the lender for one). If you are married, both of you may be sent a Tax Return; since you'll get only one copy of MIRAS 5, send it to one spouse's tax office first and tell the other Tax Inspector that this is what you have done.

At the bottom of this section on Forms 11P and 11, there is space to give details of any loan to buy or improve your home which has been paid off during the last complete tax year.

Form 11P

On Form P1, give the name of the lender and the mortgage account number. If the lender is not a building society, give the gross amount of interest paid in the last tax year (that is, the amount before tax relief) and enclose the certificate of interest paid).

If you have sold a home during the last tax year, you should enter details under *Capital gains* – see p. 324. If the home was your only or main one, write 'private residence' beside the details.

TREASURE TROVE CLUE No. 9

The state pension age for men (2 digits).

27 • PROPERTY

Letting out property can provide a steady source of income, and – over the longer term – offers the chance of a capital gain on the value of the property. The government is keen to encourage more people to let out property, and has now provided an extra incentive in the form of the rent a room scheme.

This chapter explains how income from property is taxed, whether it comes from renting out a room, taking in lodgers, renting out furnished property, letting out holiday accommodation or letting shops or offices. And it outlines the capital gains tax rules for let property.

RENTING OUT A ROOM

The income from renting out furnished rooms is normally taxed as investment income under Schedule D Case VI. Broadly, this means paying tax on the income after deduction of certain expenses – see p. 250. However, up to £3,250 a year from renting out furnished accommodation in your home is tax-free under the rent a room scheme.

The scheme applies whether you own your home or are yourself a tenant. The only requirement is that it is your only or main home (see p. 233) and in the UK. The £3,250 which can be tax-free is before deducting any expenses from the rent. So you don't even need to bother with claiming expenses under the rent a room scheme.

However, if the gross rent (i.e. before deducting any expenses) is over £3,250, there may be some tax to pay. You can choose between:

● paying tax on the gross rent less £3,250, still ignoring expenses. So if your income from this type of rent was £3,500 a year, you would pay tax on £3,500 – £3,250 = £250

● paying tax on the rent in the normal way – that is on the gross rent less allowable expenses (see p. 250 for how to work this out).

As a rule of thumb, if your gross rent is slightly over the £3,250 limit, the best bet is probably to pay tax on the gross rent less £3,250. The more the gross rent exceeds £3,250, the more likely it is that you will pay less tax by having the rent taxed in the normal way.

If you are married or share your home, the income is treated as belonging to the person who actually rents out the room. Where the income is shared (whether with your spouse or anyone else), you can each have up to £1,625 a year tax-free.

TAKING IN LODGERS

If you take in lodgers in your own home, providing meals and other services, the income is normally taxed under Schedule D Case I (that is, as business income). However, up to £3,250 a year of income from taking in lodgers (before deduction of any expenses) is tax-free under the rent a room scheme – see above for more details and for what happens if the income is somewhat over £3,250.

If the income is substantially over £3,250, you will pay tax on the income less allowable expenses. The tax, payable in two instalments on 1 January and 1 July, is based on the income you received in the preceding year. See p. 208 for how this works when you start taking in lodgers.

EXPENSES

You can claim as expenses any money you spend in finding your lodgers and providing them with services. This would include the cost of advertising for them, maintaining and repairing their rooms and buying materials such as food and cleaning products. You can't claim the cost of your time in serving your lodgers, but you can claim the cost of wages and salaries paid to other people to do the work (your spouse, for example). The payments are taxable as earnings of the person you pay; with a spouse not in paid employment, he or she can earn up to the amount of the personal allowance without paying tax on it (see p. 104).

A proportion of the following household expenses is also allowable:

● gas and electricity (unless separately metered)

● council tax and water rates

● premiums for insurance policies covering the building and its contents

● your rent if you are a tenant (note that you cannot claim a share of the mortgage interest as an expense).

You will have to negotiate with your Tax Inspector to agree the proportion of the general household bills which can be claimed. The number of rooms let as a proportion of the total number of rooms is often used. If the lodging covers only certain weeks of the year (university terms, for example), then the amount which can be claimed is further reduced in proportion to the number of weeks of letting.

You can also claim capital allowances for the cost of furniture and equipment (see p. 199).

LOSSES

If your expenses outstrip your income from lodgers in any tax year, you have made a loss. This can be used to reduce the amount of tax you pay on the rest of your income, in the same way as for any other sort of business losses – see p. 203.

FURNISHED PROPERTY

With furnished accommodation, the income is normally taxed as investment income under Schedule D Case VI, unless you provide sufficient services to the tenants for the income to count as earnings from a trade. With a hotel or guest house, for example, all the income will normally be taxed as earnings from a business (see Chapter 23, 'The Self-Employed', p. 192). If you provide services such as laundry and cleaning to tenants, then at least part of the rent may be taxed as earnings, the rest as investment income from letting the property.

However, up to £3,250 a year of income from letting out furnished accommodation in your own home can be entirely tax-free under the rent a room scheme – see p. 248. And furnished holiday accommodation has special tax treatment (see p. 254).

Under Schedule D Case VI, you will be taxed on the rents you receive (so if the rent is not paid, you do not pay tax on it). In calculating the tax due on income from furnished accommodation, you can deduct certain allowable expenses. You may also be able to deduct interest paid on a loan to buy or improve the property so long as you are not already getting tax relief on it through the MIRAS scheme (see p. 235). And losses from letting out furnished property may reduce your tax bill.

The tax is payable on 1 January, normally based on the income received in the previous tax year.

ALLOWABLE EXPENSES

The following expenses count as allowable:

● payments you make for rent (if sub-letting), ground rent, water rates and council tax if you pay it on behalf of tenants (see overleaf)

● insurance premiums on policies which cover your liabilities as property owner, the buildings and its contents (you can also claim the cost of valuations for insurance)

● the cost of materials for cleaning the rooms or providing meals

● costs of maintaining common parts of let property, including heating, lighting, porterage, gardening and cleaning

● management costs, including the costs of rent collection, legal and accountancy fees, stationery, phone bills and salaries

● costs of letting, including advertising, fees for an estate agent or accommodation agency and drawing up an inventory of the contents – but not payments to tenants for moving out of the property

● maintenance and repairs, but not the cost of improvements, additions or alterations to the property

● any other payments you make as part of the agreement with the tenant, including gardening, gas and electricity (less any amounts you recharge to the tenant and money from slot meters).

You cannot claim the cost of your own time for any of these activities. However, you can claim the cost of wages and salaries paid to other people for providing them (your spouse, for example). The payments are taxable as earnings of the person you pay; with a spouse not in paid employment, he or she can earn up to the amount of the personal allowance without paying tax on it (see p. 104).

If only part of a property is let out (one floor of your house, say), then only a proportion of the expenses incurred on the whole property will be allowable. For example, if you let out half your house, then only half the insurance premiums would normally be an allowable expense.

You can claim an allowance for wear and tear on the furnishings, in one of the following ways:

● what you actually spend on replacing fixtures and fittings during the tax year (a *renewals basis*)

● 10 per cent of the rents less service charges and standard community charge or council tax if you pay them (a *notional basis*).

Once you have chosen a method, you can't switch. If you agreed an alternative method of allowing for wear and tear with your Tax Inspector before the 1975/76 tax year, you can carry on using this.

COUNCIL TAX

Your tenant will normally be sent his or her own council tax bill by the local authority. In some cases, however, you will be responsible for paying the council tax:

● if the home is empty or the people who live there are all under 18

● the home is in multiple occupation, such as a lodging house or divided into bedsits.

If you pay the council tax on a house you let out, you can claim this as an allowable expense. If you let it out for only part of the year, or you let out part of the house you live in, you can claim a proportion of the council tax. For example, if you let out your country cottage for six months of the year, you could claim half the council tax as an expense. And if you let out half your home to lodgers, you should be able to do the same. You should include anything the tenant contributes towards council tax in your income from the letting.

Note that if you pay *business rates* on the property you let out, you can claim them as an allowable expense in the same way as council tax.

EXAMPLE

Eddie Carlisle has divided most of his house into furnished rooms which he lets out, providing cleaning. The total income per year from the lodgings is £8,640 but the following expenses can be deducted from this rental income before tax is assessed:

● a proportion of the outgoings on the house (council tax, water rates, gas, electricity and insurance) which add up to £2,400 a year – since Eddie is letting out three-quarters of his house, he could claim three-quarters of this amount

● the cost of cleaning (cleaner's wages plus materials) – £25 a week or £1,300 a year

● an allowance for wear and tear of the furniture and furnishings – Eddie claims the actual costs of replacement (£300 for this year).

Thus Eddie's tax bill would be calculated as follows:

Total rent received		£8,640
Less		
Three-quarters of the outgoings (£2,400)	£1,800	
Cost of cleaning	£1,300	
Cost of replacing furniture and furnishings	£300	
Total allowable expenses		£3,400
Taxable rental income		£5,240

Note that if Eddie does the cleaning, then no allowance can be made for his time. But if, as the above example assumes, he pays someone else to do the work (his wife, say), he could claim this cost as an allowable expense. The wages would be taxable income for whoever Eddie paid, but if he or she had no other income, there would be no tax to pay on this income since it is less than the personal allowance.

INTEREST ON LOANS

If you take out a loan to buy or improve property in the UK or Republic of Ireland which you let out, you can get tax relief on the interest – including at the higher rate of tax if you pay it. The interest you pay can be set off against any income from letting property (but not against other sources of income). There is no limit on the size of the loan and it doesn't count towards the £30,000 limit for an only or main home (see Chapter 26, 'Home', p. 231). If the interest is more than your property income in any tax year, you can carry forward the excess to later years as long as you still own the property on which the loan was used.

To qualify, the loan must be for property which is let out at a commercial rent for at least 26 weeks in any 52-week period. And when not let out, the property must either be available for letting or under repair or building work. But you won't get tax relief for interest on bank overdrafts or credit card debts. And there's no tax relief if the loan has to be repaid within a year of being taken out (unless it is from a bank, stockbroker or discount house).

If the property is your home, you can get tax relief on the interest as for any other loan on your only or main home (see p. 234), provided you are not letting out more than a third of it. If you are letting out more than a third, tell the lender and your Tax Inspector – you will no longer get the tax relief through the MIRAS scheme.

LOSSES

Losses from furnished lettings can be set off against any other Schedule D Case VI income in the same tax year or future years (this includes freelance earnings and the Enterprise Allowance – see p. 41). If the loss is created by interest payments, it can be set off only against other income from property.

Note that if you make losses on furnished property, you can reduce your tax bill immediately if you also let out unfurnished property. You can opt to have the part of the furnished property income which comes from the premises taxed under Schedule A like income from unfurnished property. You can then set the loss on this part off against Schedule A income for the same tax year – see p. 256. The income from the furnishings will still be taxed under Schedule D Case VI. To make the switch, tell your Tax Inspector within two years of the end of the tax year.

FURNISHED HOLIDAY LETTINGS

If you let out your weekend cottage or other furnished holiday accommodation, the income will be taxed under Schedule D Case VI (see above). However, if the accommodation counts as what the Inland Revenue calls 'furnished holiday lettings', the income can be treated as if it were from a trade. This means that it is treated as business earnings with the following benefits:

● tax is payable in two instalments on 1 January and 1 July

● you can claim capital allowances on purchases of plant and equipment (see p. 199)

● losses can be set off against other income for the same or next tax year – reducing your tax bill on your earnings, for example. During the first four years of the business, losses could even be set off against other income from the previous three years (p. 203)

● the income counts as *relevant earnings* for getting tax relief on personal pension contributions (p. 225)

● you can claim the special business reliefs for capital gains tax (p. 320).

To count as furnished holiday lettings, the property must be available for letting to the general public on a commercial basis (that is, with a view to a profit) for at least 140 days in any twelve-month period *and* actually let for at least 70 of those days. No letting should normally exceed 31 days in a row for at least seven months of the twelve-month period (which should include any days when the property is let commercially). If you own more than one furnished holiday letting, you can average out the letting and occupancy periods between all of them.

INCOME FROM LAND AND UNFURNISHED PROPERTY

Income from land or unfurnished property in the UK is taxed as investment income under Schedule A. This includes rents from letting property or land, ground rent, feu duties and premiums on leases.

Under Schedule A you are normally taxed on the income you are entitled to receive (whether or not you have actually received it), less certain allowable expenses. You may also be able to deduct interest paid on a loan to buy or improve the property from your rental income before working out your tax bill. And losses from letting out property may be deductible in certain circumstances.

HOW THE TAX IS CALCULATED

Under Schedule A all property income due to you in the tax year is taxable, even if you don't actually receive it. But you will not pay tax on unpaid rents if you have taken reasonable steps to enforce payment or the rent is unpaid because you waived it to avoid hardship.

Tax is payable on 1 January in the tax year in which the property income is due (that is, on 1 January 1995 for the 1994/95 tax year). This is before all the income is in, so the bill will normally be based on the property income you got in the previous tax year. After the end of the tax year, your Tax Inspector will revise the bill in the light of your actual income. If you know that your property income will be down on the previous year because you've lost a source of income (for example, sold one of the houses you let out), you can ask the Tax Inspector to reduce your provisional bill by a corresponding proportion.

If you prefer to be taxed on the income you have actually received, you can opt for the 'accounts basis' of assessment for Schedule A. This means putting your property income on a business footing, drawing up full accounts (including a balance sheet) at the same date each year. With the accounts basis, your tax bill is based on the income for the accounting period which ended in the previous tax year. Thus if you draw up your property income accounts to 30 June every year, your

Schedule A tax bill for the 1994/95 tax year would be based on your income for the accounting year ending in the 1993/94 tax year (that is, on 30 June 1993). Once you have switched to the accounts basis, you can't change back.

TYPES OF LEASE

The tax rules in some cases depend on the type of lease which is involved. The following definitions should be borne in mind when reading the rest of this chapter:

● *a full-rent lease* is one which brings in enough income to cover the expenses and interest over the years. You might make a loss in one year, but as long as over the longer term the income exceeds the outgoings, the lease can be a full-rent one

● *a tenant's repairing lease* is one where the tenant is responsible for the repairs to the property (or at least most of the repairs).

ALLOWABLE EXPENSES

You can claim much the same expenses for unfurnished lettings as for furnished accommodation. But instead of claiming an allowance for wear and tear on the furnishings, you claim capital allowances on them and on equipment you need to service the lettings (see p. 199).

In general, you must deduct the expenses for a particular property from the rental income from that property only. But if you let out two or more properties at full rent which are not on tenant's repairing leases, you can set the expenses of one against the income from another.

LOSSES

If your allowable expenses plus loan interest come to more than your property income, you have made a loss. If the loss is from loan interest, it can be carried forward and set off against property income in future years, as long as you still own the property on which the loan was spent.

If you're unable to use all your allowable expenses, the loss may be carried forward as follows:

● with a full-rent lease which is *not* a tenant's repairing lease, any unused expenses which cannot be set off against income from other properties of the same type in the same tax year can be carried forward and set off against income from the same type of property only

● with a full-rent lease which *is* a tenant's repairing lease, you can set off the unused expenses against either income in the same tax year from full-rent leases which are not tenant's repairing leases or any future income from that property or any other let on full rent which is not a tenant's repairing lease

● with a lease which is not full rent, the loss can be set only against future income from the same lease (that is, the same property and the same tenant).

PREMIUMS ON LEASES

If you receive a premium from a tenant in return for granting a lease, this will be taxable if the lease lasts less than 50 years. So, too, will be the value of any work the tenant agrees to do for you on being granted a lease.

Part of the premium will be taxable under Schedule A, and the rest will be subject to capital gains tax. The proportion on which you will have to pay income tax is calculated as follows:

$$\frac{51 - \text{number of years of the lease}}{50}$$

So if the lease is a ten-year one, the proportion of the premium which is taxable is:

$$\frac{51 - 10}{50} = \frac{41}{50}$$

Capital gains tax is payable on the remainder of the premium, that is 9/50.

If you are paid the premium in instalments, the total premium is still taxable in the year the lease is granted. But you can ask your Tax Inspector to allow you to pay by yearly instalments if paying in one go would cause you hardship. The maximum number of instalments is eight (or the number of years you are getting the premium over, if less).

There are complicated rules to stop the granting of leases being used to avoid tax.

OVERSEAS PROPERTY

Income from property overseas is normally taxed under Schedule D Case V in much the same way as other overseas investment income (p. 280 for details). Thus you are liable for tax on the income even if you do not bring it back to the UK, and tax is assessed on a *preceding-year basis*. You can deduct expenses incurred in letting the property broadly similar to those allowed for UK property income, including the cost of managing and collecting the income (for example, paying an agent).

If tax is deducted from the income in the country where the property is, this tax can normally be deducted from your UK tax bill (though you won't be able to claim it back if it is more than your UK tax bill). The Inland Revenue has signed *Double Tax Agreements* with more than 80 countries to try to ensure that income isn't taxed twice when earned in one country by a taxpayer in another country.

CAPITAL GAINS TAX ON PROPERTY

If you sell a property which you have let out, the gain will normally be subject to capital gains tax, unless the property is your only or main home and you let it while absent for one of the reasons set out on p. 242.

Similarly, if you let part of your home, then you may have to pay capital gains tax on the part that is not occupied by you. If you let two of your six rooms, for example, one-third of the gain on selling the home is taxable (less if you haven't let the two rooms for all the time that you've owned the home). But there is no CGT to pay on let property if either of the following applies:

● you take in a lodger who shares your living rooms and eats with you (that is, is treated as a member of the family)

● the gain is £40,000 or less *and* the gain from the letting is no more than the gain on the part you've lived in. If either limit is exceeded, CGT is due only on the excess (the higher excess if both are exceeded).

If your property letting counts as a business (you run a hotel or guest house, or furnished holiday lettings, for example), you will be able to put off the tax bill on selling a property if you buy another for the same business by claiming *roll-over relief* (p. 320). And you may be able to benefit from *retirement relief* if you sell after the age of 55 (p. 320).

WHAT TO PUT IN YOUR TAX RETURN

Details of your property income should be entered on your Tax Return under *Income from property* on page 4 of Forms 11P and 11. However, if your lettings are a business, and the income is to be taxed under Schedule D Case I, you should enter the details under *Income from self-employment* – see p. 212. With several properties, give all the details on a separate sheet of paper. If you are married and the property is jointly owned, write 'Joint' and enter half the income unless you have agreed a different split with the Tax Inspector (see p. 263).

The first part of the property section is for people who are letting out furnished rooms in their only or main home.

Form 11P

<table>
<tr><td>

The Rent-a-Room scheme only applies to homes in the UK. Gross income includes rent and payments for related services.

</td><td>

Furnished rooms in your only or main home (UK homes only)
Under the Rent-a-Room scheme the first £3,250 of gross income from furnished rooms in your only or main home can be tax-free. You may not then claim any expenses or capital allowances. Alternatively, you can choose not to take part in the scheme and instead declare all the income and claim expenses and capital allowances in the normal way.

The tax-free amount is reduced to £1,625 if someone else is also letting furnished rooms in your home.

Tick one of the three boxes below if you let furnished rooms in your only or main home:

1 Your gross income plus any balancing charge was no more than £3,250 (or if appropriate £1,625) and you do not opt out of the scheme.

You do not need to give any more details.

2 Your gross income excluding any balancing charge was more that £3,250 (or if appropriate £1,625) and you want to be assessed on the difference between the rents and this tax-free amount, with no claim for expenses or capital allowances.

Show:

</td></tr>
</table>

Capital allowances and balancing charges can only arise if the letting amounts to a trade. See note 11.

- Gross income (excluding any balancing charge)   £
- Tax-free amount (£3,250 if you are the only person letting furnished rooms in your home or £1,625 if someone else is letting furnished rooms in your home).   £
- Balancing charge (if any)   £

†Income from a holiday letting may affect the amount of relief due to you for Retirement Annuity Payments etc.

If the income is from a furnished holiday letting enter 'Holiday letting'. [_____]

3 Neither box 1 nor box 2 applies. Your rental income, expenses and capital allowances will be treated in the normal way. Give details under *Other rentals in the UK* on page 5 unless the lettings amount to a trade. In this case give details under *Income from self-employment* on pages 2 and 3.

The income is tax-free under the rent a room scheme (see p. 248) if it comes to £3,250 or less before deducting any expenses (£1,625 if you are jointly letting the rooms with your spouse or partner). If this applies to you, tick the first box and move on – no further details need be given.

If your income is over the limit, you have a choice:

● you pay tax on the excess – tick the next box, fill in the gross income and the tax-free amount you are claiming (£3,250 or £1,625). If the income is from a furnished holiday letting, write this in the space marked

● you pay tax on the rental income in the normal way, claiming deductions for expenses etc – tick the third box and give details under *Other rentals in the UK*.

Note that if you have been running the lettings as a business (taxed under Schedule D Case I) and you have sold or given away an asset of the business, you may have a balancing charge (see p. 201). In this case, the limit for the rent a room scheme is £3,250 less the balancing charge (or £1,625 less the balancing charge if you jointly let the rooms). You should write in the amount of this balancing charge where indicated.

With Form P1, enter details of rent a room income under *Income from furnished rooms in your only or main home (UK only)* on page 2.

Details of other UK property income, whether furnished or unfurnished, should be entered under *Other rentals in the UK*.

Form 11P

Notes
If you let more than one property give details on a separate sheet of paper. See note 23 for what counts as a holiday letting.

Other rentals in the UK
Address of the property you let

Tick to show the type of rental

Furnished holiday letting
Furnished property
Unfurnished property
Ground rents and feu duties
Land

Include rent paid in kind and profits from supplying gas and electricity but not premiums. For expenses see note 24.

Gross rents due and other income received in 1993-94 £

Expenses £

Gross income less expenses £

If your gross rents etc before expenses were £15,000 or more enclose a detailed statement for each property of how you reached your figure for expenses.

Premiums received £

Length of lease if you received a premium £

Your Tax Office will work out how much of the premium is income and how much is capital gains.

Tick the type of property income, give the address of the property, the gross rental income including profit on gas or electricity supply, allowable expenses and the net income (that is, gross income less allowable expenses). Interest should be included as an expense only with furnished holiday lettings and furnished lettings taxed under Schedule D Case VI. There are separate boxes to give details of any premiums received for granting leases. For gross rents and other income is more than £15,000, you should attach schedules setting out details of the expenses for each property.

With Form P1, give these details under *Other income from property in UK or abroad* on page 2.

Interest on unfurnished lettings and furnished lettings taxed under Schedule A should not be claimed as an expense, but under *Other qualifying loans* on page 8 of Forms 11P and 11. Give the name of the lender, purpose of the loan, address of the property, the number of weeks in the tax year in which it was let and the amount of interest. Enclose a certificate of interest paid which the lender should supply.

Form 11P

Other qualifying loans

Complete this form if you can claim tax relief on other loans. Only give details of loans not included elsewhere on this form. Enclose a certificate of interest paid from your lender. Do not include loans on your main home.

Name of lender

Purpose of loan

Give the address of the property if the loan is for the purchase or improvement of property used for letting

The number of weeks let

Amount of gross interest paid in the 1993-94 tax year £

On Form P1, enter details of loan interest on let property under *Other loans qualifying for tax relief* on page 3.

Income from overseas property should be entered under *Property abroad* on Forms 11P and 11.

Form 11P

Property abroad
Address, including country, of the property

Gross rents and other income received in 1993-94 £ Expenses £

Gross income less expenses £

Give the full address of the property, the full amount due to you during the tax year (gross rents) and the expenses. Then enter the gross income less expenses in the *Income before tax* column. If any foreign tax has been deducted from the income, give details of this in a note with the Tax Return. Give these details under *Other income from property in UK or abroad* on Form P1.

Enter details of property you have bought or sold during the tax year in the *Capital gains* section of the Tax Return (see p. 324).

28 • INVESTMENTS

The choice of investments open to the ordinary investor is wider than it has ever been. Banks and building societies offer a bewildering variety of savings accounts. National Savings sells a growing range of investments in addition to the traditional savings certificates. Many more people are dabbling in share ownership with new share issues aimed at the small investor and continuing growth in unit trusts and investment trusts. And there are special tax rules to attract investors into Personal Equity Plans (PEPs), Tax Exempt Special Savings Accounts (TESSAs) and the Enterprise Investment Scheme which has just replaced the Business Expansion Scheme (BES).

The different tax treatment of the various types of investment means that going for the highest pre-tax return is not always the best thing to do. You must consider what the return will be after two different taxes have been deducted from the proceeds:

● *income tax* – payable on interest or dividends, even if not paid out to you but added to your investment. Income from investments is added to the rest of your income for the tax year and income tax is due on the total

● *capital gains tax* – payable on realized increases in the value of the investments themselves (for example, if the value of the shares or the property rises). There's no tax to pay if your total net capital gains in the tax year are below £5,800 in the 1993/94 and 1994/95 tax years. If capital gains tax is due, the taxable gain is added to your income and taxed at the lower, basic or higher rate of tax.

This chapter looks at how income tax applies to most investments (for how capital gains tax applies, see Chapter 31, 'Capital Gains Tax', p. 301). The taxation of life insurance is a particularly complicated subject so it is dealt with in more detail in the next chapter. For details of the taxation of property investments see the previous chapter.

INCOME TAX ON INVESTMENTS

Income from some investments is tax-free (that is, there is no income tax to pay). For a list of these, see p. 264.

All other investment income is taxable. And with more and more investments, tax is deducted from the income before it is paid to you. There is no further tax to pay on such income unless you pay tax at the higher rate. If you should have paid less tax than was deducted, you will normally be able to get a refund. The tax treatment of investment income paid after deduction of tax is covered on p. 265.

Some investments still pay a taxable income without deducting any tax from it. A list of these and how they are taxed is on p. 273.

THE INVESTMENT INCOME OF MARRIED COUPLES

Married couples are each responsible for paying the tax on their own income – whether it is income from a job or income from investments. But married couples may have investment income from joint accounts, shares or unit trusts held in their joint names or property which is jointly owned. Income from jointly-owned assets must therefore be divided between husband and wife before their tax bills can be worked out.

The Tax Inspector will normally divide such joint income between husband and wife equally (the 50:50 rule). In many cases, this will be the appropriate split, but in some cases the asset may actually belong to only one partner or be owned in unequal shares. If you want the income divided between you other than 50:50 for tax purposes, you can tell your Tax Inspector by making a 'declaration of beneficial interests' on Form 17 (available from tax offices).

The new split of joint income applies from when the declaration is signed – so don't delay in filling it in. If you acquire new assets on which the 50:50 split is not to apply, you must make a further declaration.

GROSSING-UP

If you receive investment income after some tax has been deducted from it, what you receive is known as the *net income*. But you may need to work out how much the income was before tax was deducted from it (the *gross income*).

You can find the gross income by *grossing-up* the net income (i.e. the income after deduction of tax) using the ready reckoner on p. 358, or by using the following formula:

$$\text{Amount paid to you} \times \frac{100}{100 - \text{rate of tax}}$$

For example, if you receive £75 of income after tax has been deducted at the basic rate of 25 per cent, the grossed-up amount of the income is:

$$£75 \times \frac{100}{100-25} = £75 \times \frac{100}{75} = £100$$

If you receive the same amount of income after tax has been deducted at 20 per cent (as is taken to be the case with dividends paid after 5 April 1993 – see p. 269), the grossed-up amount of the income is:

$$£75 \times \frac{100}{100-20} = £75 \times \frac{100}{80} = £93.75$$

TAX-FREE INVESTMENT INCOME

The following investments are free of income tax:

● National Savings Certificates including index-linked certificates, Yearly Plan and Children's Bonus Bond

● bank and building society Save-As-You-Earn (SAYE) schemes

● the first £70 of interest in any tax year from National Savings Ordinary Account (a married couple can have up to £70 each or a total of £140 of such interest tax-free from a joint account)

● Premium Bond prizes

● loan interest paid to members of credit unions

● income from investments held in Personal Equity Plans (p. 274)

● interest paid on a Tax Exempt Special Savings Account (TESSA) – provided the capital is not withdrawn (see p. 276)

● interest paid on damages for personal injury or death

● interest paid by the Inland Revenue on overdue tax rebates.

The proceeds of qualifying life insurance policies and some policies issued by friendly societies are also free of tax (see Chapter 29, 'Life Insurance', p. 287 for details).

INVESTMENT INCOME PAID AFTER DEDUCTION OF TAX

Income on most investments is now normally paid after deduction of tax. Among the investments to which this applies are building society accounts, bank accounts, government stock (gilts), local authority loans and bonds, National Savings First Option Bonds and annuities. There is no further tax bill if you pay tax at the basic rate only on your income – which is the case for the vast majority of taxpayers. The taxation rules for each of these types of investment income are examined on p. 266.

If you pay tax at the higher rate, there will be extra tax to pay on this income – see below. And if your income is too low to pay tax, you should be able to reclaim the tax which has been deducted (you can even arrange for interest to be paid without deduction of tax – see p. 267). If you pay tax at the lower rate of 20 per cent, you can reclaim some of the tax which has been deducted (for how to do this, see p. 72.

There are special rules for income from shares and unit trusts – see p. 269.

EXAMPLE

Lionel Richards gets £300 interest credited to his building society account in the 1994/95 tax year. Tax has been deducted from the interest at the basic rate of tax (25 per cent) before it is credited to his account, but Lionel reckons he should be paying tax on it only at the lower rate of 20 per cent. He checks to see if he is due a tax rebate.

Lionel first works out the gross amount of interest – that is, the amount before deduction of tax at the basic rate. He grosses up the net amount he received to find the gross amount as follows:

$$£300 \times \frac{100}{100 - 25} = £300 \times \frac{100}{75} = £400$$

That means he has been paid a gross amount of interest of £400, from which £400 – £300 = £100 of tax has been deducted.

When this £400 of gross interest is added to the rest of his income, his taxable income comes to £1,500. So he should have paid tax on the £400 interest at the lower rate of 20 per cent, not the basic rate of tax.

Lower rate tax at 20 per cent on the gross interest of £400 is £80. Since £100 of tax had been deducted from Lionel's interest, he is due a tax rebate of £100 – £80 = £20.

HIGHER-RATE TAX ON INCOME PAID AFTER DEDUCTION OF TAX

If you get investment income after tax has been deducted and pay tax at the higher rate of 40 per cent, there will be a further tax bill to pay on the investment income, as the example below shows.

EXAMPLE

Avis Garbutt gets £75 interest on her building society account in the 1994/95 tax year. Basic-rate tax has already been deducted from the interest before it is credited to her account, so this £75 is the net (that is, after deduction of tax) amount.

To work out the gross (i.e. before deduction of tax) amount of interest, Avis must gross-up the net amount. The basic rate of tax for 1994/95 is 25 per cent, so the grossed-up amount of interest is:

$$£75 \times \frac{100}{100-25} = £75 \times \frac{100}{75} = £100$$

In other words, Avis is assumed to have paid £100 − £75 = £25 in basic-rate tax on the interest received. If Avis should pay tax at 40 per cent on this interest, her overall tax liability is 40 per cent of £100 = £40. But she has already paid the basic-rate tax (i.e. £25), so only has to pay £40 − £25 = £15 in higher-rate tax. That leaves her with £75 − £15 = £60 of interest after higher-rate tax has been paid.

The higher-rate tax on these types of investment income is normally due on 1 December after the end of the tax year in which you get the income. So if you got the investment income during the 1993/94 tax year, any higher-rate tax due on it will be payable on 1 December 1994. But if the assessment is issued after 1 November, the tax is due 30 days after the date the assessment was issued.

BANK, BUILDING SOCIETY AND OTHER DEPOSIT ACCOUNTS

UK banks, building societies, finance houses, organizations offering high-interest cheque accounts and other licensed deposit-takers all deduct tax at the basic rate (currently 25 per cent) from interest they pay UK-resident taxpayers. Tax is also deducted from interest on local authority loans before it is paid to you. If you pay tax at the higher rate there will be extra tax to pay on the interest (see above).

If too much tax has been deducted, the excess can be claimed back after the end of the tax year in which it is received. This would happen if your income is too low to pay tax at all, or if your income is taxable at the lower rate of 20 per cent. For how to claim a repayment, see p. 72.

Non-taxpayers can arrange with the bank or building society to be paid interest without deduction of tax, simply by filling in Form R85. You can get copies of this form from banks, building societies and post offices, as well as from tax offices. A copy is in the back of Inland Revenue leaflet IR110 *A guide for people with savings* – this also contains useful hints on checking whether you will pay tax or not. Arranging for interest to be paid without deduction of tax not only saves you the trouble of claiming back the tax which has been deducted, it means you get the money much earlier (but note that there are hefty penalties for making a false declaration). With joint accounts, interest can be paid without deduction of tax to just one of the two account-holders only if the bank or building society can arrange it.

Non-taxpayers who don't arrange for payment of interest without deduction of tax will have to claim the tax back after the end of the tax year in which it is paid (Inland Revenue leaflet IR110 *A guide for people with savings* has the details and includes a copy of the claim form). Where interest is paid without deduction of tax and it later turns out that you should have paid tax on it, the tax will be collected by the Inland Revenue. If you think you will start paying tax (because your income rises), tell the bank or building society in writing so that they can begin to deduct tax.

BRITISH GOVERNMENT STOCKS

Interest on most British Government stocks (commonly known as gilt-edged securities or gilts) is paid after deduction of basic-rate tax. Payments come with a tax voucher setting out the tax deducted. You can claim back some or all of this tax if you are a non-taxpayer or should have paid less tax than the amount of the tax credit.

But interest is paid without deduction of tax (i.e. gross) in three cases:

● on 3½ per cent War Loan

● on holdings producing gross income of less than £2.50 half-yearly

● where the stocks were bought through the National Savings Stock Register (you can get a leaflet from post offices about how to do this).

For how interest paid gross is taxed, see p. 273.

If you own fixed-interest securities with a nominal value in excess of £5,000 at any time during the current or preceding tax year, there are special tax rules when you buy or sell them. There may be an income tax bill to pay if you sell gilts (or other fixed-interest securities) *cum dividend*. This is because the sale price should be higher to reflect the next interest payment due (*accrued income*), so this part of the proceeds is taxed as your income. There is also an income tax bill if you buy shares *ex dividend*, since the price you pay is lower because you haven't bought the next interest payment.

Conversely, if you buy such securities *cum dividend* or sell them *ex dividend*, you should be able to claim a deduction from your tax bill. For more details of these provisions, designed to stop tax avoidance by turning income into capital gains ('bond-washing'), ask your Tax Inspector to send you Inland Revenue leaflet IR68 *Accrued income scheme*.

LOCAL AUTHORITY INVESTMENTS

The interest on local authority stocks and yearling bonds is paid after deduction of tax at the basic rate. As with bank and building society interest, you can reclaim some or all of the tax if it is more than you should have paid. Non-taxpayers can arrange for it to be paid without tax being deducted (i.e. gross).

ANNUITIES

If you buy an annuity, you pay a lump sum to an insurance company and it pays you an income for an agreed period (ten years, say, or until you die). Part of the income will be treated as interest, part as return of your capital: only the part which is treated as interest is taxed as income. The insurance company will deduct tax at the basic rate from the interest part before handing over the payment. You will get a tax voucher with each payment which tells you how much tax has been deducted. You can claim some or all of this tax back if you are a non-taxpayer or pay tax at the lower rate of 20 per cent.

Note that this treatment applies only to annuities you buy voluntarily with your own money. If you buy the annuity as part of a pension scheme, basic-rate tax will be deducted from all the income before it is paid to you.

INCOME AND GROWTH BONDS

These are lump sum investments sold by insurance companies, which provide either a guaranteed income or a guaranteed growth for a fixed number of years. Companies achieve this in different ways and some bonds can be complicated packages of insurance policies and annuities. You will have to ask the insurance company for details of what income is due under the bond each year, whether it is taxable and whether tax has been deducted. In some cases, the income is provided by cashing in part of a life insurance policy: only higher-rate tax will be due (p. 288). With growth bonds, there may even be a tax liability before the bond matures even though no income has been paid out to you.

SHARES AND UNIT TRUSTS

Dividends from UK companies and distributions from authorized unit trusts are paid with a *tax credit* which covers the basic rate tax due on the income. The amount of the tax credit is given on the tax voucher which comes with the dividend or distribution which looks something like the example shown below (different companies lay out the information differently). The grossed-up dividend for tax purposes is normally the net dividend plus the tax credit.

For dividends paid after 5 April 1993, the tax credit is 20 per cent of the gross dividend or distribution. So if you received a dividend of £75, the grossed-up amount of this dividend will be:

$$£75 \times \frac{100}{100-20} = £75 \times \frac{100}{80} = £93.75$$

The £75 dividend will have come with a tax credit of £93.75 − £75 = £18.75.

This 20 per cent tax credit covers your tax liability if you pay tax at

Tax voucher

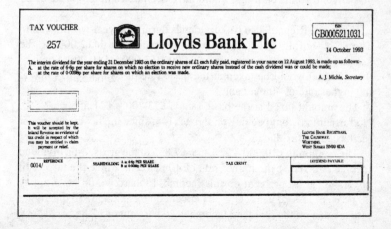

the basic rate or the lower rate. And it does not eat up any of your lower rate band: you could have, say, £500 of gross dividend income in 1994/95 as well as having £3,000 of earnings taxed at 20 per cent.

If your income is too low to pay tax, you can claim back the tax credits in the normal way (see p. 72 for how to do this). If you pay tax at the higher rate, there will be extra tax to pay on the grossed-up amount of dividends and distributions. The rate will be 40 per cent less 20 per cent = 20 per cent of the grossed-up income. So on the £75 of net dividends, you would have to pay 20 per cent of the grossed-up dividend of £93.75 = £18.75. That would leave you with £75 – £18.75 = £56.25 after tax.

Because the tax credit is 20 per cent, a higher-rate taxpayer who receives £75 of dividends or distributions therefore ends up with £56.25 after tax. With £75 of net interest, he or she would end up with £60 after deduction of higher-rate tax (see p. 266). To make matters worse, any dividends or distributions you receive are always treated as your top slice of income, taxed at the highest rate you pay. This means that higher-rate taxpayers always pay more tax on this type of income than on other types, as the following example shows.

EXAMPLE

Richard Soo earned £25,000 in the 1993/94 tax year. His only tax allowance was the personal allowance of £3,445. If his earnings had been his only source of income, his taxable income would have been £25,000 – £3,445 = £21,555. This is below the level of £23,700 at which the tax rate rises from the basic rate of 25 per cent to the higher rate of 40 per cent, so his earnings would have been taxed at a top rate of 25 per cent.

However, Richard also had dividends during the year worth £8,000. The £8,000 of dividends came with tax credits worth £2,000, so the grossed-up dividend income was £8,000 + £2,000 = £10,000. Some of this £10,000 would be taxed at the basic rate of 25 per cent, some at the higher rate of 40 per cent.

The amount taxed at the basic rate is £23,700 – £21,555 = £2,145. No further tax would be due on this £2,145, since the tax credits cover the basic rate tax due on it.

The remaining £10,000 – £2,145 = £7,855 of the grossed-up dividend income is taxed at the higher rate of 40 per cent. Since the tax credit covers tax at 20 per cent on this income, Richard would have to pay 40 per cent less 20 per cent = 20 per cent on this £7,855. So the higher rate tax due on the dividend income is 20 per cent of £7,855 = £1,571.

If Richard had received net interest of £8,000 instead of dividends worth that amount, his higher-rate tax bill would have been lower. The net interest comes after deduction of tax at 25 per cent, so the gross amount of interest is:

$$£8,000 \times \frac{100}{100-25} = £8,000 \times \frac{100}{75} = £10,667$$

£2,145 of this is taxed at the basic rate, so no further tax is due on it as basic-rate tax was deducted from the interest before it was paid. The remaining £10,667 − £2,145 = £8,522 is taxed at 40 per cent. However, since basic rate tax has already been deducted at 25 per cent, Richard would have to pay 40 per cent less 25 per cent = 15 per cent of this £8,522. So the higher rate tax due if the investment income had been interest would be 15 per cent of £8,522 = £1,278.

STOCK DIVIDENDS

If you receive new shares instead of a cash dividend, this is known as a stock dividend. The value of the stock dividend is known as the *cash equivalent* (the amount of cash dividend forgone) and you are treated as having received the grossed-up amount of the cash equivalent. For stock dividends received after 5 April 1993, the cash equivalent is grossed-up at 20 per cent.

If you pay tax at the basic rate only, there is no further tax to pay. If you pay tax at the higher rate of 40 per cent, there will be extra tax to pay, based on the grossed-up amount of the cash equivalent. But unlike with a cash dividend, you cannot claim back any tax credit if you are a non-taxpayer or pay tax at the lower rate of 20 per cent only.

UNIT TRUSTS

Income from most authorized unit trusts (known as *distributions*) comes with a tax credit in the same way as for share dividends. With accumulation unit trusts, income is automatically reinvested to increase the amount of your investment. But this income is taxable in the year in which it is reinvested, so you will still get a tax voucher with a tax credit after each distribution. You can reclaim some or all of this tax credit if you are a non-taxpayer – even though you haven't received the income.

Income from some authorized unit trusts does not come with a tax credit: this includes unit trusts which invest in government stocks and other fixed-interest investments. In these cases, tax has been deducted from the income at the basic rate before you get it in the same way as for bank or building society interest (you will get a tax voucher telling you the amount paid). You can claim some or all of this tax back if your income is too low to pay tax or you pay tax at the lower rate, in the same way as the tax deducted from interest (see p. 72).

Note that when you get your first distribution from a unit trust, this sometimes includes an *equalization* payment. This is a return of part of the amount you originally invested and isn't taxable as income.

TRUSTS AND ESTATES

If you get income from a trust, it will come with a tax credit which depends on the type of trust. You should get a certificate R185 from the trustees setting out the amount of income and tax credit.

If you have the right to the income from the trust, it is a trust with an *interest in possession*. The tax credit will be at the basic rate of 25 per cent of the grossed-up income (that is the net income you receive plus the tax credit). You can reclaim some or all of the tax if it is more than you should have paid. However, income from dividends paid out after 5 April 1993 will come with a tax credit at the 20 per cent lower rate. This can be claimed back only if your income is too low to pay tax at all – you cannot claim it back if you pay tax at the lower rate.

If the trustees have discretion about paying out the income, it is a *discretionary trust*. The tax credit will then be for 35 per cent of the grossed-up income (that is, the net income you receive plus the tax credit). If the tax credit is more than you should pay on the grossed-up income, you can claim a rebate. With a discretionary trust, even basic-rate taxpayers should be entitled to a tax rebate of 35 per cent less 25 per cent = 10 per cent.

With either type of trust, higher-rate taxpayers will have to pay extra tax on the income, in the same way as for share dividends.

Note that you can't claim back tax on trust income paid out to you if the trust was set up by your husband or wife. The same applies if the person who set up the trust will benefit in any way from its income or capital. These restrictions apply to trusts set up on or after 14 March 1989; they apply to trusts set up before 14 March 1989 only if the trust was set up by your husband or wife.

If you have received income from the estate of someone who has died, this will also come with a tax credit in the same way as a trust with an interest in possession. The same rules apply if you are a non-taxpayer or a higher-rate taxpayer.

TAXABLE INVESTMENT INCOME PAID WITHOUT DEDUCTION OF TAX

Interest on the following types of investment is taxable, but paid without deduction of tax (that is, gross):

● National Savings Ordinary Account and Investment Account (the first £70 a year of interest on Ordinary Account is free of tax – see p. 264)

● National Savings Income, Deposit and Capital Bonds, and the new Pensioners' Guaranteed Income Bond

● 3½ per cent War Loan

● British Government stocks bought through the National Savings Stock Register (you can get a leaflet from post offices about how to do this)

● interest of less than £2.50 gross overall per half year on other British Government stocks

● shares with a co-operative society or credit union.

Interest paid to you by someone to whom you personally make a loan is also taxable in this way.

The interest is taxable even if it is not paid to you (for example, if it is credited to your account). As far as the taxman is concerned, you get the interest when it is paid or credited to you, even if it relates to an earlier period. For example, if you get interest half-yearly, and it is credited to your account on 6 April 1994, it is treated as if all of it was earned in the 1994/95 tax year (even though almost all of it was earned in the 1993/94 tax year).

HOW THE TAX IS COLLECTED

This type of interest is normally taxed on a *preceding-year basis*. This means that your tax bill for one tax year depends on the interest you got in the previous tax year. The tax is collected on 1 January in the tax year or within 30 days of the date the Notice of Assessment is issued, if this is later. So on 1 January 1995, you would have to pay the tax on this type of income for the 1994/95 tax year, which would be based on what you got in the 1993/94 tax year.

But if you are just starting to get interest of this type from a particular source, there will be no previous tax year to base your tax bill on. The tax due in each of the first two tax years will therefore depend on the interest you actually get in that year (that is, a *current-year basis*). In the third tax year, you can choose between paying tax on what you got in either the second tax year (preceding-year basis) or the third tax year (current-year basis). If you do nothing, tax will be charged on a preceding-year basis, so check whether you would pay less if you opted for current-year basis – you have up to six years after the end of the third tax year to tell the Tax Inspector that this is what you want.

There are also special tax rules to cover the last two tax years before you stop getting interest from a particular source. When you close the account, the tax bill for that tax year will be based on the interest you actually got in that tax year (current-year basis). And the Tax Inspector can also increase your tax bill for the last-but-one tax year to collect the tax due on what you actually got in that tax year (that is current-year basis) if that would be more than you would have paid on the preceding-year basis.

EXAMPLE

Marcus Campbell opened a National Savings Investment Account in the 1989/90 tax year. The following table shows the interest he got and the amount he paid tax on up until the 1994/95 tax year:

Tax year	Interest	Amount he pays tax on
1989/90	£100	£100 – interest he actually got
1990/91	£200	£200 – interest he actually got
1991/92	£150	£200 – interest he got in the preceding year
1992/93	£200	£150 – interest he got in preceding year
1993/94	£250	£200 – interest he got in preceding year
1994/95	£100	£250 – interest he got in preceding year

If Marcus closed the account during the 1994/95 tax year, his tax bill for that year would be based on the interest he actually got (that is, £100, not £250). But his Tax Inspector would be able to change the basis of assessment for 1993/94 to make the tax bill depend on the interest Marcus actually got in that tax year (£250) if this is more than the interest he got in the preceding year (£200). Since it is more, his Tax Inspector would make the change.

PERSONAL EQUITY PLANS

Personal Equity Plans (PEPs) are a type of investment offered by banks, building societies, insurance companies, unit trust managers and others. Your money is invested in shares, unit trusts or investment trusts. The proceeds from a PEP, whether income or capital gain, are almost always entirely free of tax.

The only exception to this tax-free rule is where some of the investment is held as cash on deposit and earns interest which is paid out to you. If more than £180 of interest is paid out to you in a year, the plan manager must deduct tax at the basic rate of 25 per cent from it and hand this over to the Inland Revenue. The net interest is treated in the same way as any other interest you receive after deduction of tax: higher-rate taxpayers will have an additional tax bill (see p. 266).

HOW MUCH CAN YOU INVEST?

You can invest up to £6,000 in a PEP in any tax year, either by single lump sum, by regular monthly instalments or in dribs and drabs. You can also invest £3,000 in one single-company PEP (see below) in addition to the £6,000 in one general PEP.

These limits apply to individuals aged 18 and over. So a husband and wife can together invest up to £18,000 in the 1994/95 tax year if they both invest the maximum in general PEPs and single-company PEPs.

WHAT YOU CAN INVEST IN

PEPs were originally conceived as a way of encouraging individual share ownership in UK companies. So with *general PEPs*, your money must be invested in the ordinary shares of UK companies listed on the Stock Exchange or traded on the Unlisted Securities Market (USM). You can also invest in authorized unit trusts and investment trusts provided at least 50 per cent of their investments are in UK ordinary shares or in broadly comparable shares incorporated in another European Union member state. Where less than 50 per cent is invested in such shares, the maximum you can invest in such unit and investment trusts is £1,500.

Single-company PEPs invest in the shares of just one company and are normally set up by the company whose shares they invest in (they are sometimes known as 'corporate PEPs'). An employee who gets shares under savings-related share option schemes (see p. 174) and employee profit-sharing schemes (see p. 175) can transfer these shares into a single-company PEP up to the £3,000 limit. There will be no capital gains tax to pay on the transfer, no income tax on the dividends and no capital gains tax on the profits on selling the shares – provided the transfer takes place within six weeks of the shares being issued.

If you buy newly-issued shares (in a privatization, say), you can put them into your PEP, so long as your total investment in the PEP remains within the limit for the tax year. You wouldn't then have to pay income tax on the dividends and capital gains tax when you sell them. Note that you must do this within six weeks of the share allocation being announced.

TAX EXEMPT SPECIAL SAVINGS ACCOUNTS (TESSAs)

A TESSA is a special type of savings account offered by banks and building societies for lump sums or regular savings. TESSAs last for five years to encourage longer-term savings and interest is free of income tax provided the savings are left in the account until the end of the five-year period. But you can draw out some of the interest as an income without losing the tax benefits – see below. You can have only one TESSA going at a time (when one finishes, you can start another).

HOW MUCH CAN YOU INVEST?

The maximum that can be saved with a TESSA over five years is £9,000. You can build this up by regular savings (up to £150 a month), by lump sum deposits or a combination of both. But there are limits on the total amount that can be invested in any year: no more than £3,000 can be invested in the first year; the maximum in each of the remaining years is £1,800.

These limits apply to individuals aged 18 and over. So a husband and wife can each invest up to £9,000 in a TESSA, a total of £18,000.

WHAT YOU GET BACK

At the end of the TESSA, you'll get back your capital plus interest on it, without deduction of tax. There'll be no tax to pay on the accumulated interest, even if you pay tax at the higher rate. On the maximum of £9,000, this could save several hundred pounds in tax.

If you need income from a TESSA, you can draw out some of the interest. But you can't draw all the interest credited to your TESSA: some of the interest must be left invested (which means that you'll always get back more than your original capital when the TESSA comes to an end). The amount which must be left in the TESSA is the equivalent of the basic-rate tax which would normally be due on the interest earned so far. For example, if the basic rate of tax is 25 per cent and you have £100 of interest in your TESSA, you must leave 25 per

cent of £100 (£25) in the account; so you can only withdraw £100 –
£25 = £75. Provided you stick to these limits, there'll be no tax to pay
on the interest left in or the interest withdrawn (even if you pay tax at
the higher rate).

If you don't stick to these limits, or you withdraw any of the capital,
the TESSA comes to an end – and you lose the tax exemptions. Tax at
the basic rate will be deducted from all the interest added to your
TESSA: you might be able to claim some or all of this back if your
income for the tax year is too low to pay tax or you pay tax at the lower
rate; there could also be extra tax if you pay at the higher rate. If you
are over 65, the addition of this taxable interest to your total income
could reduce the amount of your personal allowance and mean extra
tax to pay (see p. 136).

INVESTMENT IN GROWING BUSINESSES

Since 1983, the Business Expansion Scheme (BES) has provided tax
relief on investments in growing businesses. In 1988, it was extended
to investments in companies providing private rented housing.
However, the BES came to an end on 31 December 1993, so that new
investments are no longer possible under it. Two new schemes were
announced in the November 1993 Budget to help growing businesses:

● the Enterprise Investment Scheme, offering tax relief on a narrower
range of investments than the BES – though, unlike the BES, it allows
investors to play an active part in the company as directors

● venture capital trusts giving tax-free income and gains to investors
in investment trusts devoted largely to investing in unquoted trading
companies.

An outline of the Enterprise Investment Scheme is given below – the
final details depend on the exact wording of the 1995 Finance Act
which will pass through Parliament after this Guide goes to press.
Venture capital trusts are not due to come in until 1995, so the rules
governing them have yet to be decided.

Details of the tax relief on BES investments made in the 1993/94 tax
year or earlier are also given overleaf.

ENTERPRISE INVESTMENT SCHEME

The Enterprise Investment Scheme provides tax relief on investments
in the shares of unquoted trading companies issued on or after 1 January

1994. Unquoted companies exclude those listed on the Stock Exchange or traded on the Unlisted Securities Market (USM) but include those traded on the Over the Counter (OTC) markets. Companies engaged in banking, insurance, share-dealing, dealing in land or property, leasing and legal or accountancy services are excluded. The company must be trading in the UK, but does not have to be registered or resident in the UK.

You can't get tax relief on investments in companies in which you work as an employee or director, or if you own over 30 per cent of the shares. In deciding how much of a company you own, you must include the holdings of *connected persons* – your spouse and you and your spouse's children, parents and grandparents (but not brothers or sisters) – and *associates* such as business partners. Once you have made your EIS investment, however, you can take part in the active management of the company as a paid director (or 'business angel').

You can get tax relief on investments of up to £100,000 in any tax year from the 1994/95 tax year onwards. For the 1993/94 tax year, tax relief is limited to a maximum of £40,000, less any investment you made in the Business Expansion Scheme in that tax year. You get the tax relief in the tax year in which the shares are issued, but if you make a EIS investment between 6 April and 5 October (inclusive), half the investment up to a maximum of £15,000 can be set off against your income for the previous tax year. With a married couple, both husband and wife can each invest up to these limits. Investors who are not resident in the UK can still benefit from the tax relief if they pay UK tax.

You can't claim the tax relief until the company has carried out its qualifying trade for at least four months. If the company ceases to qualify under the scheme within three years, you have to pay back the relief. If you sell the shares within five years, you lose relief on the amount you sell them for (that is, if you sell them for more than they cost you, you have to pay back all the relief).

If both you and the company make it through these time limits, then there will be no capital gains tax to pay when you eventually sell the shares. A loss made on selling the shares in this case can be set off against other income or capital gains – reducing your overall tax bill for the year.

BUSINESS EXPANSION SCHEME

Investments in certain types of companies and funds made on or before 31 December 1993 qualified for tax relief at your highest rate, within limits, under the Business Expansion Scheme. Three types of investment qualified under the BES:

● new ordinary shares in unquoted UK trading companies

● new ordinary shares in unquoted UK companies providing private rented housing

● approved funds investing in such companies.

You couldn't get tax relief on money you put into a company you worked for as an employee or paid director, or if you owned over 30 per cent of the shares (including the holdings of connected persons and business associates – see p. 278).

To get tax relief on BES investments, you had to be resident and ordinarily resident in the UK (p. 188) when the shares were issued. You got tax relief at your highest rate of tax on up to £40,000 of BES investments in the tax year. The investment had to be at least £500 unless made through an investment fund. With a married couple, both husband and wife could invest up to £40,000 in the BES in the tax year. You get the tax relief in the tax year in which the shares are issued, but if you made a BES investment between 6 April and 5 October (inclusive), half the investment up to a maximum of £5,000 could be set off against your income for the previous tax year.

With direct BES investments in companies, you can't claim the tax relief until the company has carried out its qualifying trade for at least four months. If the company ceases to qualify under the scheme within three years, you have to pay back the relief. And if you sell the shares within five years, you lose relief on the amount you sell them for.

If both you and the company make it through these time limits, then there will be no capital gains tax to pay when you eventually sell BES shares bought after 18 March 1986. Any losses made on selling BES investments cannot be set off against taxable gains to reduce your capital gains tax bill.

Claim the tax relief on the back of Form BES 3 (for an investment in an individual company) or BES 5 (for an investment fund). These forms will be given to you by the company or fund once they have been authorized as BES investments by the Inland Revenue. A BES investment reduces your taxable income but not your 'total income' (p. 23). So investing in the BES won't reduce your 'total income' for calculating the amount of allowance you get if over 65 (p. 135) or in calculating top-slicing relief (p. 289).

OVERSEAS INVESTMENTS

Income from overseas investments is taxable if you are domiciled and resident in the UK, even if you do not bring it back into the UK. This applies to sterling and non-sterling investments, including those made in the 'offshore' islands such as the Channel Islands and the Isle of Man. If you have got income from these offshore investments, it must still be declared on your Tax Return – even if your income is too low to pay UK tax on it.

If you do have to pay tax on overseas investment income, the rules are similar to those for UK investment income paid without deduction of tax (see p. 273). It is taxed on a preceding-year basis except in the opening and closing years. The collecting agent (probably your bank) will deduct UK income tax from most foreign investment income at the basic rate of 25 per cent. For share dividends and unit trust distributions, tax is deducted at the lower rate of 20 per cent. If this is more tax than you should pay, you can claim some or all of this back. If tax is deducted from the income in the country where the investment is held, this tax can normally be deducted from your UK tax liability (though if the overseas tax is more than your UK bill, you cannot claim back the excess).

The Inland Revenue has signed *Double Tax Agreements* with more than 80 countries to try to ensure that income isn't taxed twice when earned in one country by a taxpayer in another country. Under these agreements, tax is deducted from investment income by the foreign country at a reduced rate: this reduces the likelihood that you will pay tax abroad that can't be reclaimed in the UK.

The taxation of overseas investment income is complex and more detail is available in Inland Revenue leaflet IR6 *Double taxation relief*. Your Tax Inspector may be able to offer help, but, if not, contact the Inspector of Foreign Dividends at Lynwood Road, Thames Ditton, Surrey KT7 0DP.

OFFSHORE FUNDS

Gains on selling offshore fund investments are taxed as income unless the fund qualifies as a *distributor fund* – one which distributes most of its income as dividends. This is to stop investors rolling up income in the funds to create capital gains and reduce their income tax bills.

Note that there are other types of offshore fund, including offshore bonds, on which specialized tax advice should be sought.

WHAT TO PUT IN YOUR TAX RETURN

Considerable space is made available for entering details of investment income under various headings under *Income from savings and investments* beginning on page 5 of Forms 11P and 11 (on page 2 of Form P1, under *Other income*). If there isn't enough room in any section, make a separate list, attach it to the Return and write 'See attached schedule' in the space. If you are married, enter half the income from joint accounts and from jointly-owned assets unless you have agreed a different split with your Tax Inspector (see p. 263). Write 'Joint' beside such types of income.

The first major heading is *National Savings*, split into *Ordinary account, Investment account, Deposit Bonds, Income Bonds, Capital Bonds* and *First Option Bonds*.

Form 11P

Enter the amounts of interest paid or credited to you for the tax year, including any Ordinary Account interest which may be tax-free (p. 264). With First Option Bonds, enter the amount of interest you actually received, the amount of tax deducted before you received it and the gross (before deduction of tax) amount. These are on the tax certificate that National Savings sends you.

The next section on Forms 11P and 11 is *Income from other UK banks, building societies and deposit takers*, for all forms of interest received other than the interest from bank and building society SAYE schemes which is tax-free and should not be included. You don't need to give details of interest paid out by a TESSA unless you have closed the account before the five years are up.

Form 11P

	Income from other UK banks, building societies and deposit takers			
Your bank or building society should be able to supply the details you need, but see note 28.	Name of the bank, building society, savings bank or deposit taker. Tick box if you have registered to have interest paid gross	Interest after tax (leave blank if no tax was deducted)	Tax deducted (leave blank if no tax was deducted)	Gross interest
		£	£	£
Do not forget to include interest from current accounts and accounts closed during the year		£	£	£
		£	£	£
		£	£	£
		£	£	£

Give the name of each organization. If you have had the interest paid gross (without deduction of tax), tick the box and fill in the interest received in the final column. Most people will have received the interest net (with tax already deducted) and should enter the amount of tax deducted, the net interest (i.e. the amount you actually received) and the gross (i.e. before deduction of tax) amount of interest paid or credited to you during the tax year. You can find this information on the Tax Deduction Certificate which you can obtain for the account shortly after the end of the tax year (or after you close the account if you do this in the middle of the tax year). Enter this information on Form P1 under *Other interest from UK banks, building societies etc.*

Under *Other interest you receive in the UK* on Forms 11P and 11, give similar details of all other interest you received. This will include interest on government stocks (whether or not tax has been deducted before you receive it), bonds, loans to other people and from credit unions and friendly societies. Also give details of interest in excess of £180 paid out by a PEP (see p. 275).

Form 11P

	Other interest you receive in the UK			
Include interest on Government stocks (gilts), bonds, loans to individuals etc. See note 29.	Give the source of the interest	Interest after tax (leave blank if no tax was deducted)	Tax deducted (leave blank if no tax was deducted)	Gross interest
		£	£	£
		£	£	£
		£	£	£

On Form P1 enter these details under *Other interest from UK banks, building societies etc.*

Give details of income from UK shares under *Dividends from shares in UK companies* on Forms 11P and 11 (*Dividends from shares in UK companies and income from unit trusts* on Form P1).

Form 11P

Notes *Enter the figures shown on your dividend voucher.* *If there is not enough space put the details on a separate sheet.*	**Dividends from shares in UK companies** Do not include income from trusts, loan stock, dividends from overseas companies or stock dividends.		
	Name of the company	Tax credit	Dividend
		£	£
		£	£
		£	£
		£	£

For each share or unit trust, enter the exact amounts of the tax credit
(as set out on the tax vouchers) and the dividend.

If you have received stock dividends, enter details in the next section
on Forms 11P and 11 (give these details under *All other income* on
Form P1).

Form 11P

Stock dividends If you took up an offer of shares in place of a cash dividend (a 'stock dividend'), give the "appropriate amount of cash" notified by the company in the dividend column.		
Name of the company	Notional tax credit	Dividend
	£	£
	£	£
	£	£
	£	£

Give the notional tax credit and the value of the dividend (the cash
equivalent) which the company will give on the voucher.

Income from UK unit trusts comes next on Forms 11P and 11 (give
details of this under *Dividends from shares in UK companies and
income from unit trusts* on Form P1).

Form 11P

These figures should be on your unit trust voucher. If you have not received one, ask the unit trust manager. If there is not enough space put the details on a separate sheet.	**Income from UK unit trusts** Complete this if you received income from unit trusts, including income reinvested in units. If your voucher shows a tax credit, give the tax credit and the dividend. If your voucher shows tax deducted, give the tax deducted and the gross income.			
	Give the name of each unit trust	Tax credit or tax deducted	Dividend	Gross income
		£	£	£
		£	£	£
		£	£	£
		£	£	£

Give the name of each unit trust. If the tax voucher shows a tax credit,
give this and the amount of the distribution – don't enter the gross
income. If the voucher shows tax deducted, give this and the gross
amount of income. Do enter details of accumulation trusts, but don't
enter equalization payments.

The next entry on Forms 11P and 11 is for *Accrued income, charges*

284

and allowances whether you received it or gave it away when buying or selling stock (p. 267). Give these details under *All other income* on Form P1.

Form 11P

See note 30.	Accrued income, charges and allowances Give details of the transactions and enter the charges and allowances for the year.	Charges
		£
		Allowances
		£

Enter details of the transaction, and either enter the income you are deemed to have received, or the deduction you are claiming because of giving income away.

Give details of investment income received from abroad under *Income from savings and investments abroad* on Forms 11P and 11 (under *Foreign investment income* on page 2 of Form P1).

Form 11P

See note 31.	Income from savings and investments abroad Describe the source and state the country	Foreign tax deducted	UK tax deducted	Gross income
		£	£	£
		£	£	£
		£	£	£
		£	£	£

Enter the full amount due to you for the tax year (whether remitted to the UK or not), less any expenses. If you have paid any foreign tax on the income or any UK tax has been deducted on paying it to you, give details.

Under *Other income from savings and investments* on Forms 11P and 11, give details of income from annuities, deep discount bonds, funding bonds, company distributions and any other investment income other than that from trusts. On Form P1, give these details under *All other income*.

Form 11P

See note 32. Leave tax credit or tax deducted column blank if there was no tax credit or tax deducted.	Other income from savings and investments For company distributions give the tax credit, if any, and distribution. For all other income give the tax deducted, if any, and the gross income.			
	Describe the source	Distribution	Tax credit or tax deducted	Gross income
		£	£	£
		£	£	£
		£	£	£
		£	£	£

With annuity income, enter the gross taxable part – the company will tell you how much this is.

Details of income from trusts and estates should be given under *Other income* on Forms 11P and 11. First give details of income from trusts not set up by you or your spouse.

Form 11P

Other income – year to 5 April 1994	

See note 27 about joint income.

See note 33.

Income from trusts funded by others
Complete this item if you received or were entitled to receive income from a trust set up by someone else
Name of trust

Tick here if any income was taxed at 20% (or carried a 20% credit)   £

Tick here if the income is from a discretionary/accumulation trust

With a discretionary trust, give the gross amount of the payment for the tax year which is on the certificate R185. With a trust with an income in possession, give the amount of income you are entitled to. On Form P1, give these details under *Income from trusts or settlements funded by others*.

Income from trusts and other settlements which you have set up which is treated as yours for tax purposes comes next. This should include income from a trust you have set up which benefits you or your spouse.

Form 11P

Income and capital from a settlement will be treated as yours if certain conditions apply. See note 34.

Income and capital from settlements for which you have provided funds
Complete this item the income, or payments of capital, should be treated as belonging to you for tax purposes.
Name and/or brief details of the settlement

Tick here if any income was taxed at 20% (or carried a 20% credit)   £

Also give here details of income from capital you have given to your children under 18 and unmarried. On Form P1, enter these details under *All other income*.

Under *Income from estates* on Forms 11P, 11 and P1, give details of income paid to you by the personal representatives (or executors) of an estate.

Form 11P

See note 35.

Income from estates
Complete this item if you had a legal entitlement to income from the estate of someone who has died but whose estate was under administration. If the personal representative of the estate has given you an income tax certificate, give the amount of gross income shown on the certificate.

Name of deceased person	Nature of your entitlement to the estate	
		£

Enter the name of the person who has died. Say what type of interest you have in the estate and give the gross amount of income received – this should be on any tax certificate given to you by the personal representative.

29 • LIFE INSURANCE

Taking out a life insurance policy is a good way of providing for your dependants should you die. But life insurance can also be used as a form of investment, particularly since the proceeds of many types of policy can be tax-free. This chapter looks at the taxation of life insurance policies, whether for protecting your dependants or as an investment.

Two groups of organizations are allowed to offer life insurance in the UK. Insurance companies have the lion's share of the market and most of what follows applies to their policies. But friendly societies (a sort of mutual self-help organization surviving from pre-welfare state days) offer policies which enjoy special tax privileges and can be well worth investigating: their policies are covered in a special section at the end of the chapter.

TYPES OF LIFE INSURANCE

Life insurance policies are divided into two types for tax purposes: *qualifying* and *non-qualifying* policies. The greatest tax advantages come with qualifying policies which include most types of life insurance where you pay regular premiums, monthly, quarterly or annually. If a life insurance policy involves only a single premium or irregular premiums, it will almost certainly be a non-qualifying policy, with less favourable tax treatment.

The following policies will normally count as qualifying:

● *mortgage protection policies* which are designed to repay your mortgage if you die before it is paid off

● *term insurance* which pays out a lump sum if you die within a set term (*family income benefit* policies convert the pay-out into an income to your dependants instead)

● *whole of life* policies which pay out whenever you die

● *endowment* policies which pay out if you die during the term of the policy and pay out a lump sum at the end of the term if you are still alive.

There are various conditions to be met if these types of policy are to count as qualifying, but the insurance company will normally ensure that these are met so that you can benefit from the tax advantages.

TAXATION OF QUALIFYING POLICIES

If a policy is a qualifying one, there is normally no income tax or capital gains tax to pay when it pays out on maturity or because the person whose life is insured dies. This reflects the fact that the life insurance company has already paid tax on income and gains year by year.

However, there may be some tax to pay if you cash in a savings-type life insurance policy before the end of its term (not usually recommended, especially in the early years of a policy). If you stop paying the premiums after less than ten years or three-quarters of the term, if this is shorter, it is taxed in the same way as a non-qualifying policy (see below).

Note that some insurance companies make a deduction from the proceeds of certain types of qualifying policies (usually unit-linked) to cover capital gains tax. This deduction is your share of the company's tax bill, not a tax charge on you personally, so you cannot claim the tax back if you are not liable to capital gains tax.

TAXATION OF NON-QUALIFYING POLICIES

If a policy is a non-qualifying one, you may have to pay income tax when it pays out. There is never any basic-rate tax to pay on the proceeds – whenever it pays out. However, there will be a higher-rate tax bill if the proceeds of the policy (added to your other taxable income) are taxable at the higher rate.

The proceeds are taxable at the higher rate of income tax as a *chargeable gain*. The gain is normally the amount you get back less the total premiums paid. But if the pay-out occurs because of the death of the person whose life is insured, the gain is calculated using the cash-in value of the policy at the time of death if this is less than the amount paid out. For how the tax is calculated on this chargeable gain, see opposite.

If you draw an income from the policy by cashing in part of it each year, this too counts as a chargeable gain. But so long as the amount withdrawn each year does not exceed 5 per cent of the premiums paid so far, the withdrawals aren't taxed until the policy comes to an end (when they're added to the gain made at the final pay-out). If you use less than 5 per cent in any year, you can carry the unused allowance forward to later years. If you draw more than the 5 per cent allowance, the excess is taxed as a chargeable gain in the year in which you get it.

Note that if you sell a non-qualifying policy, there will also be a chargeable gain if you sell it for more than the premiums paid.

HOW CHARGEABLE GAINS ARE TAXED

The gain is added to your income for the tax year in which it is chargeable, but no basic-rate tax is due on the gain. Only if the gain, added to the rest of your taxable income, is taxable at the higher rate will there be any tax to pay. So for the 1993/94 and 1994/95 tax years, there will be tax to pay on a gain only if your taxable income including the gain exceeds £23,700.

Even if the gain is taxable at the higher rate, the tax charged on the gain is not the full rate of tax, but the difference between the higher rate and the basic rate. So, if the rate of tax applicable to the gain is 40 per cent, and the basic rate is 25 per cent, tax is charged on the gain at $40 - 25 = 15$ per cent.

This could mean a very large tax bill in the year in which you cash in a non-qualifying policy. But you may be able to benefit from *top-slicing relief* which spreads the gain you make over the years of the policy. Your Tax Inspector should automatically apply top-slicing relief if it means a smaller tax bill but you can check the calculations:

STEP 1 Work out the average gain made in each year on the policy, that is, the total gain divided by the number of complete years you held the policy.

STEP 2 Calculate the higher-rate tax which would be due if the average gain was added to the rest of your taxable income (you can do this by working out how much tax would be due on the gain if it was your top slice of income and then subtracting the amount of basic-rate tax which would be due on the gain).

STEP 3 Multiply the higher-rate tax due on this average gain by the number of complete years you held the policy to find the total tax due on the gain.

STEP 4 The answer will be the tax due on the gain.

EXAMPLE

Deirdre Moss buys a single-premium bond (that is, life insurance policy) for £20,000 at the age of 50, when she pays higher-rate income tax on her earnings. Each year, she can draw an income of 5 per cent of the premiums paid without paying tax in that year: thus Deirdre can draw 5 per cent of £20,000 = £1,000 a year without increasing her tax bill for the year.

When Deirdre retires at 65, she cashes in the bond for £40,000. The chargeable gain is the proceeds she has drawn from the bond (£40,000 + 15 × £1,000 = £55,000) less the premiums paid (£20,000): £55,000 − £20,000 = £35,000.

If her taxable income from her pension and other investments is £23,000 (that is, taxable at the lower and basic rate only), this gain of £35,000 will increase Deirdre's total taxable income to £58,000. A taxable income over £23,700 would be taxable in 1994/95 at the higher rate of 40 per cent. Indeed, the higher-rate tax due on the gain of £35,000 would be £5,145. But she will be able to benefit from top-slicing relief as follows:

STEP 1 Calculate the average yearly gain over the 15 years; this is £35,000 ÷ 15 = £2,333.

STEP 2 Calculate the higher-rate tax due on this average gain of £2,333 when added to the rest of Deirdre's taxable income for the year of £23,000 – that is a total taxable income of £25,333. Remember that tax is due only at the difference between the higher rate of tax and the basic rate:

Taxable income without gain	= £23,000
Amount of basic-rate tax band unused	= £23,700 – £23,000
	= £700
Tax due on gain of £2,333:	
25% of £700 £175	
40% of £1,633 £653	
Total £828	
Basic-rate tax due on gain	= 25% of £2,333
	= £583
Higher-rate tax due on gain	= £828 – £583
	= £245

STEP 3 Multiply the higher-rate tax due on the average gain (£245) by the number of years the bond was held (15) to find the higher-rate tax due on cashing in the bond:

$$£245 \times 15 = £3,675$$

STEP 4 Since the amount of tax due with top-slicing relief (£3,675) is less than if the whole gain was added to Deirdre's taxable income for the year (£5,145), the tax bill on the gain will be £3,675.

LIFE INSURANCE GAINS AND PERSONAL ALLOWANCES

If you make a chargeable gain, this counts as part of your total income for the tax year when working out whether you are entitled to the higher personal allowances for people over 65. If a chargeable gain reduces the amount of your allowance, there will be extra tax to pay on your income (p. 135). This is particularly important if you buy a single-premium bond with the intention of cashing it in after retirement when you expect your top tax rate to be lower than when at work.

LIFE INSURANCE AND INHERITANCE TAX

If a life insurance policy, qualifying or otherwise, pays out on the death of the person who took it out, the proceeds will be paid into his or her estate and be liable to inheritance tax (see p. 344). This inheritance tax bill (and the delay in getting the money while probate is sought) can be avoided if the policy is written in trust for someone else: a child, say. With policies written in trust, the proceeds go straight to the person or people for whom they are written in trust without passing through the dead person's estate. The premiums count as gifts but if they are regular are likely to be exempt from inheritance tax as gifts made out of normal income (p. 330).

Note that if a non-qualifying policy is written in trust, you will be liable for any income tax due on the gain if this becomes due during your lifetime. However, you can reclaim the tax from the trustees (that is, from the proceeds of the policy).

TAX RELIEF ON LIFE INSURANCE PREMIUMS

If you took out a qualifying life insurance policy before 14 March 1984, you got tax relief on the premiums (within limits). Provided you haven't substantially changed the policy, you can still get the tax relief on premiums for policies taken out before midnight on 13 March 1984.

The rate of tax relief is 12½ per cent for 1993/94 and 1994/95; in most cases you get it by paying reduced premiums to the insurance company. So in 1994/95, you pay 87½ per cent of the gross premium and the insurance company reclaims the 12½ per cent tax relief direct from the Inland Revenue.

There are limits on the amount of tax relief: you can get tax relief on no more than £1,500 of gross premiums in any tax year (that is, on £1,312.50 of net premiums while the rate of tax relief is 12½ per cent) or one-sixth of your total income if this is greater. If you pay more than the limit, the taxman will reclaim the tax relief you have automatically been given on the excess.

And if you change the policy so as to get more benefits, you will lose the tax relief: for example, you will lose the tax relief if you extend the term of the policy, increase the amount of cover or convert the policy into a different type of policy (for example, from term to endowment). But you won't lose the tax relief if the benefits increase automatically as part of the policy (for example, if the sum insured increases by 5 per cent every year). Check before making any changes.

FRIENDLY SOCIETIES

Friendly societies supported their members before the arrival of the welfare state by paying sickness benefit, unemployment benefit and widow's pensions. Some continue in existence and you can get tax relief on premiums you pay on certain combined sickness and life insurance policies they offer. The tax relief is at half your top rate of tax on the life part of the premium; you can also get the same tax relief on part of your trade union subscription if it includes superannuation, funeral or life insurance benefits.

Friendly societies also sell investment-type life insurance policies which can offer a tax-free return in the same way as normal life insurance policies. But the amount you can invest in them is currently limited to £200 a year in premiums. If this limit is stuck to, the policy is a qualifying one and the friendly society pays no income tax or capital gains tax on the business. But if you cash the policy in early and it becomes a non-qualifying policy, you will have to pay tax on the chargeable gain at both the basic rate and the higher rate (not just the higher rate, as with life insurance policies).

Some of these 'tax-exempt' policies offer highly competitive returns because the society doesn't have to pay tax on the investment returns. But you can't take out several policies with different societies each below the limits for tax relief to take advantage of these returns. If you take out a policy which takes all your tax-exempt policies over the limits, the policy automatically ceases to be a qualifying one and loses its tax-exempt status. However, these limits don't apply to policies taken out before 14 March 1984, so if you've already got several of these, you can enjoy the benefits on all of them.

WHAT TO PUT IN YOUR TAX RETURN

Most people don't need to enter any details of their life insurance policies on their Tax Return. However, you have to enter details of any chargeable gain you have made on a non-qualifying life insurance policy.

Enter the details under *Other income from savings and investments* on page 6 of Forms 11P and 11. With Form P1, enter details under *All other income* at the bottom of page 2. Give the name of the life insurance company and enter the taxable gain as the gross income (the company will tell you what to enter). If married, make sure you allocate the gain on a joint policy correctly between husband and wife (p. 263).

Form 11P

See note 32. Leave tax credit or tax deducted column blank if there was no tax credit or tax deducted.	**Other income from savings and investments** For company distributions give the tax credit, if any, and distribution. For all other income give the tax deducted, if any, and the gross income.			
	Describe the source	Distribution	Tax credit or tax deducted	Gross income
		£	£	£
		£	£	£
		£	£	£
		£	£	£

If you pay premiums to a friendly society on a combined life and sickness insurance policy, you should give details in the *Pension contributions* section – see p. 232.

TREASURE TROVE CLUE No. 10

The 1994/95 scale charge used to tax the benefit of free fuel for a company car with a petrol engine of 2,001cc or more (4 digits).

30 • GIVING TO CHARITY

If you want to give money to charity, there are some useful tax concessions to search out. Whether it's a regular donation to your local church, a response to a disaster appeal or a legacy in your will, you can maximize the amount the charity gets from your money by taking advantage of these concessions. This chapter looks at the income tax relief you can get through employers' payroll-giving schemes and on regular gifts under covenant. It explains the Gift Aid scheme which gives tax relief on larger gifts to charity. And there are details of the gifts you can make for various good works which are free of inheritance tax and capital gains tax.

Note that if you run a business, you can get tax relief on gifts of equipment to schools and other educational institutions – ask your Tax Inspector for details.

PAYROLL-GIVING SCHEMES

If your employer has an approved payroll-giving scheme, you can get tax relief at your highest rate of tax on donations to charity (within limits). The money goes to the charities of your choice and there's no need to draw up a covenant or agree to make donations for several years. There are limits on the amount you can give each year under a payroll-giving scheme: the limit was £600 a year for the 1993/94 and 1994/95 tax years.

To get the tax relief, your employer must have set up a payroll-giving scheme (sometimes known as Give As You Earn). This means signing up with an Inland-Revenue-approved agency which collects the money employees wish to give and passes it on to the charities of their choice. Once a scheme has been set up, you tell your employer how much you want to give and the charities you want to give it to. The money is deducted from your pay before working out how much tax is due on it, as with contributions to an employer's pension scheme. This automatically gives you the tax relief: a £100 gift out of your before-tax pay costs you £75 of your after-tax pay if you pay tax at the basic rate of 25 per cent only. Your employer hands over all the money deducted from employees' pay under the payroll-giving scheme to the agency which then acts as a clearing house, passing on the money to the charities nominated by the employees.

COVENANTS TO CHARITY

You can get tax relief at your highest rate of tax on payments you make to registered charities if you make them under *deed of covenant*. A deed of covenant is a legally binding agreement to make a series of payments and to get the tax relief on payments to charity they should continue for more than three years.

You won't get the tax relief if you get significant benefit from the payments, so you can't use a covenant to pay your children's school fees to a private school which is a charitable foundation. But you can use a covenant to pay a subscription to certain types of charity if you are allowed access to the charity's property as a benefit of membership. This allows you to get tax relief on subscriptions to charities such as the National Trust or those which conserve wildlife for the public benefit, even though you get free or reduced price entry to the charity's property. And in practice, the Inland Revenue ignores benefits if they are worth less than a quarter of the subscription.

HOW A COVENANT WORKS

Suppose you draw up a covenant to give your favourite charity a *gross amount* of £100 a year (the gross amount is what you give before deduction of the tax relief). When you make the payment, you deduct tax at the basic rate from the gross amount and hand over the *net amount*. So if the basic rate of tax is 25 per cent, you deduct £25 from the gross amount of £100 and hand over the net amount of £100 − £25 = £75.

You can keep the tax you deduct from the gross amount of your gift provided you pay at least that much basic-rate tax on your income, so the £100 gift has cost you just £75. And the charity can reclaim the £25 you have deducted, so it ends up with the gross amount of your gift of £100. This process automatically gives you the basic-rate tax relief on the gift. If you are entitled to higher-rate tax relief on the payment, you will have to claim it from your Tax Inspector (you'll get it either through PAYE or in a reduced tax bill).

If the basic rate of tax changes, you will have to change the amount you hand over: for example, if the basic rate fell to 20 per cent, you would deduct £20 from the gross amount of £100 and hand over £80. To avoid having to recalculate the amount to hand over every time the basic rate changes (and having to alter your banker's order), you can instead agree to hand over a fixed net amount.

For example, if you agree to hand over a net amount of £75 a year, this would be equivalent to a gross amount of £100 if the basic rate of tax was 25 per cent. If the basic rate fell to 20 per cent, the gross amount would become £93.75 to leave £75 after deduction of basic-rate tax. So, agreeing to pay a net amount means that you know exactly how much you have to hand over each year but the charity doesn't know exactly how much it is going to get from year to year.

Note that if you pay less tax at the basic rate than you deduct from the covenant payments, you will have given yourself too much tax relief. The same applies if you pay tax at the lower rate of 20 per cent only or are a non-taxpayer. In any of these cases, you may have to hand some of the money back to the Inland Revenue. For example, if you pay tax at the lower rate only, and make a gross payment of £100, you would deduct £25 and hand over £75. But since you will have paid only 20 per cent tax on the £100, you will be entitled to just £20 tax relief (20 per cent of £100). You would have to repay the extra £5 to the Inland Revenue (though the charity would still end up with £100).

DRAWING UP A COVENANT

Most charities have printed covenant forms for you to complete if you wish to make regular donations. These usually specify payments for four years to meet the over-three-years rule. They will probably be expressed as a net amount rather than a gross amount, so that you don't have to keep changing your banker's order every time the basic rate of tax changes. You will have to fill in your name, address, the date of the first payment and the amount you wish to give.

The deed of covenant will contain the words 'signed, sealed and delivered'. It must be signed and dated before the first payment is due (you can't backdate the covenant to cover payments already made). And the signing must be done in the presence of a witness who must also sign the deed (the witness should not be a relation). The deed should technically be sealed by sticking on a disc of paper but the Inland Revenue has said that it won't insist on this. You 'deliver' the deed, once you've completed these steps, by sending it to the charity (keeping a photocopy for reference).

If you're drawing up a covenant in Scotland, you don't need to seal or deliver the deed, nor is a witness required. But you must write the words 'Adopted as holograph' in your own handwriting above your signature and at the bottom of previous pages if the deed covers more than one.

Although a covenant may be drawn up to run for only four years, the Inland Revenue will continue to give tax relief on the payments if you continue to make them after the four years are up.

MAKING THE PAYMENTS

It is important to fulfil the promises in the deed of covenant to the letter, handing over the net amount on the stated date. After the first payment has been made, the charity will send you Inland Revenue Form R185AP to sign. This sets out the amount you have handed over and the tax you have deducted, so that the charity can reclaim the tax. Fill it in and return it to the charity when you have signed it. With small amounts, you'll have to fill in Form R185AP only after the first year's payment: but if the amount you hand over after deduction of tax is over £400 a year, you'll have to complete Form R185AP every year.

USING COVENANTS FOR ONE-OFF PAYMENTS

The tax relief on covenant payments is designed to encourage regular payments lasting over three years. But it is possible to get tax relief on single donations if you make regular payments to a charity which acts as a clearing house for passing on money to other charities.

It works like this: you sign a covenant to make regular payments to the intermediary charity. You can deduct tax at the basic rate from the payments before handing them over. The intermediary reclaims the basic-rate tax you deduct and probably makes a yearly charge to cover expenses. When you wish to give a donation to a particular charity (in response to an appeal, perhaps), you instruct the intermediary to forward the amount you wish to give.

The largest organization acting as an intermediary in this way is the Charities Aid Foundation (CAF), 48 Pembury Road, Tonbridge, Kent TN9 2JD. They give you a book of cheques which you can sign and send direct to the charities of your choice who claim the money from the CAF. Other bodies, such as local voluntary service councils, provide a similar service.

GIFT AID

You can get tax relief at your highest rate of tax on single one-off gifts to charity of £250 or more. There is no upper limit on the size of the gifts which qualify for tax relief. Gift Aid applies only to gifts in your lifetime – there's no income tax relief for bequests on death.

The tax relief works in much the same way as for covenant payments. Suppose you want to give a charity a gross amount of £1,000. You hand over the donation after deducting tax at the basic rate: so if the basic rate of tax is 25 per cent, you deduct 25 per cent of £1,000 = £250; and you hand over £1,000 – £250 = £750. The charity claims back the £250 of basic-rate tax from the Inland Revenue, and ends up with £1,000 at a cost to you of £750.

If you pay tax at the higher rate, the £1,000 gift will cost you even less. You still deduct tax at the basic rate only and hand over £750 to the charity as above. But you can claim higher-rate tax relief: if the higher rate of tax is 40 per cent, you're entitled to tax relief at 40 per cent of £1,000 = £400. You claim the extra £400 – £250 = £150 from the Inland Revenue. So your £1,000 donation costs you just £600.

Note that if you pay less tax at the basic rate than you deduct from the gift, you will have given yourself too much tax relief. The same applies if you pay tax at the lower rate of 20 per cent only or are a non-taxpayer. In any of these cases, you may have to hand some of the money back to the Inland Revenue. For example, if you pay tax at the lower rate only, and make a gift of £1,000, you would deduct £250 and hand over £750. But since you will have paid only 20 per cent tax on the £1,000, you will be entitled to just £200 tax relief (20 per cent of £1,000). You would have to repay the extra £50 to the Inland Revenue (though the charity would still end up with £1,000).

If you don't pay tax, you will have to hand over all the basic-rate tax relief you have deducted from the gift to the Inland Revenue. So if you are a married couple, make sure that any donations made under Gift Aid come from the partner who pays tax at the highest possible rate.

When you make a donation under Gift Aid, you should give the charity a tax deduction certificate (available from your tax office).

CAPITAL TAXES

Inheritance tax may be payable on gifts of money made on your death or within seven years of your death (for more details, see Chapter 32, p. 327). Gifts of things such as paintings, historic homes, *objets d'art* and other heirlooms are also taxable in the same way but, if made during your lifetime, you may have to pay capital gains tax as well (p. 301).

But gifts and legacies to UK charities are free of inheritance tax, no matter how large they are. And if you give an asset which is showing a chargeable gain to a charity, there is no capital gains tax to pay. Note that the charity must be established in the UK: with an international charity like the World Wide Fund for Nature you would have to specify that the gift is to go to its UK offshoot.

If you give an asset to charity which is showing a chargeable loss, this cannot be set off against other taxable gains. So if you wish to combine the greatest tax-saving in giving some property to charity, you should give things which are showing a taxable gain. If an item is showing a taxable loss, you would do better to sell it and give the proceeds to charity: this would create a loss which could be used to reduce your CGT bill on other disposals.

Other gifts which fall in the 'good works' category are also free of inheritance tax and capital gains tax, and include:

● gifts to certain national institutions, such as the National Trust, the National Gallery, the British Museum (and their Scottish, Welsh and Northern Irish equivalents)

● gifts for the public benefit to non-profit-making concerns like local museums

● gifts of land in the UK to registered housing associations

● gifts of certain types of heritage property (for example, paintings, archives or historic buildings).

WHAT TO PUT IN YOUR TAX RETURN

You don't have to give any details of donations made under payroll-giving schemes on your Tax Return, since the tax relief is given automatically through PAYE (see p. 294).

Details of Gift Aid donations should be given on page 9 of Forms 11P and 11 and page 3 of Form P1.

Form 11P

If you made "Gift Aid" donations give the amounts you actually paid to each charity. Use a separate sheet of paper if necessary.	**Gift aid donations**	**Net amount paid in 1993-94**
	Name of charity	£

Give the name of the charity and the amount you handed over to the charity in the tax year (the net or after deduction of tax amount).

There is also space for similar details of covenants to charity. Give the date you signed the covenant.

Form 11P

	Covenants to charity	Net amount paid in 1993-94
Give the amounts you actually paid to each charity. Use a separate sheet of paper if necessary. See note 47.	Name of charity	£

There is no need to report gifts which are exempt from inheritance tax (p. 328). But if you give something to charity which would normally be liable to capital gains tax on disposal, you should enter the details under *Capital gains* on your Tax Return (see p. 324 for what to enter).

31 • CAPITAL GAINS TAX

If you own items which increase in value, you may find yourself paying capital gains tax (CGT) at some time. For example, shares and unit trusts, land, property and antiques can increase in price, giving you a capital gain. If you sell them, or even give them away, you may be faced with a tax bill on the gain.

The teeth of CGT have been getting blunter over the last few years. Gains clocked up before 1 April 1982 are no longer taxable. You won't have to pay tax on increases in value which are simply the result of inflation. The first £5,800 of taxable capital gains in any year is tax-free. If you make a loss on one asset, you can deduct this from the gains made on other assets. And there are various allowances and exemptions for businesses. The average taxpayer is unlikely to be faced with a CGT bill.

But if you do have to pay capital gains tax, the rate is the same as you would pay on your income: this could be a hefty 40 per cent of the taxable gain for a higher-rate taxpayer. It is all the more important, therefore, to take advantage of the allowances which can reduce the amount of CGT you pay. And because the first £5,800 of taxable capital gains is tax-free, it is still tax-efficient for all taxpayers to consider investing to get a capital gain rather than income, so as to use up that tax-free band.

WHEN CAPITAL GAINS TAX IS CHARGED

You may have to pay CGT when you dispose of an asset. What is meant by 'dispose' is not defined by law. But, for example, if you sell an asset, swap one asset for another or give something away, you might find yourself caught up with CGT. Indeed, if an asset is lost, destroyed or becomes valueless, this can count as a disposal (though not if you replace or restore it by claiming on an insurance policy).

There is a long list of assets which are free of capital gains tax on disposal – see overleaf for details. There are also some occasions when there is no CGT to pay, regardless of what is being disposed of or how much it is worth. These occasions are when:

- you die

- you give something to your husband or wife, unless separated (p. 110)

- you donate an asset to charity.

TAX-FREE GAINS

There is no CGT to pay on a gain you make on any of the following assets:

- your home (though not a second home in most cases – see p. 242)

- personal belongings sold for less than £6,000 (see p. 309)

- a wasting asset with a useful life of 50 years or less (for example, a boat or caravan), so long as you could not have claimed a capital allowance on it. Gains on leases are not tax-free

- British money, including sovereigns dated after 1837

- foreign currency for your personal spending abroad (including what you spend on maintaining a home abroad), but not foreign currency accounts

- proceeds of an insurance policy, unless you bought it and were not the original holder (though you may have to pay part of the insurance company's CGT bill – see p. 288)

- betting or lottery winnings

- various National Savings investments, such as National Savings Certificates, Save-As-You-Earn and Capital Bonds

- Personal Equity Plans (PEPs) – see p. 274

- Business Expansion Scheme (BES) shares bought after 18 March 1986, provided you have owned them for at least five years and they carried on their qualifying activity for at least three years (see p. 278)

- Enterprise Investment Scheme (EIS) shares, provided you have owned them for at least five years and they carried on their qualifying activity for at least three years (see p. 277)

● British Government stock and any options to buy and sell such stock

● certain corporate bonds, such as company loan stock and debentures, issued after 13 March 1984 and options to buy and sell such bonds

● interest in a trust or settlement, unless you bought it

● a decoration for bravery, unless you bought it

● certain gifts for the public benefit (see p. 298)

● damages or compensation for a personal injury or wrong to yourself or in your personal capacity (for example, libel).

Disposals of land to housing associations may also be free of CGT.

WHO HAS TO PAY?

Capital gains tax applies to you as an individual in your private life or in your business, if you are self-employed or in partnership. Companies may also pay CGT, though some organizations do not have to pay tax on all the gains they make: charities, certain friendly societies, housing associations and pension funds, for example. Trustees may also have to pay CGT on the assets held in trust (see p. 323).

If you owe CGT it must be paid on 1 December after the end of the tax year in which you make the gain, or 30 days after the issue of a Notice of Assessment if this is later. It is important to give information about any possible capital gains to your Tax Inspector by the end of October at the latest if you are to avoid paying interest on the CGT which would be due on 1 December. Be sure to appeal against a Notice of Assessment if you disagree with it within 30 days of the date on it (see p. 61).

MARRIED COUPLES

A husband and wife are each treated as two single people for capital gains tax purposes, and each is responsible for paying their own CGT bills. They each have their own tax-free allowance (£5,800 for 1993/94 and 1994/95), and losses carried forward from previous years can only be set against their own gains.

Many assets may be jointly owned by husband and wife – second homes, shares, valuables and so on. Your Tax Inspector will assume that joint assets are owned equally by the two of you, so any gain or loss will be split 50:50 between you. However, you can make a 'declaration of beneficial interests' on assets held in your joint names using Form 17 (see p. 263) if the asset actually belongs to one of you or is owned in unequal shares – this will alter the split of the gain or loss.

If you have already filled in a Form 17 for the income of the asset, there is no need to fill in another one for capital gains. But many assets which produce capital gains do not produce an income – so make sure that you complete Form 17 for such assets if not owned in equal shares.

HOW TO WORK OUT THE GAIN OR LOSS

To work out the gain or loss on an asset, follow these steps:

STEP 1 Find the *final value* of the asset (see below).

STEP 2 Find the *initial value* of the asset (see opposite). Deduct the initial value from the final value to find the gross capital gain or loss.

STEP 3 If there are any *allowable expenses* (opposite), deduct these from the gross capital gain to give the net capital gain or loss.

STEP 4 Work out the *indexation allowance* (p. 306). Deduct this from the net capital gain to give the chargeable gain (or allowable loss) on the disposal. Note that for disposals on or after 30 November 1993, indexation allowance cannot turn a gain into a loss, or reduce a loss further – see p. 307.

STEP 5 If the asset was owned before 1 April 1982, you'll have used its market value at that date as the initial value, but in some cases, you should use the original purchase price instead (see p. 305). There's an opportunity to simplify the taxation of gains on such assets – see p. 308.

The figure you end up with after making these adjustments is known as the *chargeable gain* (or *allowable loss,* if the deductions are greater than the final value).

FINAL VALUE

The final value of an asset is normally what you get for selling it. If you give it away, the final value is its market value: what anyone selling it at the time of the gift would get for it on the open market.

The market value is also the final value if you dispose of an asset to a *connected person,* however much you sell it for. For capital gains tax, a connected person includes your husband or wife, your business partner and their spouse, a relative of yours or these others (brother, sister, parents, child, grandchild) and the spouse of one of these relatives.

THE INITIAL VALUE OF THE ASSET

The initial value of an asset is normally what you paid for it. With something you inherited, the probate value is its initial value. If you were given it, the initial value is normally the market value at the time of the gift (unless you agreed at the time of the gift to take over the giver's capital gain – see p. 313).

There are special rules for working out the initial value of shares and unit trusts where you have bought more than one batch of particular shares or unit trusts – see p. 314.

ASSETS OWNED BEFORE APRIL 1982

If you owned an asset on or before 31 March 1992, only the gain since that date is liable to capital gains tax. Any gain made before 1 April 1982 is tax-free. With such assets, the initial value is normally its market value on 31 March 1982. You may need to produce proof of its value on that date if it cannot be easily found out (for example, from catalogues or valuations at the time).

EXAMPLE

Herol Burton bought a seaside flat for a holiday home in June 1979. He paid £21,000 for it. He sold it in October 1993 for £50,000.

Any gain made before 1 April 1982 is tax-free, so Herol has to find out the market value of the flat on 31 March 1982. After consulting a valuer, he puts this at £26,000 and this becomes the initial value. His unindexed gain is £50,000 – £26,000 = £24,000.

In some circumstances, using the 31 March 1982 value could artificially inflate your gain or loss. Suppose, for example, you bought something in 1978 which fell in value before 31 March 1982, and has risen in value since. Basing the gain on the 31 March 1982 value would make it larger than the gain you've actually made. In such cases, there are special rules to make sure that you do not pay too much tax (or clock up too big an allowable loss) – see p. 308.

ALLOWABLE EXPENSES

You can deduct certain allowable expenses in computing the gain for capital gains tax. These include:

● acquisition costs, such as payments to a professional adviser (for example, surveyor, accountant, solicitor), conveyancing costs and stamp duty, and advertising to find a seller

- what you spend improving the asset (though not your own time)

- what you spend establishing or defending your rights or title to the asset

- disposal costs, similar to acquisition costs, but including the cost of valuing for CGT.

If the asset was owned before 1 April 1982, don't at this stage, deduct any expenses incurred on or before 31 March 1982.

EXAMPLE

Benny Barber bought a painting for £2,000 in April 1982. He paid an additional fee to the auction house of £200. In July 1982, he spent £500 having the painting cleaned. The painting was sold for £20,000 in May 1993, with a fee of £2,000 for the auction house.

The gain before indexation allowance is worked out as follows:

Final value		£20,000
less allowable expenses:		
original cost	£2,000	
cleaning	£500	
buying cost	£200	
selling cost	£2,000	
		£4,700
Unindexed gain		£15,300

INDEXATION ALLOWANCE

Once you have deducted the initial value and the allowable expenses from the final value, you have the unindexed gain or loss. Because many gains will include increases which are simply the result of inflation, you can claim indexation allowance to further reduce the unindexed gain to compensate for inflation.

To calculate indexation allowance, multiply the initial value and each allowable expense by the following:

$$\frac{\text{RPI in disposal month} - \text{RPI in expenditure month}}{\text{RPI in expenditure month}}$$

RPI stands for Retail Prices Index (figures for the RPI since March 1982 are given on p. 360). The expenditure month is the month in which the payment of the initial value or the allowable expense became due.

If you owned the asset before 1 April 1982, use the RPI for March 1982.

Work out this sum for the initial value and each allowable expense to three decimal places, and add together the answers.

EXAMPLE

Benny Barber works out the indexation allowance he can claim on his painting (see above).

First, he works it out for the original cost and the buying fee (£2,200), both of which were spent in April 1982. This comes to:

$$£2,200 \times \frac{\text{RPI May 1993} - \text{RPI April 1982}}{\text{RPI April 1982}}$$
$$= £2,200 \times \frac{141.1 - 81.04}{81.04}$$
$$= £2,200 \times 0.741$$
$$= £1,630.20$$

Now he works out the indexation allowance for the cost of cleaning:

$$£500 \times \frac{\text{RPI May 1993} - \text{RPI July 1982}}{\text{RPI July 1982}}$$
$$= £500 \times \frac{141.1 - 81.88}{81.88}$$
$$= £500 \times 0.723$$
$$= £361.50$$

Benny's total indexation allowance is £1,630.20 + £361.50 = £1,991.70. His taxable gain is therefore £15,300 − £1,991.70 = £13,308.30.

For disposals on or after 30 November 1993, indexation allowance cannot create or increase an allowable loss. So if the indexation allowance is bigger than the unindexed gain, the gain is reduced to nil. If there is already a net capital loss on the disposal, no indexation allowance can be claimed.

For disposals before 30 November 1993, you can claim the full indexation allowance – even if it turns a paper gain into an allowable loss or increases a loss still further. The example below shows how it worked.

EXAMPLE

Jayne Bennett acquired a piece of antique silver in January 1984 for £8,000. When she sold it in September 1993, she received only £9,000, making a small unindexed gain of £1,000.

Jayne works out the indexation allowance she can claim:

$$£8,000 \times \frac{\text{RPI September 1993} - \text{RPI January 1984}}{\text{RPI January 1984}}$$

$$= £8,000 \times \frac{141.9 - 86.84}{86.84}$$

$$= £8,000 \times 0.634$$

$$= £5,072$$

Jayne's unindexed gain of £1,000 turns into a loss of £4,072 when £5,072 indexation allowance is deducted from it.

SPECIAL RULES FOR ASSETS OWNED BEFORE 1 APRIL 1982

The initial value of assets owned before 1 April 1982 is taken to be their market value on 31 March 1982. However, this could mean a bigger gain than you really made if you dispose of something bought before 1 April 1982 which had fallen in value before that date. Similarly, if you dispose of something which rose in value while you owned it before 1 April 1982 and fell in value afterwards, this could produce a bigger loss than you actually made.

In such cases, the market value of the asset when you originally acquired it becomes its initial value. If this basis applies, you can also deduct expenses incurred before 1 April 1982 (these cannot normally be deducted). But indexation allowance still runs from March 1982 only, both for the initial value and for expenses prior to 1 April.

It is even possible that you could make a gain using the value at 31 March 1982 and a loss using what you originally paid for the asset (or vice versa). If using the alternative basis turns a loss into a gain or a gain into a loss, then your Tax Inspector will treat the disposal as if there was neither a loss nor a gain.

Basing the gain on the market value when you acquired a pre-1 April 1982 asset means producing records of what you paid for it and spent on it in allowable expenses before 1 April 1982, as well as since that date. If you want to dispense with all the record-keeping (or it's got into a mess), you can choose to have *all* your pre-1 April 1982 assets treated as if they were acquired on 31 March 1982. Tell your Tax Inspector within two years of the first disposal of such an asset after 6 April 1988 – but remember it is irrevocable.

EXAMPLE

Herol Burton sold his seaside flat for £50,000 in October 1993, having owned it since June 1979 when he had paid £21,000 for it. The example on p. 305 shows how its value at 31 March 1982 (£26,000) became its initial value for CGT purposes.

But suppose that Herol's flat had fallen in value between 1979 and 1982, so that it was worth only £16,000 on 31 March 1982. The gain using this value as the initial value would be £50,000 − £16,000 = £34,000. The gain based on what he paid for it in June 1979 would be £50,000 − £21,000 = £29,000. Since using the 31 March 1982 value would produce a bigger gain for Herol to pay tax on, the market value at June 1979 would be used instead (unless Herol opted for all his pre-1 April 1982 assets to be treated as if they were acquired on that date).

SPECIAL RULES FOR PERSONAL BELONGINGS

Personal belongings, known as *chattels* by the Inland Revenue, enjoy special treatment for CGT. If sold for less than £6,000, the gain is tax-free. Chattels are defined as 'tangible, movable property' and include furniture, silver, paintings and so on. A set (for example, a silver tea-set) counts as one chattel for this exemption.

If a chattel is sold for more than the tax-free limit, the size of the taxable gain is restricted to $\frac{5}{3}$ of the amount of the disposal over the limit. So when the limit is £6,000 the *maximum* gain on a chattel sold for £7,200 would be $\frac{5}{3}$ of £7,200 − £6,000 = $\frac{5}{3}$ of £1,200 = £2,000.

EXAMPLE

Caroline Burns bought a piece of furniture for £4,000 and sold it for £7,500 in the 1994/95 tax year. This produces a gain of £7,500 − £4,000 = £3,500. The sale price is over the £6,000 chattels limit so the gain is not tax-free. But for CGT purposes, the gain cannot be more than $\frac{5}{3}$ of £7,500 − £6,000. This is $\frac{5}{3}$ of £1,500 = £2,500, thus reducing the taxable gain by £1,000.

WORKING OUT THE TAX BILL

To work out your capital gains tax bill for the tax year, add together all your chargeable gains for the year, and subtract allowable losses on any disposals in the same tax year. This gives you the *net chargeable gain* (or *net allowable loss* if your allowable losses outstrip your chargeable gains).

You won't have to pay CGT on the whole amount of the net chargeable gain, however. The first slice of net chargeable gains in any tax year is free of capital gains tax. For the 1993/94 and 1994/95 tax years, the first £5,800 of net chargeable gains is free of tax. And if your net chargeable gain is bigger than the tax-free slice, you may be able to deduct losses from previous tax years (see p. 312 for more about this).

If there is anything left after all these deductions, it is added to your taxable income for the year and income tax is charged on it:

● if you are a basic-rate taxpayer, you'll pay tax on the gain at 25 per cent, so long as your taxable income and gains together add up to less than £23,700 for the 1993/94 and 1994/95 tax years

● if your taxable income and gains add up to more than £23,700 for the 1993/94 and 1994/95 tax years, you'll pay tax on the excess at 40 per cent

● if your taxable income is less than £3,000 in 1994/95 (£2,500 in 1993/94), then you'll pay tax on your taxable gains at the lower rate of 20 per cent until your combined taxable income and gains exceed this limit when the excess will be taxed at the basic rate.

As well as these general rules, there are special rules for calculating the CGT bill in particular circumstances. For example, with gifts of business assets, you can pass the CGT bill on to the recipient, rather than paying it straightaway (p. 313). There are allowances to reduce the bill when you retire from a business or sell it (p. 319). And trusts have their own tax rates and allowances (see p. 323).

CAPITAL GAINS AND DIVIDENDS

Capital gains are normally taxed as if they were your top slice of income. However, there is a special rule for taxing capital gains where you receive share dividends or unit trust distributions which come with a tax credit of 20 per cent of the gross dividend (see p. 269). These special rules apply if your income before adding the grossed-up share dividends is less than the upper limit of the lower rate band (£2,500 for 1993/94 and £3,000 for 1994/95). In this case, any capital gains are taxed first at 20 per cent until the lower rate band is fully used up, with the balance being taxed at whatever the top rate of tax is.

EXAMPLE

Eleanor Rose earns grossed-up interest of £1,600 in the 1993/94 tax year, receives grossed-up dividends worth £2,500 and has chargeable gains worth £10,000 after deducting all losses and the tax-free slice. She works out the tax bill on the gains as follows.

For the 1993/94 tax year, the first £2,500 of taxable income is taxed at the lower rate of 20 per cent. All of the grossed-up interest of £1,600 falls into this band, leaving £2,500 – £1,600 = £900 of the lower rate band unused. So the first £900 of the capital gains is taxed at the lower rate of 20 per cent.

The £2,500 of grossed-up dividends is taxed at the basic rate of 25 per cent, as is the remaining £10,000 – £900 = £9,100 of capital gains. So the tax due on the £10,000 of capital gains is calculated as follows:

£900 is taxed at the lower rate of 20 per cent	£180
£9,100 is taxed at the basic rate of 25 per cent	£2,275
Total CGT bill on £10,000 of gains	£2,455

HOW TO REDUCE OR DELAY YOUR CAPITAL GAINS TAX BILL

There are a number of ways to reduce or delay a CGT bill:

● make sure you claim all the *allowable expenses* you can (p. 305), and your *indexation allowance* (p. 306)

● take advantage of the special rules for disposing of assets owned before 31 March 1982 (p. 308)

● make sure you use the band of tax-free gains you can make each year (see below) – and that of your husband or wife

● don't overlook *losses* which you can set off against gains (see p. 312)

● pass the tax bill on gifts of business assets and certain other gifts on to the recipient if possible, or pay it in instalments if not (p. 313)

● if you are disposing of a business, take advantage of the special reliefs which can reduce your tax bill – see p. 319.

Minimizing your CGT bills means taking advantage of all these deductions and allowances. It will help in claiming these if you keep a record of the assets you have acquired which may fall into the CGT net, together with relevant receipts (for example, for allowable expenses).

THE TAX-FREE BAND

The first slice of net taxable gains in any tax year is free of capital gains tax. For the 1993/94 and 1994/95 tax years, the first £5,800 of net chargeable gains is free of tax. If you know that you are going to dispose of a number of items, try to space the disposals out over the years to take advantage of the tax-free band. If you dispose of them all in one year, there is only one tax-free band to be used.

A husband and wife each have their own tax-free allowance to set off against their own net chargeable gains only. Since there is no capital gains tax on gifts between husband and wife (p. 110), you can effectively double your tax-free band if you are married by giving assets to your spouse to dispose of.

If you do not use up all the tax-free band in one tax year (because your net taxable gains are too small), you can't carry the unused portion forward to another year.

LOSSES

Losses you make on disposing of assets are deducted from gains before working out the net chargeable gains on which you pay CGT. So if you are facing a CGT bill, one option is to sell something which is showing a loss to set against the gain. If you don't really want to get rid of it, you can buy it back some time later: with shares, this is called 'bed and breakfasting'.

But having too much in the way of losses may not be helpful: you have to deduct losses from gains made in the same tax year, even if this reduces your net gains below the tax-free level. If your losses are greater than your gains, the excess can be carried over to the next tax year and beyond. Losses from previous years can be used to reduce your net taxable gains in any tax year, but you do not have to reduce them below the tax-free band.

EXAMPLE

Hattie Wilson has made taxable gains of £4,500 in the 1993/94 tax year and allowable losses of £7,000 in the same year. She has to set off losses of £4,500 against her gains, even though she would not have to pay CGT on £4,500 of gains which is within the £5,800 tax-free band for that year. She can carry £7,000 − £4,500 = £2,500 of losses forward to future tax years.

In 1994/95, Hattie makes taxable gains of £7,200. She can use part of her losses carried over from the previous year to reduce her net taxable gains to the tax-free limit. So she sets off £1,400 of her losses to bring her net taxable gains for 1994/95 to £7,200 − £1,400 = £5,800. This reduces her CGT bill to zero; it leaves £2,500 − £1,400 = £1,100 of losses to carry forward to 1994/95 and beyond.

A loss made when you dispose of an asset to a connected person

(p. 304) can only be set off against a gain made to a connected person. This applies even if the loss was made when you disposed of the asset for a genuine commercial value.

Losses can never be carried back to an earlier tax year, except in the year when you die. Your executors will be able to carry back these losses to set against gains you made in the three previous tax years.

GIFTS

You can avoid paying CGT on certain assets if you give them away and do not receive the full commercial payment for them. By claiming *hold-over relief,* the gain is passed on to the recipient. Hold-over relief is available only for the following gifts, however:

● business assets (see p. 320)

● heritage property

● gifts to political parties

● gifts which result in an immediate inheritance tax bill (mainly gifts to certain trusts and companies).

If you give the asset away without receiving anything for it, hold-over relief means that your gain is taken to be nil. But for the person you give it to, the initial value of the gift is its market value at the time of the gift, less the gain you made on it. So when the recipient disposes of the asset, their gain will include the gain made while you owned it. Thus the CGT bill is passed on to the recipient.

Hold-over relief could be claimed on almost any gift made before 14 March 1989. If you dispose of something you were given on which hold-over relief was claimed, you will need to take this into account in working out the gain.

EXAMPLE

In December 1988 Lucy Warden gave a brooch valued at £8,500 to her favourite niece, Rebecca. Lucy had bought the brooch herself four years previously at a cost of £4,000. They claimed hold-over relief.

In December 1993 Rebecca sold the brooch for £12,000. Because hold-over relief had been claimed on the gift, her gain (ignoring indexation allowance) was not £12,000 – £8,500 = £3,500. Instead, Lucy's original purchase price of £4,000 is taken as the initial value. So Rebecca's gross gain was £12,000 – £4,000 = £8,000.

There is no point in claiming hold-over relief if your net taxable gains for the year, including the gift, will be within the tax-free band (£5,800 for 1993/94 and 1994/95).

Claiming hold-over relief on a gift to someone else requires both you and the recipient to tell your Tax Inspector within six years of the tax year in which you make the present. The relief is available only if the person receiving the gift is resident or ordinarily resident in the UK. If that person later becomes non-resident without having sold or given away the gift, you could find yourself having to pay a CGT bill.

If you make a gift which doesn't qualify for hold-over relief, you may be able to pay the CGT in ten annual instalments. This applies to gifts of land, a controlling shareholding in a company and minority holdings in unquoted companies. Interest is charged on the unpaid tax, except with agricultural property.

SHARES AND UNIT TRUSTS

Shares and unit trusts are treated in the same way as other assets for capital gains tax. But there are complications where you own more than one batch of shares in a particular company or units in a particular unit trust. If you sell part of a batch bought at different times, how can you decide which shares or units have been sold to calculate the capital gain?

The answer is that shares of the same class in the same company are normally treated as a single asset, even if they were acquired at different times – this is known as pooling. If one share from a pool of ten is disposed of, the gain is taken to be a tenth of the gain of the whole pool. A similar procedure applies to unit trusts.

The gain made on the whole pool is worked out by comparing its value at the time of the sale with the indexed cost of buying the shares or units that went into it. The following example shows how it works in practice.

EXAMPLE

Danny Singh bought 2,000 ordinary shares in Tudor Myles PLC in June 1983 at a cost of £7,000. In December 1988, he added another 1,000 Tudor Myles shares at a cost of £5,000. That gave him a pool of 3,000 such shares. He sold 1,000 of them in July 1993 for £7,500.

Since he has sold a third of his pool of Tudor Myles shares, Danny's taxable gain on the sale will be a third of the taxable gain he would have made if he had sold the lot in July 1993. He works out the taxable gain on the whole pool at July 1993 using the following figures for the RPI on the dates of transactions:

> June 1983 – 84.84
> December 1988 – 110.3
> July 1993 – 140.7

First Danny calculates the indexed cost of the pool at each stage in buying and selling the shares. This involves adding indexation allowance to the value of the pool at each transaction.

The first purchase in July 1982 started off the pool with a value of £7,000. The next transaction was the purchase of a second batch of shares in December 1988. By this date, the value of the first batch had increased by the amount of indexation allowance due since July 1982. This is worked out as follows:

$$£7,000 \times \frac{\text{RPI December 1988} - \text{RPI July 1982}}{\text{RPI July 1982}}$$
$$= £7,000 \times \frac{140.7 - 84.84}{84.84}$$
$$= £7,000 \times 0.300$$
$$= £2,100$$

The indexed cost of the July 1982 shares was therefore £7,000 + £2,100 = £9,100 in December 1988. The second purchase of shares at £5,000 took the indexed value of the pool to £9,100 + £5,000 = £14,100.

No more Tudor Myles shares had been bought by the time of the first sale in July 1993. So the indexation allowance due on the pool since December 1988 was as follows:

$$£14,100 \times \frac{\text{RPI July 1993} - \text{RPI December 1988}}{\text{RPI December 1988}}$$
$$= £14,100 \times \frac{140.7 - 110.3}{110.3}$$
$$= £14,100 \times 0.276$$
$$= £3,892$$

The indexed cost of the pool was therefore £14,100 + £3,892 = £17,992 in July 1993. However, Danny sold only 1,000 of the 3,000 shares in July 1993 – a third of the pool. So the indexed cost of the shares he sold was one-third of £17,992 = £5,997. Since he sold the shares for £7,500, his taxable gain is:

$$£7,500 - £5,997 = £1,503$$

The indexed cost of the remaining 2,000 shares in Danny's pool in July 1993 is:

$$£17,992 - £5,997 = £11,995$$

SHARES BOUGHT ON OR BEFORE 5 APRIL 1982

Shares owned on or before 5 April 1982 and on or after 6 April 1965 are kept in a separate pool, and treated like other assets owned before 1 April 1982:

● the gain is normally based on their value on 31 March 1982 (unless it is to your advantage to base it on their cost when you bought them – see p. 308)

● indexation allowance runs only from March 1982 – so all these shares have the same allowance.

If you have shares in a company bought after 5 April 1982 and some bought on or before that date, any shares you sell are assumed to come from the pool of shares acquired after 5 April 1982 first. Only when all those have been sold do you start to sell shares in the pool acquired on or before 5 April 1982.

EXAMPLE

Suppose in the example above that Danny Singh also had 1,000 Tudor Myles shares he bought in November 1980. These would be held in a separate pool from the 3,000 shares bought after 5 April 1982 (the two batches dealt with above). The 1,000 shares sold in July 1993 would come from the post-April 1982 pool – so the gain would be as worked out above.

If Danny sold another 2,000 of his Tudor Myles shares, those would also come from his post-April 1982 pool. Any further sales would then come from his pre-April 1982 pool: the initial value of the shares from that pool could be their value on 31 March 1982, and indexation would run from that date.

SHARES BOUGHT BEFORE 6 APRIL 1965

Any shares acquired before 6 April 1965 are kept completely separate. They are the last to be sold if you have bought batches since that date – all shares bought after that date are sold first. When you come to sell pre-April 1965 quoted shares, it is 'last in, first out' (the last to be bought are the first to be sold).

However, you can elect for your shares acquired before 6 April 1965 to be added to your pre-April 1982 pool. This is usually to your advantage, as their value on 31 March 1982 is likely to be higher than what you paid for them more than 17 years before.

SELLING SHARES WITHIN TEN DAYS OF BUYING THEM

If you sell shares in a company within ten days of buying shares in the same company, there are special rules for calculating the gain on them. The shares you sell are assumed to be the most recently acquired ones, in the following order:

- any bought on the same day as the sale are the first to be sold

- any others bought in the ten days before the sale are assumed to go next

- only if you sell more than you have bought in the previous ten days do you have to dip into the pool for the rest.

Note that there is no indexation allowance if you sell shares within ten days of buying them.

RIGHTS ISSUES

If you get extra shares through a rights issue or a bonus issue, they are allocated to the relevant pool. So if half your shares are in the post-April 1982 pool and half in a pre-April 1982 pool, the rights issue is split 50:50 between the two pools. Whatever you pay for the rights issue is similarly added to the initial costs of the two pools, with indexation allowance from the time the payment is made.

STOCK DIVIDENDS AND ACCUMULATION UNIT TRUSTS

If you get extra shares instead of dividends, this is known as a stock dividend (or scrip dividend). The value of the new shares is the same as the value for income tax purposes (see p. 271), excluding the value of the tax credit. Indexation allowance runs from the date of the dividend.

Accumulation unit trusts work in a similar way, with extra units instead of a dividend allocated to the appropriate pool.

TAKE-OVERS AND MERGERS

Shareholders of companies which are taken over often get shares in the new parent company in exchange for their old shares. This exchange does not count as a disposal: the new shares are assumed to have been acquired at the cost of the old ones and on the same dates.

If part of the price for the old shares is cash, then this is a disposal. For example, if you get half cash, half shares, you are assumed to have disposed of half the old shares.

PAYMENT BY INSTALMENTS

If you have bought newly issued shares – particularly as part of the privatization of a former state-owned company – you may have paid for the shares in instalments. With a privatization issue, indexation allowance runs from the date that you acquire the shares (even though you hand over some of the money months or even years later).

With other new issues, indexation allowance on the full purchase price runs from when the shares were acquired only if all the instalments were paid within twelve months of acquisition. If instalments are paid more than twelve months after the shares were acquired, indexation allowance on those instalments runs from when the payments were made.

MONTHLY SAVINGS SCHEMES

If you have invested in unit trusts or investment trusts through a monthly savings scheme, working out your gains and losses could be very complicated. You would have to work out the gain and indexation allowance for each instalment you invested in the savings scheme when making a disposal from the pool.

If you want to avoid the detailed calculations, you can opt for a simplified way of working out the initial costs and indexation allowances. This assumes that all twelve monthly instalments for a year are made in the seventh month of the year (the year is the accounting year of the fund). So if you invested £100 a month in a fund with an accounting year that runs from 1 January to 31 December, you could assume that you invested $12 \times £100 = £1,200$ in the seventh month – July.

You may have to add in or deduct extra amounts:

● any distribution or dividend reinvested during the year is added to your investment. So if there was a £50 dividend added to your fund in the above example, you would be treated as having invested £1,200 + £50 = £1,250 in July

● extra savings over and above the regular instalments are included, provided you don't add more than twice the monthly instalment in any month (if bigger than this, it is treated as a separate investment)

● if you increase the monthly instalments, the extra is added to the year's investment so long as the increase is in or before the seventh month (if after, it is added to next year's fund)

● small withdrawals are deducted if they are less than a quarter of the amount invested in the year by regular instalments (if withdrawals exceed this amount, the simplified calculation cannot be used).

To opt for this simplified method, you must write to your tax office within two years of the end of the first tax year after 6 April 1988 in which you dispose of the units or shares and any of the following applies:

● you face a capital gains tax bill

● the disposal proceeds are more than twice the amount of the tax-free band for the year (£5,800 for 1993/94 and 1994/95)

● your other disposals in the year create net losses.

UNIT TRUSTS AND INVESTMENT TRUSTS

The gain on disposing of unit trusts and investment trusts is worked out in the same way as for shares.

If you receive an *equalization* payment with your first distribution from a unit trust, this is a return of part of your original investment. It should therefore be deducted from the acquisition price in working out your gain or loss.

BUSINESS RELIEFS

In addition to the hold-over relief available for gifts of business assets (see p. 313), there are several special reliefs for businesses:

● *roll-over relief* if you replace business assets (overleaf)

● *retirement relief* when you retire from your business (overleaf)

● *reinvestment relief* if you reinvest capital gains in unquoted trading companies (p. 322).

Brief details of each of these reliefs is given below. However, the rules are complex, and you should take professional advice from your accountant if you hope to benefit from them.

REPLACING BUSINESS ASSETS

If you sell, or otherwise dispose of, assets from your business, there could be CGT to pay on any gain you make. But if you replace the certain types of business asset in the three years after the sale or the one year before it, you can claim *roll-over relief* and defer paying CGT. You can also claim the relief if you do not replace the exact asset, but use the proceeds to buy another qualifying business asset.

You usually get the relief by deducting the gain for the old asset from the acquisition cost of the new one. So when you come to sell the new asset, the gain on it has been increased by the gain on the old asset. However, if you replace again, you can claim further roll-over relief, and so on. CGT will not have to be paid (under the current legislation) until you fail to replace the business asset.

Assets which qualify include land or buildings used by the business, goodwill, fixed plant and machinery.

RETIRING FROM YOUR BUSINESS

If you are disposing of a business because you are retiring, a large CGT bill could eat into the proceeds which you hoped to live on in retirement. *Retirement relief* reduces the CGT on a business if you dispose of it when aged 55 or more (less if retiring due to ill-health).

If you dispose of a business you have owned for at least ten years, up to £250,000 of capital gain can be tax-free (£150,000 if the disposal was before 30 November 1993). And only half the gain between £250,000 and £1,000,000 is taxable (between £150,000 and £600,000 for disposals before 30 November 1993). If you have owned the business for less than ten years, the amount on which you can get relief is reduced by 10 per cent for each year less than ten.

The relief applies to business assets, and to shares in a company in which you have at least 5 per cent of the voting rights, provided you have been a full-time director or an employee of the company for the past ten years. A husband and wife can each claim retirement relief if they are eligible – effectively doubling the limits for a married couple who share ownership of a business.

EXAMPLE 1

Doreen Butler, aged 65, started a business 15 years ago and sold it in March 1994. The gain after indexation allowance was £300,000. She is entitled to the maximum retirement relief as she had the business for more than ten years.

She can claim full relief on the first £250,000 plus relief on half the gain between £250,000 and £1,000,000:

£250,000 + 50% of (£300,000 – £250,000)
= £250,000 + 50% of £50,000
= £250,000 + £25,000
= £275,000

Doreen's taxable gain is:

£300,000 – £275,000 = £25,000

The first £5,800 of taxable gains in 1994/95 is free of CGT, so tax is charged on:

£25,000 – £5,800 = £19,200

Doreen's taxable income is £15,000 on which she pays tax at the lower and basic rate only. On the first £23,700 – £15,000 = £8,700 of her gain on the business, the tax will be at the basic rate of 25 per cent (£2,175). On £19,200 – £8,700 = £10,500 of the gain, the rate of tax will be 40 per cent (£4,200). The total tax bill is:

£2,175 + £4,200 = £6,375

EXAMPLE 2

Rupert Foot sells his business in July 1994 when he is 62. He started the business five years before. His gain after indexation allowance is £600,000. He claims retirement relief. As the business has been going for less than ten years, he cannot claim the maximum relief. He can claim 10 per cent of it for each year the business has been owned by him; as this is five years, he can claim 50 per cent. He can get all the relief on 50 per cent of the first £250,000 of his gain, that is, £125,000. He gets half relief on 50 per cent of the rest of his gain up to £600,000, that is, 50 per cent of £600,000 – £250,000 = 50 per cent of £350,000 = £175,000.

The total amount of relief is:

£125,000 + 50% of £175,000
= £125,000 + £87,500
= £212,500

Rupert's taxable gain is:

£600,000 – £212,500 = £387,500

Rupert has already used his tax-free band for 1994/95 for other investments, so the full £387,500 is added to the rest of his income. He pays tax on his income at the higher rate of 40 per cent, so this is the rate of tax he will pay on his capital gain. His tax bill will be:

40% of £387,500 = £155,000

Note that although this relief is called retirement relief, you do not have to retire to claim it. But you must be retiring to claim the relief if you are selling or disposing of your business before the age of 55 because of your ill-health (which is strictly defined). If you wish to claim this relief because of ill-health, you must do so within two years of the end of the tax year in which you dispose of the business.

REINVESTING GAINS IN A SMALL BUSINESS

The tax on capital gains tax for disposals made on or after 30 November 1993 can be deferred by reinvesting the gains in the shares of certain types of small companies. *Reinvestment relief* works rather like roll-over relief (see p. 320): there is no capital gains tax to pay if you reinvest the gain in eligible investments. The gain will be taxed only when you eventually sell the shares in the small company (though you could defer the tax bill again by reinvesting the proceeds in another small company and claiming further reinvestment relief).

You can make the investment any time between one year before the disposal and three years after. Eligible investments are ordinary shares in unquoted trading companies or in the holding company of a trading group. Investments in companies holding more than half their chargeable assets as land, farming companies, subsidiaries and certain financial concerns are excluded from the relief. The deferred gain will be taxed only if you emigrate, sell the shares without replacing them with other qualifying shares, or the company ceases to be a qualifying one.

Reinvestment relief was introduced in the March 1993 Budget and applied to disposals after 15 March 1993. However, until the November 1993 Budget, it could be claimed only on gains from selling your own business. To get reinvestment relief on disposals before 30 November 1993, the following conditions had to be met:

● you sold shares in a qualifying unquoted trading company, broadly defined in the same way as for the Enterprise Investment Scheme (see p. 277)

● you had to have been a full-time working director or employee in a managerial or technical capacity with the company

● for at least one year you had owned more than 5 per cent of the shares in the company

● you reinvested in a qualifying unquoted trading company so that you own at least 5 per cent of its shares at any time between one year before selling the original shares and three years after.

TRUSTS

Where assets are held in trust (see p. 337), the trustees are liable for capital gains tax on disposals of the assets in the trust, in much the same way as individuals. However, the slice of net taxable gains which is free of capital gains tax in any tax year is half the figure which applies to individuals. So for the 1993/94 and 1994/95 tax years, the first £2,900 of net chargeable gains is free of tax for a trust.

The rate of capital gains tax for trustees is equivalent to the basic rate of income tax (25 per cent for 1993/94 and 1994/95). For a discretionary trust (including accumulation trusts), there is a single flat rate of tax on gains, of 35 per cent for the 1993/94 and 1994/95 tax years.

Note that if you are the beneficiary of a trust which is not resident in the UK, or is also resident in another country (a *dual resident trust*), you may be liable to capital gains tax on anything you receive from the trust – whether it be cash, a loan or an asset. And if you have set up a trust from which you or your spouse may benefit, any chargeable gains made by the trust will be taxed as if they were yours. The same applies if you have set up or given money to a non-resident trust after 18 March 1991.

Trusts are one of the most complex areas of the law and you should always seek professional advice from a solicitor or accountant if you are involved in trusts.

WHAT TO PUT IN YOUR TAX RETURN

Information about capital gains should be entered on your Tax Return under *Capital gains* on page 10 of Forms 11P and 11, page 3 of Form P1. For the Tax Return 1994/95, for example, this refers to gains made in the year ending on 5 April 1994.

However, you don't need to give detailed information about gains and losses for the 1993/94 tax year if both the following conditions are met:

● your gains on taxable assets for the year were within the tax-free limit of £5,800

● the total value of the chargeable assets disposed of for the year was less than £11,600.

If both these conditions apply, tick the box at the top of the *Capital gains* section on Forms 11P and 11. No further information is required.

Form 11P

Complete this section if you have sold or given away any assets which are subject to capital gains tax, or in any	**Capital gains – year to 5 April 1994**	
	Tick here if the total value of any assets you have disposed of in 1993-94 was £11,600 or less and your chargeable gains were £5,800 or less. You do not then need to give any further details.	☐

With Form P1, if both the above conditions apply, you do not need to enter anything. No further details are then needed in this section.

If your assets or gains exceed the limits above, you will have to give details of each taxable asset disposed of on Forms 11P and 11, under *Chargeable assets disposed of*.

Form 11P

liable, see notes 49 and 50. See note 50 for reliefs.	**Chargeable assets disposed of** Describe the asset and give the amount of chargeable gain		
See notes 51 and 52 for information about calculating capital gains.		£	
	Total chargeable gains (before annual exemption)	£	

Give details of each asset and the amount of the taxable gain or allowable loss on it. Write 'gain' or 'loss', whichever is appropriate. Put the total chargeable gain or loss in the final column.

There is a calculator to work out the gain or loss on page 20 of the booklet that comes with the Tax Return (make photocopies if more than one asset is involved).

You might have made a chargeable gain in 1993/94 without having disposed of an asset. For example, if you became non-resident in the UK after receiving a gift on which hold-over relief had been claimed (see p. 313). Give the amount of such gains under *Chargeable gains from other sources* on Forms 11P and 11, together with the date the gain became chargeable, and the reason why it came into the tax net.

Form 11P

See note 53.

Chargeable gains from other sources
Complete this item if you have made gains which became subject to tax in 1993-94 but are not gains from the disposal of chargeable assets in 1993-94 or gains dealt with in the next two sections, "If you benefit from a non-resident or dual resident settlement" and, "If you are the settlor of a settlement.".

Date gains became subject to tax   /   /19

Reason gains became subject to tax

Gains accruing in 1993-94   £

If you are the beneficiary of a non-resident or dual resident trust (see p. 323), you may be liable to capital gains tax on anything you receive from the trust if it is not subject to income tax. Give details of the value of any cash, a loan or assets received under *If you benefit from a non-resident or dual resident settlement* on Forms 11P and 11. Enter the name of the trust and the Inland Revenue's file reference for the trust if you know it.

Form 11P

See note 54.

If you benefit from a non-resident or dual resident settlement
Name of the settlement

Inland Revenue reference

Value of any cash payment, loan, asset or other benefit received from the settlement not subject to income tax.   £

Date received   /   /19

If you have set up a trust from which you or your spouse may benefit, you must give details of any chargeable gains made by the trust under *If you are the settlor of a settlement* on Forms 11P and 11. The same applies if you have set up or given money to a non-resident or dual resident trust after 18 March 1991. Enter the name of the trust and the Inland Revenue's file reference for the trust if you know it.

Form 11P

See note 54.

If you are the settlor of a settlement
Name of settlement

Inland Revenue reference

Amount of any chargeable gains by reference to which you, as settlor, are chargeable.

£

TREASURE TROVE CLUE No. 11

The higher rate of income tax, as a percentage (2 digits).

32 • INHERITANCE TAX

Inheritance tax is the latest in a line of three taxes designed to tax wealth passed on at death (or shortly before). The first, estate duty, started in 1894; in 1974 it was succeeded by capital transfer tax (CTT), which also covered wealth passed on during your lifetime. Since 18 March 1986 CTT has been replaced by inheritance tax: this largely ignores gifts made in your lifetime, unless they are made in the seven years before death.

Nonetheless there is much that you can do in your lifetime to reduce the inheritance tax bill that will be due on your death. Tax is payable on quite modest estates: if you leave just £175,000 (not improbable for anyone owning a home in London or the south-east), there could be £10,000 to pay in inheritance tax or more if you've made taxable gifts in the seven years before your death.

A little planning now can ensure that as much as possible of your worldly wealth goes to your heirs and as little as possible to the taxman.

WHAT YOU PAY TAX ON

Inheritance tax is payable on the value of what you leave on death and anything you have given away in the previous seven years (these are called *transfers of value* by the taxman). It may also be due on gifts made outside this seven-year zone to certain types of trust or to a company. But many gifts and bequests are free of inheritance tax: for example, gifts to your husband or wife are always tax-free, whether made in your lifetime or on death (for a full list of tax-free gifts, see p. 328).

Because inheritance tax may have to be paid on a gift if you die within seven years of making it, lifetime gifts are often described as *Potentially Exempt Transfers (PETs)*: they are potentially free of inheritance tax but you must survive for seven years after they are made for the tax to be avoided.

THE TAX RATES

For deaths on or after 10 March 1992, inheritance tax is payable at the nil rate (0 per cent) if taxable gifts total £150,000 or less. If total taxable gifts exceed £150,000, inheritance tax is payable at 40 per cent on the excess.

So if taxable gifts total £175,000, tax is payable on the excess over £150,000: £175,000 – £150,000 = £25,000. This gives a tax bill of 40 per cent of £25,000, that is £10,000.

TAPERING RELIEF

The inheritance tax payabℓe on gifts made between three and seven years before your death is reduced on the following scale (this is known as *tapering relief*):

YEARS BETWEEN GIFT AND DEATH	% OF INHERITANCE TAX PAYABLE
0 – 3	100%
3 – 4	80%
4 – 5	60%
5 – 6	40%
6 – 7	20%

GIFTS FREE OF INHERITANCE TAX

There are three different types of gift which are free of inheritance tax:

● gifts that are always free of inheritance tax, whether made in life or on death

● gifts that are free of inheritance tax on death only

● gifts that are free of inheritance tax only if made during your lifetime.

GIFTS THAT ARE ALWAYS FREE OF INHERITANCE TAX

There is no inheritance tax to pay on gifts *between husband and wife*, whether made on death or during their lifetime. This applies however large the gift and even if the couple are legally separated. But gifts totalling more than £55,000 from one partner domiciled in the UK (p. 347) to a partner who is not domiciled in the UK are taxable.

This is by far the most important category of gift which is free of inheritance tax, and the one most likely to be available to readers of this Guide. But the following gifts which can be loosely classed as 'good works' are also free of inheritance tax:

- gifts to UK charities

- gifts to certain national institutions such as the National Trust, the National Gallery, the British Museum (and their Scottish, Welsh and Northern Irish equivalents)

- gifts for the public benefit to non-profit-making concerns like local museums

- gifts of certain types of heritage property such as paintings, archives or historic buildings

- gifts of land in the UK to registered housing associations

- gifts of shares in a company into a trust for the benefit of most or all of the employees which will control the company.

Quaintly, the politicians who drew up the rules for inheritance tax believed that their own parties were also worthy of charity. Thus gifts to political parties (or at least established ones) are also tax-free.

GIFTS THAT ARE FREE OF INHERITANCE TAX ON DEATH ONLY

There is no inheritance tax to pay on lump sums paid out on your death by a pension scheme provided that the trustees of the scheme have discretion about who gets the money. Also free of inheritance tax is the estate of anyone killed on active military service in war or whose death was hastened by such service.

GIFTS THAT ARE FREE OF INHERITANCE TAX IN
LIFETIME ONLY

Anything given away more than seven years before your death is free of inheritance tax unless there are strings attached to the gift (see p. 344) or it is to certain types of trust (p. 338). And many routine gifts made in your lifetime are free of inheritance tax even if you die within seven years of making them. Although there are limits on the size of these tax-free gifts, they can add up over the years and allow you to give away tens of thousands of pounds free of inheritance tax during the seven-year period before death. (Note, however, that gifts in your lifetime, other than cash, may mean a capital gains tax bill – see p. 301.)

For example, gifts worth up to £250 to any number of people in any one tax year are free of inheritance tax. This *small gifts exemption* applies to the total that you give each person in the year. So if you give someone £500, you can't claim the exemption on the first £250 – the whole £500 will be taxable.

Regular *gifts made out of your normal income* are also free of inheritance tax. The gifts must come out of your usual after-tax income and not from your capital: after paying for the gifts, you should have enough income left to maintain your normal standard of living. Even if you have made only one payment, it can be tax-free provided that there is evidence that there will be further payments (for example, a covenant or letter of intent). Paying the premiums on a life insurance policy which will pay out to someone else on your death is usually a tax-free gift under this heading (it can also provide some cash to pay any tax which is due on taxable bequests you leave on death).

Gifts on marriage to a bride or groom are exempt from inheritance tax, within limits:

● £5,000 if you are a parent of the bride or groom (that is, £10,000 in all if both parents make such gifts)

● £2,500 if you are a grandparent or remoter relative of the bride or groom

● £2,500 if you are either the bride or groom yourself (once you're married, of course, all such gifts are free of inheritance tax)

● £1,000 for anyone else.

The gift must be made 'in consideration of marriage', so it should be made before the great day. If the marriage is called off, the gift becomes taxable.

There are other gifts which aren't really gifts at all and are therefore free of inheritance tax. For example, if you hand money over to your divorced spouse under a Court Order, there will be no tax to pay on the gift. Similarly money used for the *maintenance of your family* in the manner to which they've become accustomed is not taxable: this exemption covers spending on your spouse, certain dependent relatives and children under 18 or still in full-time education. The children can be yours, step-children, adopted children or any other children in your care.

After all these tax-free gifts have been made, you can make further gifts worth up to £3,000 in total each year free of inheritance tax. If you don't use the whole £3,000 *annual exemption* in one year, you can carry forward the unused part to the next tax year only. But note that you can't use the annual exemption to top up the small gifts exemption:

if you give someone more than £250 in a year, all of it must come off the annual exemption if it is to be free of inheritance tax.

NIL-RATE BAND

Even if a gift or bequest is taxable, the rate of tax on the first slice of taxable transfers is nil per cent, so transfers within this nil-rate band are effectively free of inheritance tax. For deaths on or after 10 March 1992, taxable gifts of £150,000 or less are taxable at the nil rate. So if you give away £150,000 in taxable gifts, and survive for seven years, you can then give away another £150,000 without incurring tax since the first £150,000 drops out of the reckoning.

EXAMPLE

Hugh James wants to give away as much as possible free of inheritance tax before he dies. He is married and he and his wife Queenie have more than enough income to live on for the foreseeable future.

Anything Hugh gives to Queenie is free of inheritance tax. And both Hugh and Queenie are entitled to make the tax-free gifts outlined above. So Hugh gives half his spare wealth to Queenie so that they can each make the maximum of tax-free gifts.

First, Hugh and Queenie each make £250 gifts every year to all of their ten grandchildren – a total of £5,000 a year free of inheritance tax as small gifts. Both also divide £3,000 among each of their three children under the annual exemption – another £6,000 a year free of tax.

Hugh and Queenie can afford to pay the premiums on insurance policies on their own lives out of their normal income. So both take out three policies, one in favour of each of their three children. The total premiums come to £120 a month each and will be tax-free as gifts made out of their normal income (when they die, the money from the insurance policies will be paid straight to the children without being taxable).

Overall, Hugh and Queenie manage to give away almost £14,000 a year free of inheritance tax. This is nearly £100,000 in a seven-year period, and even if they die within seven years of starting this programme of gifts there will be no inheritance tax to pay on them. If they want to give away more than this, they could also make gifts of £150,000 each to take advantage of the nil-rate band, repeating this every seven years when the last £150,000 gift drops out of the reckoning.

HOW THE TAX BILL IS WORKED OUT

In working out the amount of tax due on your estate and taxable lifetime gifts, the taxman starts with the earliest taxable gifts first, which are therefore taxed at the lowest rates. The tax on a lifetime gift is charged on its value at the time of the gift. But the tax rates to be used are those which apply at the date of your death, not when the gifts were made.

Use the following steps to calculate an inheritance tax bill:

STEP 1 Work out the tax due on the first taxable gift.

STEP 2 Then add the second gift to the first gift and work out the tax due on the cumulative total. Subtract the tax due on the first gift from the tax due on the cumulative total to find the tax due on the second gift.

STEP 3 Add the third gift to the cumulative total so far and work out the tax due on this new cumulative total. Subtract the tax due on the previous gifts from the tax due on the new cumulative total to find the inheritance tax due on the third gift.

STEP 4 Repeat step 3 for all taxable gifts made before death to find the tax due on each.

STEP 5 Finally, add the taxable value of your estate to the cumulative total of your taxable lifetime gifts and work out the inheritance tax due on what you leave on death.

STEP 6 If any of the tax due is on a lifetime gift made between three and seven years before your death, the amount payable will be reduced by tapering relief (see the scale on p. 328).

EXAMPLE

Every year Eileen Dover gives her grandchildren the maximum possible in tax-free gifts, always taking care to use up the £3,000 annual exemption in full. As part of a programme of larger gifts, she gives her three children taxable gifts of £80,000 each: to her son Ben in September 1989, her daughter Angela in April 1991 and her daughter Ruth in December 1993. Eileen dies in June 1994, leaving an estate valued at £160,000.

The inheritance tax bill due on Eileen's death is worked out as follows (using the tax rates in force in 1994/95):

STEP 1 All the taxable gifts were made in the seven years before Eileen's death and are therefore subject to inheritance tax. The first

£80,000 gift to Ben is taxed at the nil rate – that is, no tax to pay.

STEP 2   The second taxable gift of £80,000 to Angela is added to the £80,000 gift to Ben to produce a cumulative total of £160,000. The tax due on this £160,000 is worked out as follows:

£150,000 is taxed at the nil rate	£0
The remaining £10,000 is taxed at 40%	£4,000
TOTAL TAX	£4,000

Since no tax was due on the first gift, all £4,000 of this total is due on the gift to Angela.

STEP 3   The gift of £80,000 to Ruth is added to the cumulative total of £160,000 to produce a new total of £240,000. The tax due on this new cumulative total is calculated as follows:

£150,000 is taxed at the nil rate	£0
The remaining £90,000 is taxed at 40%	£36,000
TOTAL TAX	£36,000

£4,000 of this total tax was due on the gift to Angela, so the tax due on Ruth's gift is £36,000 – £4,000 = £32,000.

STEP 4   There are no other taxable gifts made before Eileen's death, so we can move straight to the next step.

STEP 5   The taxable value of Eileen's estate of £160,000 is added to the cumulative total of £240,000 to produce a total of £400,000. The inheritance tax due on this is worked out as follows:

£150,000 is taxed at the nil rate	£0
The remaining £250,000 is taxed at 40%	£100,000
TOTAL TAX	£100,000

£36,000 of this total tax was due on the lifetime gifts, so the tax due on Eileen's estate would be £100,000 – £36,000 = £64,000.

STEP 6   The tax bills due on gifts between three and seven years before death are reduced by tapering relief, using the scale on p. 328. The gift to Ben was made five years before Eileen's death but as no tax is due on it no reduction is necessary. The gift to Angela was made between three and four years before death, so only 80 per cent of the £4,000 tax bill is payable – £3,200 in all. The gift to Ruth was made within three years of Eileen's death and so all the £32,000 tax bill is payable (as is the £64,000 on Eileen's estate).

The tax bills on the lifetime gifts must be paid by the children who got them. So, although Eileen gave £80,000 to each of her three children, they ended up with different amounts once the tax was paid. Ben would have got and kept £80,000; Angela would have £76,800 after paying the £3,200 inheritance tax bill; Ruth would have just £48,000 after paying inheritance tax of £32,000.

If Eileen had lived for at least seven years after making the last gift to Ruth, no inheritance tax would have been payable on her gifts. If she wanted her children to get and keep all £80,000 each, she could have taken out special life insurance policies designed to cover the tax bills on her death within seven years of making the gifts.

SPECIAL INHERITANCE TAX RULES

Applying the rules above to gifts and legacies of money is fairly straightforward but special rules are needed to value non-cash goods. And there are special tax reliefs to help those who own shares, small businesses and farms (though these are not normally available for businesses which consist mainly of dealing in stocks and shares, land and buildings or investments).

VALUABLES

Bequests of valuables such as antiques, jewellery, cars, boats, heirlooms and the like – and gifts within seven years of your death – will all fall into the inheritance tax net. The rule for valuing such gifts is that their value is the amount by which your wealth (or estate) is reduced by the gift: in most cases, this will be the market value of the item in question.

But the value may be somewhat higher if the item is part of a set or group whose collective value is greater than the sum of its parts. For example, a set of antique silver cutlery may be worth more than the value of the individual pieces. If a single piece worth, say, £500 is given away, the value of the remaining pieces may fall by more than £500. It is the fall in value of the remainder which is the value of the gift for inheritance tax purposes, not the £500 the single piece would fetch at auction.

HOUSES AND LAND

The value of your home and any other real estate that you own is the market value at the date of your death or the gift. This value must be agreed with the District Valuer (an employee of the Inland Revenue).

LISTED SHARES

For stocks and shares listed on the Stock Exchange, the value is found from the prices recorded in the *Official Daily List* (which can be supplied by a stockbroker or bank) on the date of the gift or bequest. If the Stock Exchange was closed, you can choose between the prices on the last working day before and the first working day after the transfer. The value for inheritance tax purposes is the lower selling price, plus a quarter of the difference between the selling price and the (higher) buying price: this is known as the 'quarter-up rule'.

In the rare event that gift or bequest of shares is a controlling interest in a listed company, *business relief* will be available for gifts made on or after 10 March 1992, and inheritance tax bills which arise out of deaths on or after that date. This will reduce the value of the shares by 50 per cent.

SHARES ON THE UNLISTED SECURITIES MARKET (USM)

Gifts or bequests of shares quoted on the Unlisted Securities Market (USM) will be eligible for *business relief* if passed on or given away on or after 10 March 1992. The value of a holding of 25 per cent of the shares or less will be halved for inheritance tax purposes. But if the holding is more than 25 per cent of the shares, no inheritance tax will be due on them.

For gifts and bequests of USM shares made before 10 March 1992, the value is halved only if the holding is a controlling interest in the company – that is more than 50 per cent of the shares.

USM shares are valued in the same way as listed shares.

UNIT TRUSTS

Authorized unit trusts are valued at the price you could sell them for (that is, the bid price) on the day of transfer or the most recent date such prices were quoted before then.

UNQUOTED SHARES

Gifts or bequests of unquoted shares or shares quoted on the Over the Counter (OTC) markets are also eligible for *business relief*. Unless the holding is more than 25 per cent of the shares, their value will be halved for inheritance tax purposes. But if the holding is more than 25 per cent of the shares, no inheritance tax will be due on them.

The value of a gift or bequest of unquoted shares or shares quoted on the Over the Counter (OTC) markets depends on the size and importance of the holding. If the holding is a controlling interest (for example, 55 per cent of the voting shares), they might be valued as a proportion of the value of the assets the company owns. A minority holding (30 per cent, say) might be valued using the price/earnings ratio (or even, if the shares are quoted on the OTC, related to their market prices). Whatever the solution, it must be agreed with the Share Valuation Division of the Inland Revenue: this cannot be negotiated in advance and reaching agreement can be a lengthy business.

The valuation becomes more complicated still if the gift or bequest turns a majority shareholding into a minority one. Since the value of a transfer is measured by the loss to the giver rather than the gain of the receiver, the value of such a share transfer is more than the value of the shares alone: the giver loses not only the shares but also control of the company. Professional advice from an accountant or solicitor is essential in these circumstances.

YOUR OWN BUSINESS OR FARM

If you own or have an interest in a small business or a farm, it is essential to seek professional advice on inheritance tax, since there are substantial concessions which can reduce or eliminate the tax:

● *business relief* means that there will be no inheritance tax to pay on business assets such as goodwill, land, buildings, plant, stock, patents and the like (reduced by any debts incurred in the business)

● if the business is a company, you can also get *business relief* on transfers of the shares of up to 100 per cent of the tax

● *agricultural relief* can mean no inheritance tax on the agricultural value of owner-occupied farmlands and farm tenancies (including cottages, farm buildings and farm houses). There are also reliefs for landowners who let farmland.

RELATED PROPERTY

In working out the value of a bequest or gift, the taxman treats as yours property which he reckons is related to yours. Suppose, for example, you own 30 per cent of the shares in a company and your spouse owns another 30 per cent. The taxman will value your 30 per cent as worth half the value of a 60 per cent controlling interest, which is generally higher than the value of a 30 per cent minority interest. Property will be treated as related if it belongs to your spouse or if it has been owned at any time in the previous five years by a charity, political party or national institution to which you or your spouse gave it.

TRUSTS

Trusts (sometimes called settlements) are independent legal bodies set up to look after money or other property such as shares or a home. They do so on behalf of *beneficiaries,* who may be a single individual (such as your daughter) or a class of individuals (such as your children, or unmarried women over 18 in the parish of Deptford). The person or people who put the assets into trust are called *settlors*: once in the trust, the property is administered on behalf of the beneficiaries by *trustees*.

There are several types of trust, including:

● *trusts with an interest in possession:* with this type of trust someone has the right to the income from it or to use property it owns (for example, to live in a house belonging to it)

● *discretionary trusts:* the trustees have discretion about what to pay out, the amount to pay out and which of the possible beneficiaries should receive the pay-out

● *accumulation and maintenance trusts:* a special type of discretionary trust designed to provide for children and grandchildren under 25. The beneficiaries must be entitled to the capital in the trust or to the income from it (that is, to an interest in possession) on or before their 25th birthday.

The advantages of setting up a trust can be purely administrative. It is a way of providing for someone after your death or while you are unable to look after them yourself. Trustees control the property in the trust but they must do so in accordance with the wishes of the settlor, which are usually set out in the document setting up the trust known as a *trust deed.* Trustees are governed by Acts of Parliament which aim to protect the interests of beneficiaries from unscrupulous behaviour. For example, trustees must invest in specified low-risk investments like government securities and shares in certain 'blue chip' companies unless the trust deed gives them wider powers (most modern trust deeds generally give trustees these powers).

But there are also tax advantages in using trusts to hold family property. The property can be used for the benefit of the family but, since no one ever owns it, it is never passed on by gift or bequest. This doesn't mean that inheritance tax is never paid: there are special rules to tax trusts because of this very fact. But the amount of inheritance tax is likely to be much less with trusts than with individual ownership.

However, trusts are one of the most complex areas of the law and professional advice should always be sought from a solicitor or accountant if you think that trusts might suit your needs. What follows is no more than a summary of the tax position to show the advantages of using trusts and outline the professional advice you might get.

GIFTS TO TRUSTS

If you make a gift to a trust, you may have to pay inheritance tax on the gift at the time you make it, even if it is more than seven years before you die. But no inheritance tax is payable at the time of gifts to the following types of trust:

- an accumulation and maintenance trust

- a trust for disabled people

- a trust with an interest in possession provided the gift was made on or after 17 March 1987.

If the gift is to one of these types of trust, there will be an inheritance tax bill only if you die within seven years of making the gift (worked out in the same way as for any other gift).

If you make a gift to any other sort of trust, there is an immediate inheritance tax bill. The gift is added to the value of other such gifts made within the previous seven years and tax is charged on the cumulative total at half the normal rate. If you survive for another seven years, then no further inheritance tax is due but if you die within seven years or leave property to a trust on your death, then the gifts to trusts are included in the reckoning for inheritance tax on your death. The full rate of tax is payable (reduced by tapering relief if made between three and seven years of death): any tax already paid on the gift (including any capital transfer tax paid before inheritance tax was introduced) is deducted from the tax due on death. But if the tax paid when the gift was made is greater than that due on death there is no refund of the excess.

PROPERTY HELD BY TRUSTS

The trustees must pay income tax on the income of the trust (see p. 272) and capital gains tax if chargeable gains arise (see p. 323). The inheritance tax treatment of property held by trusts depends on the type of trust:

● *trusts with an interest in possession:* the property owned by the trust is treated as the property of the person who has the interest in possession. If he or she dies or gives away the right within seven years of death, inheritance tax is due as if it was their property (but the trustees pay the bill, not the beneficiary's estate)

● *discretionary trusts:* there are complicated rules designed to collect inheritance tax from the trustees as if the property belonged to a single individual and was passed on at death once every 30 years

● *accumulation and maintenance trusts:* no inheritance tax is payable on the property until it is disposed of by the beneficiary.

PAYMENT OF INHERITANCE TAX

In most cases inheritance tax will have to be paid because of the death of someone whose taxable estate and taxable gifts during the previous seven years exceed the nil-rate band. This could create two sets of tax bills: on the executors or personal representatives of the dead person for the tax due on the estate; and on people who got taxable gifts from the dead person during the seven years before their death on which tax is now due.

Inheritance tax is due six months after the end of the month in which the death happened. In practice, it can often take longer for the executors to sort out the will and tidy up the dead person's affairs. As part of the process of seeking probate, they must submit an Inland Revenue account, listing the value of the dead person's property (including property owned jointly with anybody else) and the amounts of any debts. Probate will not be granted until the tax has been paid. Interest is charged if the tax is paid after the six-month deadline (see below).

INTEREST ON UNPAID TAX

Interest is charged on inheritance tax which is paid late, from the time that the tax was due. Likewise, if you pay too much inheritance tax, you will get interest on the over-payment from the Inland Revenue. The rate is currently 4 per cent per annum.

PAYMENT BY INSTALMENTS

With certain gifts and bequests, inheritance tax can be paid in ten equal yearly instalments rather than as a lump sum. This option is allowed only with bequests on death and lifetime gifts where the recipient still owns the property when the death occurs. Interest may be due on the instalments in some cases but this may be preferable to having to find the tax in one go (if it would mean selling the family home, for example).

Two groups of assets qualify for payment of tax by instalments:

● *land and property* – but interest from the date the tax was due is payable except with business property and agricultural land

● *a business, including certain holdings of unquoted shares* – with shares, no interest is payable on the deferred tax unless the instalments are paid late.

If you want to pay in instalments, tell the taxman before the normal payment date for the tax. The first instalment is due on the date the whole tax would have been payable.

If you take out a loan to pay inheritance tax before probate is granted, you can get tax relief on the interest on it for up to twelve months.

LOSSES ON INVESTMENTS OR LAND

There are special rules which can reduce the inheritance tax bill on inherited investments and land which fall in value after being passed on.

The rules for investments apply to quoted shares (including those quoted on the USM) and authorized unit trusts which fall in value or become worthless in the year after death:

● if sold during this period for less than they were worth on death, the sale price can be used to value them for inheritance tax purposes instead of their value on death

● if cancelled without replacement, they are treated as having been sold immediately before the date of cancellation for the nominal sum of £1

● if suspended and remaining suspended a year after the death, their value at the first anniversary can be used for inheritance tax purposes instead of their value on death.

When this relief is claimed, however, all such investments sold in the year after death are revalued in this way. So if some shares or unit trusts have been sold for more than they were worth on death, this would offset any loss made on other shares or unit trusts.

EXAMPLE

Eleanor Tomkins is acting as executor of her father's estate, which included quoted shares and unit trusts worth £50,000 on his death. During the year after her father's death, she sells all the shares and unit trusts to distribute the proceeds according to his wishes. Some go for less than they were worth on her father's death – £15,000 less. The rest go for £5,000 more. For inheritance tax purposes, the value of the shares left on death is reduced by £10,000: £15,000 – £5,000. So the value of the shares is £50,000 – £10,000 = £40,000.

Similar rules apply to sales of land or buildings within four years of the death. If the sale is for less than the value of the land or buildings on death, the inheritance tax bill can be worked out on the actual sale proceeds instead. Again, if this relief is claimed, all land or property sold during the four-year period is revalued for inheritance tax purposes at what it was sold for, rather than what it was worth on death.

QUICK SUCCESSION RELIEF

Inheritance tax is largely designed to tax wealth when it changes hands on death. Normally this would happen once a generation but family fortunes could be cruelly hit if two deaths in quick succession meant two inheritance tax bills in a few years. Quick succession relief helps reduce the tax impact of deaths within five years of each other.

If you die within a year of receiving a gift on which inheritance tax has been paid, the inheritance tax due on your estate is reduced by a fraction of the tax previously paid. The fraction is calculated as follows:

$$\frac{\text{Value of gift at the time of first transfer}}{\text{Value of gift at transfer} + \text{tax paid on first transfer}}$$

If you die between one and five years after receiving the gift, the fraction is reduced by 20 per cent for each complete year since the first transfer.

EXAMPLE

Larry Morris inherited £40,000 from his parents, a legacy on which inheritance tax of £10,000 had been paid. Three and a half years later Larry dies leaving an estate on which £20,000 inheritance tax is payable.

Because his death is within five years of receiving the legacy from his parents, quick succession relief reduces the inheritance tax bill on Larry's estate. The fraction of the previous tax bill which can be taken into account is worked out as follows:

$$\frac{£40,000}{£40,000 + £10,000} = \frac{£40,000}{£50,000} = \frac{4}{5}$$

This, expressed as a decimal, is 0.8, which is reduced by 20 per cent for each complete year that Larry received the legacy before his death. Since he received the legacy three and a half years before his death, the 0.8 is reduced by 3×20 per cent = 60 per cent. Sixty per cent of 0.8 is 0.48. Thus the tax on Larry's estate is reduced by 0.48 of the tax due on the legacy when he got it (£10,000) – that is, £4,800. That means a tax bill of £20,000 – £4,800 = £15,200.

PLANNING FOR INHERITANCE TAX

There is much that you can do to reduce the inheritance tax bill on your estate by making gifts which are free of tax or making taxable gifts more than seven years before your death. But it's worth bearing in mind that your heirs will be better off as a result of the bequests and legacies you make, even if inheritance tax is due on them. Don't give away so much that you or your spouse are left impoverished in old age, merely to cheat the taxman of every last penny of tax. Allow a good margin in deciding how much to keep for yourself – even modest rates of inflation can make generous provision look inadequate after a few years. And remember that many people enjoy considerably more than three score years and ten: it is not unusual for retirement to last 25 years or more.

If you do have some resources to spare, make as full use as possible of the tax-free small gifts, gifts on marriage and the like. And make sure that your spouse has enough to make similar gifts free of inheritance tax.

If you want to make larger gifts, the earlier you make them the better. If you live for seven years after making the gifts, there is no inheritance tax to pay. Even if you die within seven years of making a gift, the inheritance tax will be reduced if the gift is made more than three years before your death.

Again, a married couple can share their wealth and each make gifts; the inheritance tax on each partner's estate depends only on what they own or have given away. And if each partner has a share of the family wealth on death, each is entitled to £150,000 taxable at the nil rate. In practice, it may not be easy to split your worldly goods and give them away during your lifetime: it may make more sense to pass all or most of them on to the survivor of the two of you, so that he or she has enough to live on. But the principle of 'estate-splitting' is a basic strategy to be followed where possible.

'Estate-freezing' is another technique for reducing inheritance tax by freezing the value of some of your wealth now and allowing any increase in value to go to someone else. Trusts offer one way of doing this, as assets are taken out of your possession and used for the benefit of someone else. But the tax treatment of trusts is complex (p. 337), so don't attempt this without professional advice.

YOUR HOME

If your home is jointly owned with someone under a *joint tenancy,* it automatically goes to the survivor when one of you dies. There will be no inheritance tax to pay if the joint tenant is your spouse, since bequests to a husband or wife are tax-free. With a joint tenancy between two people who are not married to each other (a mother and daughter, say), the half of the tenancy which is transferred to the other person on death counts as a taxable gift.

If your home is jointly owned with someone else as a *tenancy in common,* you can bequeath your share to anyone you please (with a liability to inheritance tax if the share is not bequeathed to a spouse). You could bequeath a half of your half-share to your spouse and the other half to the next generation. This would reduce the size of your spouse's estate but leave him or her in control of the home.

One thing which won't save tax is to bequeath your home to your children on condition that your spouse can continue to live in it. This counts as a gift with reservation of benefit (see overleaf), and the home will be treated as your spouse's.

There are other ways of reducing the inheritance tax due on a home. But unless you've got a particular reason to want it to pass intact to the next generation (it's the family seat, say), it may be best to avoid doing anything which could jeopardize your future life in it and leave your heirs to pay the tax.

LIFE INSURANCE

If you want to make sure that there is enough money to pay an inheritance tax bill on a large gift (for example, a home or business), you can take out a *term* life insurance policy which pays out if you die within seven years of making the gift. And if you plan to leave a large asset on death, *whole life* insurance policies pay out whenever you die, again providing cash to pay the inheritance tax.

When the insurance policy pays out, the money will be added to your estate and inheritance tax charged on it (there will also be a delay before your heirs can get their hands on it until probate is granted). But if the policy is written in trust to the person you want to have the money, the proceeds will be paid directly to that person on your death and be free of inheritance tax. The premiums for a policy written in trust count as gifts, but will be free of inheritance tax if the policy is for your spouse. And if you pay the premiums out of your normal spending, they will be tax-free, whoever is to benefit (p. 330).

ASSOCIATED OPERATIONS

You might think that there are some rather obvious wheezes to get round the inheritance tax rules and avoid tax. For example, you might give tax-free gifts of £250 to several friends, taking advantage of the small gifts exemption, on condition that they pass the money on to someone else (your adult child, say). But there are provisions for the taxman to 'see through' such associated operations and treat them as direct gifts.

GIFTS WITH STRINGS ATTACHED

Another tempting wheeze might be to give something away but reserve the right to use it for yourself. For example, you might think about giving your home to a child on condition that you can go on living in it until your death. This would, however, count as a *gift with reservation of benefit*. In this case, the gift would not be recognised for inheritance tax purposes and its value would be added to your estate when you died.

This could apply even if there was no formal agreement that you go on living in the home. If the gift was made after 17 March 1986, it counts as subject to a reservation if you go on using it.

WHAT TO TELL THE INLAND REVENUE

There's no space on your Tax Return for details of transfers which are liable to inheritance tax. But you are expected to tell the Inland Revenue if you make lifetime gifts which are liable to inheritance tax at the time of the gift (broadly, gifts to certain trusts).

And if someone dies within seven years of making taxable gifts to you, you may have to tell the taxman. However, there is no need to send details if the gifts do not add up to more than £10,000 in any tax year or £40,000 over seven tax years.

Inheritance tax is dealt with by the three Capital Taxes Offices:

● **England and Wales:** Minford House, Rockley Road, London W14 0DF

● **Scotland:** 16 Picardy Place, Edinburgh EH1 3NB

● **Northern Ireland:** Law Courts Building, Chichester Street, Belfast BT1 3NU.

If you want to claim tax relief on interest for a loan to pay inheritance tax until probate is granted, enter details on page 8 of Forms 11P and 11 under *Other qualifying loans*. On Form P1, give details under *Other loans qualifying for tax relief* on page 3. Give the name of the lender, the purpose of the loan and the amount of interest paid. Enclose a certificate of interest paid, which the lender will supply.

Form 11P

Notes

For details of loans on which you can claim tax relief see note 40. For details on loans to buy or improve rental property see notes 24 and 25. If you have more than one qualifying loan, give details on a separate sheet of paper.

Other qualifying loans

Complete this form if you can claim tax relief on other loans. Only give details of loans not included elsewhere on this form. Enclose a certificate of interest paid from your lender. Do not include loans on your main home.

Name of lender

Purpose of loan

Give the address of the property if the loan is for the purchase or improvement of property used for letting

The number of weeks let

Amount of gross interest paid in the 1993-94 tax year £

GLOSSARY

Your Tax Inspector, tax advisers and others offering advice (objective or otherwise) will all tend to slip into jargon, if given half a chance. Many of the terms they use can be found in the Index to this Guide. But you may find that words in common usage, which you think you understand, are being used in a particular sense when applied to your tax affairs. This brief Glossary explains the meaning of some everyday words used in a tax context.

ALLOWABLE

Anything which a Tax Inspector is likely to agree is acceptable. For example, if you spend money in the course of your business, you will be able to deduct it from the takings in working out your taxable profit if the expenses are allowable.

ASSESSMENT

An assessment is a calculation of your tax bill. Your Tax Inspector may send you a copy of the calculation, a Notice of Assessment (p. 72).

BASIC RATE

The basic rate of income tax is 25 per cent for the 1994/95 tax year, payable on taxable income between £3,000 and £23,700. It is called the basic rate, because most people's taxable income falls between these two limits – so that the basic rate is the rate of tax they pay on each extra £ of income. For this reason, tax is deducted from most types of interest at the basic rate by the bank or building society, and handed over direct to the Inland Revenue so that the taxpayer does not need to pay the tax separately.

BENEFITS

May be used in two ways: to refer to social security benefits; and to group together fringe benefits such as a company car, low interest loans and free travel.

CAPITAL ALLOWANCE

A tax allowance against the cost of buying plant and equipment like business vehicles, computers and machinery (p. 199).

CASE

Schedule D income tax is divided into six Cases, each with somewhat different tax rules (p. 38).

CONSIDERATION

Anything you get in return for a service or a possession. For example, if you exchange your house for a luxury yacht, the Tax Inspector will say that you have sold it for the consideration of the yacht (the price being the value of the yacht).

DEDUCTIONS

Certain payments you make which can be deducted from your income before working out how much tax you have to pay (see Chapter 5, p. 43).

DEDUCTION AT SOURCE

Some types of income are paid after tax has been deducted from them: for example, earnings under PAYE and building society interest. The tax deducted 'at source' is paid directly to the Inland Revenue; if further tax is due on the income, it will normally be collected direct from you. In some cases, you will be able to claim back some or all of the tax if it is more than you should have paid or you are a non-taxpayer.

DISPOSAL

If you sell, give away or otherwise part with a possession, this counts as a disposal for capital gains tax purposes (p. 301).

DOMICILE

The country you regard as your natural home. For most people, their domicile is the place of their birth, and while it is possible to change your domicile, it can be a lengthy process.

DUE DATE

The date by which you must do something: for example, pay tax, send in a Return.

EARNED INCOME

Income from a job or business, earned by your own work. Some pensions are also taxed as earned income; they can be seen as deferred earnings.

EMOLUMENTS

The rewards of working which are taxable, including salary, fees, wages, fringe benefits, expense allowances, bonuses, etc.

EMPLOYMENT

A job working for someone else or a company.

EXEMPTION

Another word for tax relief or tax allowance: an exemption is an amount of income, a gain or a gift on which tax is not payable.

FISCAL YEAR

See *Tax Year*.

GROSS

Before deduction of tax.

GROSSED-UP

The amount before deduction of tax. For example, if you get income after tax has been deducted, adding back the tax which has been deducted gives you the grossed-up amount.

HIGHER-PAID

People earning at more than a set rate (currently £8,500 a year) face tougher rules on the taxation of their fringe benefits and expense allowances (p. 162). People in this bracket were, until the 1989 Budget, described as 'higher-paid employees'.

HIGHER-RATE TAX

People with a taxable income over the top limit for the basic rate of tax (£23,700 for the 1993/94 and 1994/95 tax years) pay tax at the higher rate of 40 per cent.

INDEPENDENT TAXATION

Since 6 April 1990 a married couple have been treated as separate individuals for tax purposes (see p. 104).

INVESTMENT INCOME

Income which is not earned from a job or a business, such as income from shares, property and deposits in a bank or building society.

LIABILITY

Tax bill.

LIABLE

Taxable. Something which is liable to tax must be taken into consideration when working out your tax bill. But you may not have to pay tax on it: for example, you may be liable to income tax on casual earnings you receive but there will be no tax to pay if your income is too low to pay tax.

LOSS

If you lose money in a business, or on selling something you own, you may have made a loss for tax purposes and this can usually be used to reduce your overall tax bill. There are special rules for working out whether you have made a loss (see Index) and you may make a tax loss without having made a loss in a business sense (or *vice versa*).

LOWER RATE

The lower rate of tax is 20 per cent, payable on the first £2,500 of taxable income in the 1993/94 tax year, and on the first £3,000 of taxable income in the 1994/95 tax year.

NET

After deduction of tax. If you get £100 after £25 tax has been deducted from it, you receive a net amount of £100 − £25 = £75.

NET RELEVANT EARNINGS

You can get tax relief on personal pension contributions provided they do not exceed a certain proportion of your net relevant earnings (see p. 225 for how these are defined).

OUTGOINGS

Certain payments you make which can be deducted from your income before working out how much tax you have to pay, now known as 'deductions' (see Chapter 5, p. 43).

PENSION AGE

Pension age is normally the age at which you can draw the state pension: 65 for men, 60 for women. But in some cases, it may have a different meaning: for example, the age at which you can draw a personal pension or a pension from your employer.

PENSIONABLE

Earnings are pensionable if they come from a job where the employer has a pension scheme and you are a member of the scheme.

RELIEF

Anything which reduces your tax bill may be described as a relief: for example, a tax allowance or a payment which counts as an outgoing reduces your taxable income. If some or all of a particular type of income can be left out of your reckoning for tax, this is also a relief.

RESIDENCE

The country you are treated as living in for tax purposes (p. 188).

RETURNS

The Inland Revenue forms on which you are asked to give information on your income, capital gains and gifts on which inheritance tax may be due are known as Returns.

SCHEDULES

Income tax is divided into five different types (A, C, D, E and F) each with its own rules and with restrictions on how they may be related to each other (p. 38).

SEPARATE ASSESSMENT

Until 5 April 1990, husband and wife were treated as a single tax unit and jointly assessed. If they preferred to fill in their own Tax Returns, receive their own tax bills and account for their own tax, they could opt for separate assessment (though their tax bill remained the same: it was merely shared out between them). Since 6 April 1990, all married couples have been separately assessed as independent taxpayers.

SEPARATE TAXATION

Until 5 April 1990, a married couple were taxed as a single unit unless they opted for separate taxation (technically, *the wife's earned income election*). Since 6 April 1990, independent taxation has done away with this option as husband and wife are separately assessed as independent taxpayers.

TAX CREDIT

If you receive income with a tax credit, you are taken to have paid tax equal to the amount of the tax credit. Your total before-tax income is the amount of income you get plus the amount of the tax credit.

TAX-FREE

Income which is described as tax-free should be free of all income tax and capital gains tax, that is, no further tax is due on it whatever your rate of tax. Sometimes erroneously used to describe income which is *tax-paid* (see below). Also misleadingly used to describe income drawn from a single-premium life insurance bond by cashing in up to 5 per cent of it each year; although no tax is due when the income is drawn, there may be a tax bill later (p. 288).

TAX-PAID

Tax-paid income comes after deduction of tax, which normally covers you for any basic-rate tax on the income. Further tax may be due if you pay tax at the higher rate. If your income is so low that you should pay no tax at all or tax at the lower rate, in many cases you can claim back some or all of the tax deducted.

TAX YEAR

Tax years run from 6 April to 5 April of the following calendar year. So the 1994/95 tax year runs from 6 April 1994 to 5 April 1995.

TOTAL INCOME

All your income for a tax year, less certain deductions (p. 23).

UNEARNED INCOME

See *Investment Income*.

FIFTY WAYS TO SAVE TAX

Here are 50 tips to cut your tax bill. They are all relatively straight-forward and do not involve reorganizing your life in search of tax savings.

1   Investigate the past. It may not be too late to claim an allowance or deduction you have forgotten about. Some of the more important deadlines for claims are given on p. 26.

2   Always check your tax forms. As soon as you receive a Notice of Coding or a Notice of Assessment make sure your Tax Inspector has got the sums right. You only have 30 days to do it for a Notice of Assessment (see p. 61). If you get a statement of taxable benefits, you must appeal against it within 60 days (see p. 182).

3   Don't delay in sending back a Tax Return – it should be sent back within 30 days unless you have won an extension from your Tax Inspector. You may have to pay interest on tax you owe if you delay in sending back your Tax Return until after 31 October following the end of the tax year for which it asks for details of income – see p. 63.

4   Keep your records well organized. Take copies of your Tax Returns. Note down all the expenses you could claim: if you are an employee, see p. 144; if you are self-employed, look at the checklist on p. 195; if you let out property, see p. 249 and p. 251.

5   Do not pay tax before you have to. If your Tax Inspector wants to collect tax on some income through the PAYE system, and this is earlier than you have to pay it by law, ask to pay it at the later due date. Chapter 3, p. 25, tells you when income tax is due.

6   If you are married and one of you has too little income to pay tax, consider reorganizing your investments so that your investment income is paid to the partner who does not pay tax (see p. 108). The same applies if one of you pays tax at the lower rate of 20 per cent only – you'll pay less tax if interest on your savings is paid to that partner.

7 Married couples where one of you has a low income and can't use up all your allowances should consider transferring them to the other partner. This can apply to married couple's allowance and blind person's allowance (see p. 106).

8 If you are married and one of you pays tax at the higher rate of 40 per cent, consider reorganizing your investments so that the income is paid to the other partner who will pay less tax on it (see p. 108).

9 If you are elderly, watch out for the income trap – that is, the region of income where, because of the withdrawal of age allowance, you are effectively taxed at a high rate. Chapter 17, p. 136, explains why. Consider tax-free investments if that is the case.

10 Married couples with one or both partners over 65 may be able to save tax by switching investments between them to avoid the income trap – see p. 136.

11 If you are single and there is a child living with you, you may be able to claim the additional personal allowance, the same amount as the married couple's allowance (£1,720 for 1994/95). You may also be entitled to claim this allowance if you are married but separated, or a married man whose wife is totally unable to look after herself – see p. 100.

12 If you are an employee, see if you can negotiate the introduction of profit-related pay (p. 141) and share option schemes (p. 174). These forms of earnings can be free of income tax.

13 There is a long list of fringe benefits which are tax-free whatever your level of earnings (p. 163). Try to take advantage of them in your negotiations with your boss. Fringe benefits which are not tax-free can still be a tax-efficient way of being paid. The taxable value put on them may be much lower than the value to you. There is a rundown of how they are taxed in Chapter 19, p. 161.

14 If you have a company car, make sure you use it for at least 2,500 miles a year on business, as it cuts your tax bill on the car by a third. If you do lots of business mileage, see if you can get it above the 18,000 miles level, as this halves your tax bill on it. Keep very good records of your business mileage so you can substantiate your claims.

15 Working parents should try to persuade their employers to provide childcare facilities, as this fringe benefit is tax-free. Your private childcare arrangements are not eligible for tax relief (see p. 164).

16 These perks of your job are still free of tax: entertainment by your suppliers or customers at cultural or sporting events (within certain rules), Air Miles (which enable you to make cheap flights) and gifts costing up to £100 (not cash) from a third party (within rules). See Chapter 19, p. 163.

17 If you leave a job to become self-employed, ask your Tax Inspector for a rebate. It will help your finances, although not cut your actual tax bill.(see p. 177).

18 If you are unemployed and not claiming social security benefits, ask your Tax Inspector for a rebate (see p. 181).

19 If you are self-employed or in partnership and your turnover is less than £15,000 a year, take advantage of the ability to send in three-line accounts (see p. 192). This won't save you any tax, but it may cut your book-keeping and accountancy fees.

20 You can still claim as an expense for your business something you use partly for business and partly in your private life, for example, using your home for work, sharing the car (p. 193).

21 When you first start your business, claim capital allowances on any equipment you already own but take into the business, for example, a car, desk, etc. (see p. 202).

22 You do not have to claim all the capital allowances you are entitled to. It may save you more tax to claim less and carry forward a higher value to the next year when your profits may be higher or your personal allowances lower (p. 199).

23 If you are married and run your own business, consider employing your spouse if he or she does not work. It could save money if you pay your spouse just under the lower earnings limit for National Insurance contributions (p. 211).

24 Consider leasing cars rather than purchasing outright. VAT can be reclaimed on leasing payments, but not on the cost of a purchased car.

25 If you are in business and buying assets, see if they can be treated as short-life assets. The cost can be reclaimed over five years, whereas the writing-down allowance of 25 per cent allows you to write off 90 per cent of the cost over around eight years (see p. 201).

26 If you are working abroad, you can get tax relief on all your earnings there if you observe a few simple rules about the length of time you spend in the UK – see p. 189.

27 The government offers lots of tax incentives to persuade you to save for a pension. Take advantage of them. Chapter 25, p. 219, tells you how to take them up.

28 If you're approaching retirement, consider making extra contributions towards a pension. If you work for an employer, you can get tax relief on additional voluntary contributions (AVCs) to your employer's scheme (p. 221). With contributions to a personal pension scheme, you can get tax relief on a higher proportion of your earnings as you get older (p. 224).

29 If you took out a life insurance policy before midnight on 13 March 1984, the chances are that you get tax relief on the premiums (12.5 per cent for 1994/95). However, altering the policy (for example, increasing the benefits unless this is done automatically under the policy) could mean losing the tax relief (see p. 291). Consider carefully before altering – perhaps you can achieve your objective in another way.

30 If you want to give money to charity, try to use the available ways in which you can save tax. These are covenants, payroll-giving schemes and Gift Aid. There are more details in Chapter 30 on p. 294.

31 Look closely at any charitable covenants you make. If you are a non-taxpayer or pay tax at the lower rate, you will not be able to keep all the tax relief you deduct at the basic rate from the covenant payments (p. 296). If your husband or wife will pay tax, it may be better for them to make the covenant payments (and any donations under Gift Aid).

32 Borrowing money to buy a home can be cheap because you get tax relief on loans of £30,000 or less. Chapter 27, p. 233, tells you the rules so you can ensure you get the maximum relief.

33 A married couple can choose to share the tax relief on mortgage interest however they like. If some split other than an equal one would save you tax, make an 'allocation of interest' election (see p. 236 for examples of when it would pay to do this).

34 If you have a home improvement loan taken out before 6 April 1988, consider carefully before you replace it with another loan with a lower rate of interest. You would not be able to claim tax relief on the interest paid on the replacement loan (see p. 239).

35 More than one home? You may have to pay capital gains tax when you sell your second home (p. 242). But you can choose which of your homes counts as your main one – make sure you nominate the home which is likely to incur the biggest CGT bill.

36 Want an income of over £60 a week tax-free? If you let out a room in your home under the rent a room scheme (see p. 248), you can take £3,250 of gross rent a year tax-free.

37 If you let out your second home, try to make sure you meet the conditions for the rent to be taxed as income from furnished holiday lettings (p. 254). You can claim a wider variety of deductions against tax, and you may be able to avoid capital gains tax when you sell the home.

38 Personal Equity Plans (PEPs) now offer you the chance to build up a portfolio of shares and unit trusts free of income tax and capital gains tax. If you buy shares in a privatization issue, you can transfer these into your PEP (see p. 276).

39 If you belong to an employee profit-sharing scheme or a savings-related share option scheme, you can transfer shares you receive under the scheme into a single-company PEP – see p. 275. This will mean no income tax on the dividends and no capital gains tax when you eventually sell the shares.

40 Investing in a Tax Exempt Special Savings Account (TESSA) means tax-free interest on up to £9,000 of savings – so long as you can leave the money for the full five years (p. 276).

41 Non-taxpayers investing in banks, building societies and other investments where basic-rate tax is deducted from the income should be sure to claim it back from the Inland Revenue. With interest from banks and building societies, you can arrange for it to be paid without deduction of tax if you are a non-taxpayer (see p. 267).

42 If you pay tax at the lower rate of 20 per cent, you can reclaim part of the tax deducted from interest from banks, building societies and other investments where basic-rate tax is deducted from the income (see p. 265).

43 Investors should consider having some investments which give a capital gain rather than income. There is a tax-free slice of net capital gains (£5,800 in the 1994/95 tax year) which you can make each tax year – see p. 301.

44 Husband and wife each have a separate limit for tax-free net capital gains of £5,800 (see p. 311). Consider reorganizing your possessions so that each of you can use up the limit before either starts paying capital gains tax.

45 Do not forget to claim losses if you dispose of something like shares or valuables at a loss. Losses can be set off against taxable gains, and carried over to later years (see p. 312).

46 If you own valuable things like antiques, a second home or collectables, you could face a capital gains tax bill when you dispose of them. Keep careful records of what they cost you to buy and maintain; claiming these as allowable expenses can reduce the tax bill (p. 303).

47 If you are going to dispose of some assets, try to split the disposals over a number of years, so that you can make full use of your tax-free slice of net capital gains.

48 Draw up a will: it should help you to start thinking about inheritance tax. There are simple steps you can take to minimize the tax payable on your estate when you die and to reduce the complications for those you leave behind (see Chapter 32, p. 342).

49 Make as full use as possible of the gifts you can make which do not fall into the inheritance tax net – for example, on marriage or out of normal income (p. 330). And if you can afford it, use the nil-rate band to make further tax-free gifts to your loved ones (p. 331)

50 If you own a small business or farm, take professional tax advice. There are extensive tax reliefs which can mean little or no capital gains tax (p. 319) or inheritance tax (p. 336) – but they are complicated and need careful planning.

GROSSING-UP TABLES

Here is a ready reckoner to help you gross-up income and deductions quickly at the 25 per cent basic rate. Opposite is a similar reckoner for grossing-up at the 20 per cent lower rate (for share dividends and unit trust distributions).

GROSSING-UP WHEN TAX IS DEDUCTED AT 25 PER CENT

Net amount £	Gross amount £	Net amount £	Gross amount £	Net amount £	Gross amount £
1	1.33	10	13.33	100	133.33
2	2.67	20	26.67	200	266.67
3	4.00	30	40.00	300	400.00
4	5.33	40	53.33	400	533.33
5	6.67	50	66.67	500	666.67
6	8.00	60	80.00	600	800.00
7	9.33	70	93.33	700	933.33
8	10.67	80	106.67	800	1,066.67
9	12.00	90	120.00	900	1,200.00
				1,000	1,333.33

EXAMPLE

Pete Elliott has received net income of £1,469 in 1993/94, from which tax has been deducted at 25 per cent. He finds the gross income as follows:

	net	gross
	£1,000	£1333.33
	£400	£533.33
	£60	£80.00
	£9	£12.00
TOTAL	£1,469	£1,958.66

GROSSING-UP WHEN TAX IS DEDUCTED AT 20 PER CENT

Net amount £	Gross amount £	Net amount £	Gross amount £	Net amount £	Gross amount £
1	1.25	10	12.50	100	125.00
2	2.50	20	25.00	200	250.00
3	3.75	30	37.50	300	375.00
4	5.00	40	50.00	400	500.00
5	6.25	50	62.50	500	625.00
6	7.50	60	75.00	600	750.00
7	8.75	70	87.50	700	875.00
8	10.00	80	100.00	800	1,000.00
9	11.25	90	112.50	900	1,125.00
				1,000	1,250.00

EXAMPLE

Pete Elliott receives share dividends worth £1,297 in 1994/95. He must gross-up the net dividends at 20 per cent for this tax year:

	net	gross
	£1,000	£1250.00
	£200	£250.00
	£90	£112.50
	£7	£8.75
TOTAL	£1,297	£1,621.25

RETAIL PRICES INDEX

	1982	1983	1984	1985	1986	1987	1988	1989	1990	1991	1992	1993
January		82.61	86.84	91.20	96.25	100.0	103.3	111.0	119.5	130.2	135.6	137.9
February		82.97	87.20	91.94	96.60	100.4	103.7	111.8	120.2	130.9	136.3	138.8
March	79.44	83.12	87.48	92.80	96.73	100.6	104.1	112.3	121.4	131.4	136.7	139.3
April	81.04	84.28	88.64	94.78	97.67	101.8	105.8	114.3	125.1	133.1	138.8	140.6
May	81.62	84.64	88.97	95.21	97.85	101.9	106.2	115.0	126.2	133.5	139.3	141.1
June	81.85	84.84	89.20	95.41	97.79	101.9	106.6	115.4	126.7	134.1	139.3	141.0
July	81.88	85.30	89.10	95.23	97.52	101.8	106.7	115.5	126.8	133.8	138.8	140.7
August	81.90	85.68	89.94	95.49	97.82	102.1	107.9	115.8	128.1	134.1	138.9	141.3
September	81.85	86.06	90.11	95.44	98.30	102.4	108.4	116.6	129.3	134.6	139.4	141.9
October	82.26	86.36	90.67	95.59	98.45	102.9	109.5	117.5	130.3	135.1	139.9	141.8
November	82.66	86.67	90.95	95.92	99.29	103.4	110.0	118.5	130.0	135.6	139.7	141.6
December	82.51	86.89	90.87	96.05	99.62	103.3	110.3	118.8	129.9	135.7	139.2	141.9

Note that from January 1987 the RPI was reorganized and became 100 again. These figures in the Table are recalculated for you

USEFUL LEAFLETS

You can get these leaflets free from your tax office.

IR1   Extra-statutory concessions (plus supplement with latest concessions)
IR6   Double taxation relief
IR14/15   Construction industry tax deduction scheme
IR16   Share acquisitions by directors and employees
IR20   Residents and non-residents – liability to tax in the UK
IR24   Class 4 National Insurance contributions
IR26   Changes of accounting date
IR28   Starting in business
IR33   Income tax and school leavers
IR34   Pay As You Earn
IR37   Income tax and capital gains tax – appeals
IR40   Construction industry: conditions for getting a sub-contractor's tax certificate
IR41   Income tax and the unemployed
IR42   Lay-offs and short-time work
IR43   Income tax and strikes
IR45   Income tax, capital gains tax and inheritance tax: what happens when someone dies
IR46   Income tax and corporation tax – clubs, societies and associations
IR51   The Business Expansion Scheme
IR53   Thinking of taking someone on?
IR56   Employed or self-employed? A guide for tax and National Insurance
IR57   Thinking of working for yourself?
IR58   Going to work abroad?
IR60   Income tax and students
IR64   Giving to charity – how businesses can get tax relief
IR65   Giving to charity – how individuals can get tax relief

IR133	Income tax and company cars from 6 April 1994: a guide for employees
CGT4	Capital gains tax and owner-occupied houses
CGT6	Retirement relief on disposal of a business
CGT11	Capital gains tax and small businesses
CGT13	Capital gains tax – the indexation allowance for quoted shares
CGT14	Capital gains tax – an introduction
CGT15	Capital gains tax – a guide for married couples
CGT16	Capital gains tax – indexation allowance, disposals after 5 April 1988
480	Notes on expenses payments and benefits for directors and certain employees
P7	Employer's guide to PAYE
IHT1	Inheritance tax (only from Capital Taxes Offices – see p. 345)
IHT2	Inheritance tax on lifetime gifts
IHT3	An introduction to inheritance tax
IHT8	Alterations to an inheritance following a death

The Inland Revenue also publishes Business Economic Notes about particular businesses (for example, travel agents, road haulage, lodgings, hairdressing, waste-disposal and funerals). These can give useful information on what the Tax Inspector is looking for in those particular businesses. You can get them from:

> The Reference Room
> Inland Revenue Library
> Room 8, New Wing
> Somerset House
> London WC2R 1LB

They cost 60p or £1 each.

INDEX

Bold numerals indicate main entry

THE LLOYDS BANK TAX GUIDE
TREASURE TROVE
– ENTRY FORM

Write your solutions to the eleven Treasure Trove clues scattered through the Guide in the spaces provided overleaf – each is a number. Add up all the numbers to find the total. Then explain why the total should be of interest to every taxpayer (in not more than 20 words). The best 20 answers will scoop the prizes!

Then send your entry on this page to arrive by 31 March 1995, to the following address:

Lloyds Bank Tax Guide Competition
Penguin Books
27 Wrights Lane
London W8 5TZ

For terms and conditions of entry, see p. 8.

YOUR FULL NAME: . . . .

ADDRESS: . . . .

. . . .

. . . .

POSTCODE: . . . .

THE TREASURE TROVE SOLUTIONS

Clue 1   £ __ __

Clue 2   £ __ __ __ __

Clue 3   £ __ __ __

Clue 4   £ __ __ __ __

Clue 5   __ __ per cent

Clue 6   £ __ __ __ __

Clue 7   __ __ years

Clue 8   __ __ per cent

Clue 9   __ __ years

Clue 10   £ __ __ __ __

Clue 11   __ __ per cent

TOTAL   __ __ __ __

Finally, give your explanation of why this total should be of interest to every taxpayer, in not more than 20 words:

. . . .

. . . .

. . . .

. . . .

. . . .